BROWN-OUT

by the same author

THINK: *A Biography of the Watsons and IBM*

ROCKEFELLER'S FOLLIES

BROWN-OUT
The Power Crisis in America

WILLIAM RODGERS

STEIN AND DAY/*Publishers*/New York

First published in 1972
Copyright © 1972 William Rodgers
Library of Congress Catalog Card No. 73-127228
All rights reserved
Published simultaneously in Canada by Saunders of Toronto Ltd
Designed by David Miller
Printed in the United States of America
Stein and Day/*Publishers*/7 East 48 Street, New York, N.Y. 10017
ISBN 0-8128-1380-4

Contents

BROWN-OUT

1

Cascade: The Loss
of
Power

FIRE WAS neither discovered nor invented. Only in mythology was it smuggled from heaven for delivery to mortals. It was hurled to earth in a discharge of electric energy formed in the sky and leaping across an intervening arc to enflame combustible matter. Electricity created fire.

In the late years of the nineteenth century, this invisible energy, generated and transmitted by techniques long in the making, burst upon the world from the tips of conductive wires to emerge as incandescent light. It changed the planet forever in immeasurable ways. No development in all history, not even nuclear fission (at least not yet), has ever equaled the harnessing of electricity in terms of universal significance and application.

In the years that span one lifetime, what had not previously existed to serve mankind grew and proliferated on a scale of such magnitude that people and industry became its slaves. Dependence on electric energy became so pervasive and exclusive—first supplanting, then making obsolescent, other modes of power—that life itself could not long endure without it. There are no alternatives to electricity because it has all but destroyed them, rendering nearly impotent those it did not eliminate.

With dependence on electricity nearly absolute, reliance on it for life and well-being became the inescapable condition for much of the human race. It is the heart of every industrial system, and when it falters or fails, so does the system it fuels. Yet, electric power is both volatile and vulnerable, often treacherously uncontrollable, unreliable, unstable

9

in its man-made universe of generators, turbines, transmission networks, circuit breakers, fuse boxes, and the wires that carry it to the light bulbs, the gadgets, and the motors of the land. When electric power fails, the heart of the world it serves stops beating.

Somewhere in the United States, which produces nearly 40 percent of all the electric energy in the world, there is a loss or reduction of power almost every day, generally of short duration and with minor consequences. But now and then, a blackout of major proportions occurs, and whole regions are subjected to the crippling experience that characterizes a *cascade*, a progressive and at times sustained loss of power. It is at such times that the significance of the energy crisis in America is appreciated and the helplessness of a power-starved society is recognized.

Twilight, on a clear November day that was chilled but not yet assaulted by advancing winter, flung five-o'clock shadows across the quitting-time congestion, the rush-hour frustration, the swarms of crawling automobiles, the surge to trains and buses in the large cities. Beyond the urban centers, from the placid dairy farms in open country, from Ontario, Canada, out through the mountain villages of New England, down the Atlantic coast, into Pennsylvania and Ohio, 30 million people were about to be taught a lesson in the perils of overdependency on technology in the nervous nuclear age.

Along the Niagara River, which extends on a north-south line from Buffalo on Lake Erie to Lake Ontario, separating and joining the United States and Canada, the great Ontario Hydro-Electric system maintained its Number 2 plant, named for an obscure notable, Sir Adam Beck. Five main transmission lines conveyed the electricity generated at the Beck plant, plus a portion of power produced at the Niagara plant of the Power Authority of New York, into Ontario.

At quarter after five on Tuesday evening, November 9, 1965, the Beck plant was operating at 1,500 megawatts, which means that it was generating an output of 1,500 million watts of electric energy.*

To the east, at the border town of Massena, New York, the only other line linking the two nations carried 200 megawatts into Canada. It was now sixteen minutes after five, and all seemed to be well in the interconnected system.

Eleven seconds later, something unbelievable occurred. An "interruption of the operation of a backup relay on one of the five transmission lines" † to Canada caused what power engineers call a "disturbance." The

---

* *Watt, dyne, erg, and joule* are terms in physics and in the centimeter-gram-second (cgs) system. Each is a unit of work, or energy. A watt is a unit of power equal to 1 joule per second. A joule is equal to 10 ergs.
† Quoted from findings published by the Federal Power Commission in 1967.

relay had been inexplicably set too low for the load surging through the line, and the interruption, in response to design function, caused the line to be disconnected. Power, which was still being generated but which was refused entry into the dead conductor, spread into the remaining four operating lines in sufficient volume to overload their transmitting capacity; and each of them tripped out, just as they were, in such circumstances, sensibly supposed to do.

Now the electrons, moving with the speed of light, unable to escape or to continue their path along any of the lines—all 1,500 million watts of them—reversed their flow and sought release by piling in on the 200-megawatt channel at Massena. Obedient to the laws of physics and system design, the overburdened line opened, breaking the intertie, leaving 1,700 million watts of power with no way to reach what was by then the electrically isolated island of Ontario. The power, already generated and locked into a closed system, surged toward every outlet, all of which led to the United States. Each line open to such an onslaught of energy collapsed as it was struck by a volume of power it was incapable of containing.

It was a cascade, a progressive blackout that enveloped one power system after another as too much current sought conveyance along electronic highways unable to handle the traffic. Electrons, however, unlike motorcars congested before an expressway access, do not wait in line until they insert themselves into an ongoing flow. Unless the transmission channels are broken off (opened), this energy of power and heat can quickly destroy whatever gets in the way. Hence, the tripping out must be automatic and fast when an imbalance occurs between what is generated and what can be transmitted for use.

The cascade spread at flash speed across widening circles of territory. As turbines slowed, electric power in transmission lines failed to flow. The surge of energy stopped in other lines that tripped out when generators received signals to produce loads beyond their capacity. Everywhere in the interconnected systems, there was either too little or too much electron movement, and the wildly imbalanced network shut itself down and died.

It took twelve minutes from the time the operational interruption knocked out the relay in a little box at the Sir Adam Beck facility to produce the worst power failure in the age of electricity, engulfing 30 million people over an area of 80,000 square miles in one form or another of dark reality.

Yet there was nothing unique or even new about the cascade. Blackouts had occurred, sometimes with maddening frequency, in the past, although not usually for as trivial an oversight as an uninspected relay. The distinction that accompanied this one was its magnitude—the geo-

graphical extent of it—and the publicity it provoked. It did not cause the
cruel and extensive suffering, the evacuation from uninhabitable homes,
the broken and frozen water lines that accompany prolonged power failures in the bitter cold of winter. It did not even last very long as power
failures go.* Most of Ontario was back in service within three hours,
and part of the area along the New York–Canadian border endured the
loss of power for scarcely more than fifteen minutes. But in both the rural
and the congested urban sectors of southern New England, it was eight
hours before current again coursed through the lines, long enough, to be
sure, to exhaust dairy farmers and whatever emergency hands they could
commandeer to work through the night to relieve thousands of bawling
cows when electrically manipulated teat cups fell inert at milking time.

   Worst of all, the power failure lingered longest in the metropolitan
New York territory of America's largest and generally most damned
public utility, the Consolidated Edison Company. That hapless and staggering giant among power companies was still struggling to restore current in full when the dawn of the next day, November 10, broke thirteen
hours after the debacle began.

   Because New York City is the hub of the nation's communications
network and sometimes designates itself as the center of the universe,
there is inevitably a good deal more publicity about anything that happens there than in regions not as relentlessly served by mass media.
Earlier power failures, some of them continuing for a week, had gone
more or less unnoticed, except in the affected areas, in nearly every state
of the Union. Even instances in which people had fled their homes in the
dead of winter to live in motels or double up with relatives while utility
workmen labored to restore electricity had generally been treated with
something of the remote and offhand detachment of an earth slide in the
Andes or a regional flood along the Nile.

   At times, however, even isolated local power breakdowns have attracted an inordinate measure of attention, depending on the circumstances surrounding them. Once, in the winter of 1961–1962, when Nelson
Rockefeller was serving his first of four terms as governor of New York,
and when the citizens of the state were being pressed to build bomb
shelters with public money, a civil defense demonstration was organized

---

* Late in February, 1969, the eastern and southern United States were plagued by
power failures and winter storms. Severe suffering followed six days of blackout
in North and South Carolina towns where more than 100,000 people were cut
off from electricity. Many made their way to National Guard armories for shelter
until service was gradually restored over the following week. At Rainsville, Alabama, fifteen National Guard troops manned portable generators to keep baby
chicks, important to the local economy, alive. In the Northeast, the heaviest snow-
falls in a century, combined with recurrent power failures, produced disaster
conditions lasting for days in hundreds of communities.

to dramatize the necessity, or at least the alleged necessity, of protecting the populace from nuclear warfare, which governor seemed to think might be imminent. Along the Hudson valley, the defense drill invoked the participation of a good many civilians, largely volunteer firemen and ladies from local service organizations, wearing arm bands and hard hats and communicating with one another on such matters as widespread simulated casualties, disposition of corpses, prevention of imagined panic, and excessive migration along public roads reserved for military use. The demonstration broke down when the power in one key area suddenly went dead. Subsequent investigation revealed that a couple of squirrels had found a warm transformer an ideal place in which to hole up for the winter. They had stashed away a supply of provender, in the course of which they chewed and pulled out of contact one of the hot lines carrying current. This ill-timed bit of sabotage on the part of prudent rodents unnerved some of the citizens in the defense corps, who suggested in shocked letters to the newspapers that the region seemed extraordinarily vulnerable on the matter of preparedness for the impending Russian bombardment.

Although news of power failures seldom spreads beyond the victimized region, over the years concern has mounted in inner utility circles and among federal agencies; but it was that formalized, bureaucratic, just-between-ourselves kind of concern that long characterized the relationship between public utilities and the agencies under mandate to regulate them. In hindsight studies made by the Federal Power Commission (FPC) at the direction of President Johnson *after* the 1965 cascade, the regulatory bodies administered by men sworn to preserve and protect the public interest discovered, to what might have been their embarrassment had they dwelt on the matter in depth, that they really did not know much about previous power failures. Their concern had been general, characterized by sympathy and worry, but unfettered by resolute action.

Detailed information on the subject over the twelve-year period from 1954 to 1966 was, said the Federal Power Commission in its report, "meager." Detailed information was less than that; it was all but nonexistent, since prior to that time, the agency had not required utilities to jot down data about those occasions when no power was delivered, except in extraordinary circumstances. This oversight was corrected thirteen months after the 1965 breakdown, when the commission, as usual moving smartly to secure the stable door upon discovering its horses missing, issued Order No. 331, which required all electric utilities "to report any interruption in bulk power supply which involves transmission facilities of 69 kilovolts or above and causes load interruptions of 25,000 kilowatts or more for a period in excess of 15 minutes." For larger "interruptions" of 200,000 kilowatts, which is the output of a small generating plant, a utility was required to notify the FPC by telephone "as soon as practicable" after the lights went out.

As a result of Order No. 331, fifty-two power failures had to be reported in the five-month period between January 15 and June 12, 1967, the first reporting period covered by the firm new policy of the regulatory commission. Only four of these failures were big enough to qualify for the mandatory telephone call to the FPC, but one of them affected 13 million people in Pennsylvania, New Jersey, Maryland, and Delaware, and left an area of 15,000 square miles without electricity for as long as ten hours. A dozen generating plants suffered damage during the disturbance, which was caused by a short circuit in a high-voltage line that knocked out 10 million kilowatts of power.

Two of the fifty-two blackouts (one on March 14 and another on April 20) struck the same customers of the publicly owned Bonneville Power Administration in the western United States and Canada, and although in each case the utility had everything in operating order again within twenty-four minutes, the interim loss of power was extensive.

The fourth failure exceeding the 200,000-kilowatt level shut power off from 163,000 customers of the Gulf Coast Utilities Company, in southeastern Texas, which lost its entire load for a period ranging from forty-five minutes to seven hours on May 11 when a lightning arrester failed.

One of the more peculiar blackouts was somewhat under the limit for a telephone call, but it deprived 78,000 customers of the Pennsylvania Power and Light Company of 163,000 kilowatts for fifteen to twenty-four minutes on June 12. The blackout cascaded outward from the Frackville substation on a calm and clear summer day that should have made no particular demands on another lightning arrester which, possibly in a pique at having nothing to arrest, reacted abnormally to bad vibrations and started all the trouble.

Two failures were caused by birds, the squirrels apparently being inactive during this period. One bird caused a short circuit in an El Paso, Texas, substation when a metal necklace it had filched from somewhere dangled, in the course of a getaway flight, across an exposed transmission bar. The other bird settled on a line in Mayfield, Kentucky, in a way (possibly by straddling it) that severed a conductor when an arc leapt across an insulator. While the 250,000 kilowatts of service in El Paso were interrupted for forty-five minutes, and 52,000 in Mayfield for fifty-nine minutes, the interruption for the birds in flight was permanent.

Seventeen of the failures were caused by "natural phenomena," meaning for the most part that weather conditions such as lightning, wind, and storms were too much for transmission systems; twenty-two, by equipment failures; two, by small planes striking wires (in one case causing only the public utility, not the plane, to lose power, but in the second case, interrupting the flight of a crop-dusting plane and damaging it); four, by what the FPC called "human errors"; one, by vandals tripping circuit breakers; and one, by the malicious destruction of insulators.

The cascade of 1965 set the Federal Power Commission to digging into whatever "meager" records it could find to determine the nature and frequency of power failures in the past, and it was able to prepare for the president a list of 148, or an average of about 1 a month for the twelve years studied. This was admittedly a poor comparison with the 10 failures a month cited in the first five months after the new orders went into effect in 1967, but in the absence of records covering power failures, the list included only "those interruptions which were sufficiently important to gain some measure of public notice." This was the language of bureaucracy; in translation, it meant those blackouts reported in the newspapers or about which some other information could be located and documented.

More than half of the 148 failures were attributed to storms and floods; 32 percent, to equipment breakdowns; 6 percent, to errors in operation; and 9 percent, to other causes, which included assaults on utility poles by motorists, who are forever knocking out electric service in the course of maiming themselves or terminating their own lives. Little varmints and critters contributed a small share to the twelve-year history of power failures. In Jacksonville, Florida, in April, 1964, a frog jumped simultaneously into a relay box and eternity and, by extension, into the FPC's report to the president. And again, the following April, a thing of no less fragility and no more substance than a bird's nest falling across a power line put out the lights and halted the production of energy in Chester, Pennsylvania.

Such reports, following the lesson-learning impact of the Black Tuesday cascade, have shown that although operational errors are comfortingly uncommon, every once in a while someone forgets to do something quite simple, such as read a gauge correctly or oil the machinery, and the mysteriously coursing electrons subdue the electrical system that is their closed universe.

In many respects, the nightlong experience of November 9–10, 1965, was, at least in retrospect, more of a lark than a disaster for some of the 30 million deprived of power. But had it struck in a blizzard accompanied by fifteen or twenty inches of snow, had the lasting and cumulative effects of the disaster been more tragic, the resulting public insistence on public-utility reforms might have been more sustained. As it was, some half-hearted attempts to induce the Congress to pass legislation bearing on the issue did not survive debate. Proposed reforms to guarantee reliability of power lost support when the utilities promised to accomplish voluntarily some measure of the perfection that proposed legislation sought to force upon them.

Inconvenience and suffering endured by consumers of electric power are, like corruption and tax inequities, conditions of modern life, conditions to which the populace seems to adjust. The 30 million victims of darkness did not persist in their cry for legislative guarantees for the future as long and as effectively as the electric utility companies persisted in their demand to be given another chance, free of government regulation, to make their systems cope with overloaded relays, falling bird's nests, uncomprehending squirrels, and self-asserting lightning arresters. Outrage, as every harassed urban dweller knows, is not generally sustained from one crisis to another.

Electric power, although as vital to modern life as any technology ever developed, never evoked anything resembling the response and passion that characterized, for instance, such issues as prayer in the schools, the sanctity of the flag, fear of bolshevism, sex education, fluoridation, and similar matters that perennially agitate office seekers and the populace. It remained for the historic blackout of 1965 and the rash of others that followed to focus attention on the sorry state of the electric utilities industry. The fact that the outbreak of public interest and attention was ineffectual in terms of the inconsequential reforms it produced had a good deal less to do with the question of its merit than with political mechanisms of government and their incapability of responding to clearly manifested public concern.

Like the great oil companies and automobile manufacturers, to which the electric utilities are politically and economically related in the business of producing energy, the privately owned power corporations are enormously experienced in deflecting attempts at government intervention in their affairs. Operating as franchised monopolies, with their customers deprived of options in choosing suppliers or shopping around for better rates and service, the utilities have traditionally operated as conventional, competitive businesses—which they are not. It is true, of course, that large oil and auto corporations over the years achieved dominance sufficient to share, rather than compete for, markets open to them. In this respect, their vast domains and the power exercised over them were comparable in some measure to franchised monopolies. But they were monopolies acquired through attrition, arrangement, and marketplace warfare, not, as in the case of utilities and television networks, by formal government gift and sanction.

The very least that any utility reform ought to accomplish might be the guaranteed reliability of a service that has become for most people in an industrial society an absolute necessity all the time. Fearful of power breakdowns in the future, the electric utilities would like to achieve a level of performance perfection, if only to keep their ratepayers quiescent, but they have been restrained by other priorities, some of them conflicting. It has been difficult for them to put a tired, creaky old industrial system in order, committing vast sums to catch up with current demands while scrambling around in the money markets—where they do, indeed, confront competition—for $10 to $20 billion a year in capital to build the nuclear plants and new generating units they need to furnish the increased power they have themselves promoted.

Some glimpses into the inner recesses of the power companies' dilemma were permitted in the official studies and dialogue stimulated by the blackouts and voltage reductions of the 1960s. Moreover, in the thirteen-state power failure of 1965 and in the brownouts that continued six and seven years later, a measure of the extent to which electricity encompasses nearly every aspect of life can be taken by many of the millions of people who have endured them. People in the inner cities in 1965 did not have to recruit hired hands to substitute for the loss of suction in the dairy farmers' milking-machine cups, but something memorable or sobering or frightening or amusing happened to nearly everyone. For many, until they could be assured that the dark and powerless night was not the starting signal for that long-threatened and half-promised nuclear attack, it was a time of paralyzing horror. Those trapped under rivers, in tunnels, locked in stalled underground trains, concluded, many of them, that they would be left to their isolated fates.

In New York, where the once-city-owned subway power system had been sold to the Consolidated Edison Company, rush-hour travelers were compressed in what seemed to be a black and bottomless pit. With guidance from subway personnel, passengers formed single-file lines and shuffled step by cautious step along the tracks to escapeways. The sight of ashen-faced people disgorged in disarray from the subsurface recesses was only slightly less unnerving than being part of the liberated passenger list. The refugees were then free to walk the unlighted and, for that night at least, strangely safe streets to their homes.

Surface railroad transportation, most of it supplied with private commercial power to operate signal and switching devices, stopped functioning generally until the light of morning brought deliverance to marooned travelers. Buses and automobiles, with their own generating support systems for heat and light, took aboard without fare or question all they could carry, only to be caught and immobilized in traffic jams caused by blocked intersections where no signal lights functioned. Wherever cars ran out of gas, they were abandoned or refueled from others, since electrically operated gas pumps were useless.

In gay camaraderie, walking throngs mingled on sidewalks and in traffic lanes, a wave of friendship encompassing all in an unintended urban preview of a later Woodstock. Lightness of heart, generosity, open-handed courtesy, and affability found easy expression in place of the usual detachment and the scarcely concealed combativeness that were the more commonplace characteristics of mass movement in illuminated hours. It had been a long time since there had been singing in the streets and warm and open good will among strangers in the congested urban world. When the lights went out, something nice in people seemed, in this instance, to turn on.

It was in the elevators that life took on new and narrow dimensions for those thousands of people whose descent from upper floors was suddenly arrested. In this claustrophobic world of suspended cages, people were wedged against one another in prolonged darkness, until building attendants or police could break through side and ceiling panels to rescue them.

Yet, all was not gloom in the dark of night. Families were brought close together in unheated quarters where, for once, no television dulled or excited the senses. People went to bed early, and couples made love so copiously and, it appeared, so carelessly that toward the end of the following July and the early days of August, the press gleefully reported a sharp, above-average increase in the birth rate.

Radio newscasters, their voices transmitted by stand-by generators, assured listeners in automobiles and those possessing the ubiquitous transistor and battery-powered sets, that no enemy saboteur had defiled the land but that the cascade originated in a trivial, isolated mechanical failure. Twelve television stations resumed operations with emergency generators, but the current to transmit television was meaningless to a powerless audience.

Gas heat served the people best that night but only when electricity was not required to operate thermostats. Oil and electric heaters were useless. In multiple dwellings where pumps were needed to fill tanks, no water flowed once stored supplies were exhausted, even for flushing toilets. In the suburbs, where electric pumps often dispatch sewage into leaching fields, the disposal systems did not dispose.

In an overdesigned society, overpowered people could not in their usually accustomed ways brush their teeth, carve a roast, stay warm in bed, or out of it, sharpen a pencil, heat the baby's formula, open a can, mix an eggnog, tell what time it was, read anything, make ice cubes, chill beer, wash or iron clothes, start an exhaust fan, have a massage, use a scalp vibrator, hear a doorbell, open a garage door or shut it, close or open draperies, make coffee, dispose of coffee grounds, play the family organ, squeeze orange juice, make toast, shine shoes, sew, look at home movies, turn on the television, use a power tool, listen to the radio, listen to records, type a letter, take a hot bath, shave, set the burglar alarm, or leave town.

In an analysis of the American passion for buying anything that consumes electricity, Jay Dolbin, an industrial designer from Chicago, determined that the average household had 168 options, or outlets, for doing so.* Most of them, said Mr. Dolbin, were not essential. In his judgment, this was altogether too many and represented waste, a shoddy scale of values, and often a contradiction to the convenience such devices and energy converters were intended to serve. Dependency on a single source of power did not produce options, safety, or convenience. It tended to make people careless about planning alternatives where opportunities existed to do so—as they do in one's own home—if impossible in offices, apartment buildings, and on the streets, where the ordinary person has little influence over the environmental conditions that surround and sometimes engulf him.

Individually, those injured or inconvenienced least by the collapse of electric power were those who by contrivance or frugality avoided exclusive dependency on the utility company for the energy and services they required. The dairy farmer with an emergency generator could get his cows milked. Oil lamps, candles, and battery-powered lights illuminated the darkness for those who chose to keep them in reserve. Alternative sources of heat, such as fireplaces or portable fueled heaters, and stored water for use when electrically driven pumps fail were protection against the failure of power.

Yet, these alternatives are difficult, often impossible, for city dwellers to provide for themselves. Inconvenience and suffering will continue to be the lot, and increasingly so, of people who demand or buy into or tolerate a technologically oriented society without demanding and enforcing, as a condition of acceptance, that it function reliably on the human scale. Since the American populace appears easily persuaded to buy, discard, and buy again virtually anything and everything—products, systems, services, and policies—that promises convenience, status, or pleasure, while remaining insensate to the larger problems thus produced, the accelerated expansion of energy usage and waste is foreordained.

For many months after the 1965 blackout on what became known as

---

* Five years after Mr. Dolbin's summary, forty-three additional gadgets and appliances were on the market. In an article in *Look* magazine, December 1, 1970, D. Bruce Mansfield, president of Ohio Edison Company and former Utilities Division lawyer with the Securities and Exchange Commission, somewhat proudly pointed out that "there are 211 electrical appliances now available for the household."

Black Tuesday, an advisory panel of eminent utility executives, corporation leaders, and government officials studied the power failure with the
view of providing policy guidance for the future. The panel found that
the simultaneous loss of five transmission lines "was not the type of
occurrence normally considered in engineering investigations concerning
planning or operating studies."

Such a statement could be amusing, perhaps, delivered by a professional comedian. Yet, it was an exercise in candor. The trivial, unbelievable tripping of a backup relay was indeed "not the type of occurrence"
that could be given credibility by sensible engineers not given to fantasy.
Nor was it credible in February, 1971, that one person could feed the
wrong code card into a complex nuclear warning system, thereby trigger-
ing the first of a series of developments to launch an intercontinental
atomic war. The latter was infinitely more horrifying than the former,
but both were distinguished by a single awesome characteristic: one inconsequential deviation from perfection and performance, which in one
case was capable of destroying power generation over 80,000 square miles
and in the other, of setting off a nuclear holocaust. One of the capabilities was realized, and the other was not. In each case, so much depended
on so little.

The Federal Power Commission, at the direction of President Johnson,
prepared a three-volume report on the Black Tuesday blackout, and in it
appeared this statement: "The initial reaction of the Northeast failure
was one of general disbelief that such an incident could happen."

Two hundred major power failures later, disbelief in such incidents
had become thoroughly dispelled.

Turning to their computers, technicians reconstructed electrical-sys-
tem behavior and devised, the public was assured, measures to anticipate
and prevent the recurrence of vast power failures from minor incidents.
And although procedures for detecting the symptoms of system failures
were considerably improved, no computer could independently *imagine*
or simulate an unpredictable minor operational incident if the engineers
and programmer overlooked it. Computers are incomparably marvelous
in helping engineers to comprehend and plan for anything that has a
capacity for disclosure. But in the absence of the human consciousness
that any given incident can occur, it has to happen once in order to
make subsequent computer simulations possible and predictable.

The electric power industry is the largest on earth, with a capital
investment (in 1971) in the United States of $104.2 billion. It has become
the prime consumer, aside from the United States and Soviet Union war
machines, of nuclear materials. As more and more uranium and, in the
1980s, the improbably dangerous plutonium become commonplace fuel

in reactors sited all over the nation and the world, the need for perfection in power performance will become absolute. An inadvertent incident is likely then to cause a good deal more inconvenience than putting out lights, stopping elevators, chilling households, and paralyzing transportation. It is theoretically capable of obliterating life and property over vast ranges by both violent and quietly insidious means. The fact that, as presently imagined, the likelihood of such occurrences is slight, cannot be taken as reason for confidence. Like the little relay at the Sir Adam Beck plant on the Niagara River, the unexpected lurks within all complex systems, and the more harm it is capable of causing, the more absolute is the perfection required. Since perfection is dependent thus far on man, and since man is by universal acknowledgment an imperfect creature, the kind of safety required for the commonplace production of nuclear power may not be obtainable with the resources now available on earth.

This does not mean that the risks will not be taken. It simply means that unless there is an extraordinary alteration in the nature of man and his commercial goals, the risks will be defined as less important than the benefits derived from taking them. At the same time, it means that they will be separated to the extent that the concentrated power of technology and economics permit, so that the risks and the benefits will be dispersed among different people.

Among the heralded, if rationalized, benefits to be conferred on the largest number of people in the phenomenal advances being prepared for the populace by the energy industry will be an increase in the number of ways consumers can use electricity. There will be many more options than the 168 enumerated and deplored by the Chicago designer, and they will burn up so much power, on the average, that the utilities have planned to deliver 30,000 kilowatt-hours a year per person by the year 2000. This is 500 percent more kilowatt-hours than the per capita usage of 1965, and the staggering increase cannot be considered fanciful. It is based on a steady, uninterrupted expansion of kilowatt-hour usage that, as the industry and the government see the issue, demands that the American capacity to generate power be doubled every nine or ten years.

This increased use of power is constantly advertised and promoted as beneficial and desirable, something explicitly equated with civilized progress, something to be sacrificed and done without only during those hours when for one reason or another the utilities cannot generate or transmit it.

It is widely believed, and probably was true historically even if it has become a cliché, that the development of civilization parallels exactly the increase in energy consumption. But this belief took little account of the uses to which energy was directed. It suggested that energy and power conferred civilized development on armed might and denied that a subsistence nation dependent upon bicycle, sampans, guerrilla warriors, and borrowed armaments had somehow achieved a relatively advanced and stable level of civilization on very little electrically produced energy. Civilization in Iceland is something of a world model, but it is not measurable, not in comparison with the United States anyway, in terms of energy expended. It is true that industrial development and energy consumption are closely related regardless of the goals sought in the application of energy. But no cause-and-effect evidence supports the arrogant thesis that the possessors of power and energy are the stewards of civilized progress, which at times has reached reasonable stages of development with little more than animal, water, wind, and people power.

Nevertheless, the industrialized nations do possess nearly all the world's capacity for producing energy, electricity included, by virtue of their access to the fuels, the processing facilities, and the essential technology to produce and transmit it to consumers prepared to pay for it.

In those areas of the world where electric power production is minimal or moderate, the doubling of power every decade could not do much harm for many years; but these are not the areas in which the proliferation of energy production will occur. It is the United States that is committed—perhaps it is doomed—to go on doubling and redoubling its power capacity, not those retarded countries that would not have much power in twenty years if they did succeed in achieving the same rate of advancement.

The United States seems bent on developing infinitely more of what it already has the most of because the markets for power exist or can be developed. Except for the money to be made in the process, it probably is not necessary. And the depletion of resources in accomplishing the goals of power production by methods presently proposed offers depressing risks out of all proportion to the glittering promise of benefits not necessarily associated with convenience or with need.

A good deal of redesigning of the electric power system, reappraising the human goals it is meant to serve, and protecting it so that it can function under pressure and unexpected conditions would seem to have priority over forced growth. The senseless promotion of the use of energy, with the resources it consumes and the destruction and pollution that follow, is a scandalous exercise in mismanagement. And individually, a few people in the power industry have begun to concede that the course they are driven (as they see it) by economic realities to pursue is wrong and inevitably dangerous. Although scarcely pausing in their forced march to expansion, some high management executives in the power industry suspect that the pursuit of money for their investors, increased production in each of several hundred large franchised domains, the acquisition of land and waterfront sites for generating facilities and transmission lines, the whole feeding of the insatiable energy giant cannot go on indefinitely. Some force or authority larger than the power industry—an uprising among the populace, the reality or imminence of terrible danger, the sudden functioning of a moribund and often corrupt government, some miracle of technology that will allow limitless and absolutely harmless growth—is depended upon to rescue the country and the industry. For the way a small and not-very-audible corps of power executives may feel personally is not the way a gigantic and nearly monolithic industry is going to act. The policy and objectives of the industry are to grow, expand, produce, promote, and profit, whatever the result and whatever the cost, which it is hoped will be less than the desired benefits. It is a capitalistic, industrial reality, and in the absence of strong governmental intervention determined to support a system of values in drastic contradiction to unrestrained expansion, no voluntary deviation from the pursuit of maximum sales and profits can be expected.

In theory, much of the harm inflicted by the incalculable expansion of electric power is capable of correction or stabilization at levels that, without more expansion, might be tolerated. The theory, however, is dependent on a condition of stability in energy usage and in the economy. Yet, neither the distribution of wealth, resources, and comforts nor political realities that confer power on the party and its leadership which most convincingly promises material benefits and the rewards of economic growth permit stability. Stability is seen, simply, as no growth, or very little. No growth in an industrial nation dependent on an increasing population as a market and on providing more material goods for a maximum of the populace is seen as stagnation and death.

In terms of ecology and conscience, the electric power industry depends most of all on new technology to render harmless, or at least acceptable, its contribution to ruin while it enlarges its contribution to industrial enterprise. Yet, it has made pitifully small investments on its own in research and development. It has concentrated on opportunism, sales, promotion, and growth and has got itself caught, with the rest of the country, in a dangerous trap where disaster looms if its present policies are reversed—and if they are not. Dependence on a miracle of some sort almost has logic in it.

The electric power industry is a highly fragmented network of individual monopolies; there is little cohesion or unity within it. A very few large utilities dominate policy. Reform in the electric utilities business

that would bring it into closer conjunction with human values not directly associated with profit and growth cannot and will not happen independently of major reforms required of government.

Unwilling or unable to exercise restraint in a political and economic
system to which it has become captive and which has conferred enormous rewards upon it, the electric utilities industry has itself become
a power that corrupts.

2

Lawlessness
and
Power

THE INDUSTRIAL revolution of the nineteenth century was an energy explosion. With the invention and application of steam-generated power, industry was propelled into technological advances measured in terms of enormously increased production. Energy originating in the movement of the wind, in gravity, water, and the muscles of beasts and people became uneconomic with the passing of time. Individuals could not compete favorably with mechanically generated energy, and in their desperate need and desire to do so, they were commonly exploited, overworked, and underpaid. The emergence of the steam-powered reciprocating engine, which was the invention of Englishman James Watt, and the development by the American, Robert Fulton, of the first money-making steamboat launched an era of manufacturing and trade increasingly dependent on mechanical rather than manual energy. The rail transport industry was born, and the era of the commercial sailing vessel, which had reached its highest level of development in fast transoceanic clipper ships, came to an end.

The explosion never subsided. When Thomas Alva Edison established the world's first central power station in New York in the 1880s, electric energy was used exclusively for incandescent lights. Then it was extended to light the darkness all over the world, to power industry, and in time to energize the gadgets and appliances that people became convinced were required for safety, comfort, and status. The release of energy in unimaginable volume, which in the beginning promised—as the combustion engine subsequently promised—to exalt mankind, diminish drudgery, and extend the range of man's mobility, did indeed change his world. But within eighty years, what liberated and improved human well-being, in combination with other forces that electricity unleashed, clearly threatened it.

Collectively, the generation and distribution of electric power is the largest business in the world. In the United States, it is second only to the government itself in size. Capital investment in the industry in 1971 was averaging $3 million a day, increasing on a scale that is expected to achieve a total capital value of $200 billion before 1980. Gross income from the sale of power alone, independent of business enterprises a number of utilities companies are running on the side, will reach $25 billion in 1972, in part with the help of $700 or $800 million worth of anticipated rate increases.

Of the 3,279 power systems operating in the United States, fewer than one-tenth of them (296, to be precise) are privately owned corporations producing 77 percent of the nation's electric power. Their share of the whole industry's 1971 electric bill was about $19 billion. Another $3 billion or so went to 10 federal agencies, 1,927 municipally owned utilities, 107 county and district systems, and 939 rural electric cooperatives. Together, they generated an estimated 1.6 trillion kilowatt-hours of electricity for 73 million customers.* The United States generates more than half as much electricity as all the other countries in the world. Its production equals that of the Soviet Union, the United Kingdom, Japan, West Germany, and Canada combined. By the end of the century, the power industry in America expects (and the federal government expects) the 1971 production of 1.6 trillion kilowatt-hours to increase to 10 trillion. Beyond that, growth is projected to levels difficult to project in coherent language.

By common agreement among private utility and federal power authorities, the growth of the industry is inseparable from that of the American economy; "one nourishes the other." † The thesis is inarguable within its own limitations, but it is the confinement of the argument to economic limitations that has caused rancor and anxiety in the country. A nation traditionally committed to expanding technology and production as its index of accomplishment has remained equally committed to finding ways to consume the energy it intends to develop, even if it appears

---

* In nearly all instances, figures and estimates cited are taken from documents and compilations of the Edison Electric Institute, the Federal Power Commission, and the American Public Power Association. The estimate of a $200-billion capital investment in the power industry before 1980 and the estimate of $25 billion in gross sales in 1972 are the author's own projections based on the same sources.
† Quoted from the Federal Power Commission, *National Power Survey, 1964:* Volume 1, page 39.

to be killing itself in the process. No political or social mechanisms exist to stand effectively against the thrust of power.

As the prime producer for the energy market in the United States, the electric power industry was under assault in the late 1960s, however, for arrogant disregard of public sensibilities; and it had begun to respond to mounting outrage against the polluted environment and its own expansion, to which the public itself, scarcely less than industry, had also contributed.

More than 95 percent of all electricity generated, excluding only hydroelectric installations, pollutes and otherwise damages the nation's air and water by both noxious emissions and heat discharge. Of all thermal generation in 1970, 60 percent was produced by coal-burning plants; 39 percent, by fuel oil, and gas; and 1 percent, by nuclear reactors.

In the outbreak of public questioning and hostility toward the major producers of energy and pollution, the largest corporate empires in the land, along with the government itself, were called upon to justify their conduct, their plans for the future, and their policy—or lack of it. It was the first time in American history that the aftereffects of industrial expansion, the destructive impact of energy production and consumption, were subjected to scrutiny and review.

Across the continent, in one bitter confrontation after another, electric utilities were in some instances persuaded, in others all but bludgeoned, into examining and altering plans for commandeering plant sites, heating the waters of lakes and rivers, fouling the air with outpourings from smokestacks, and frightening people with prospects of irradiating them with effusions from nuclear-fueled boilers.

Upper-echelon executives of power corporations, hardened by success and sometimes sanctified by it, responded with increases in their advertising and public relations programs to assure people that they were, and always had been, committed to environmental protection and the wise use of power. The promotion techniques of patting the public on the head and issuing syrupy statements of reassurance, of substituting the *impression* of responding to criticism for actually confronting it, had worked for many years. Little Disney-like characters, engaging make-believe fellows named Redi Kilowatt and Willy Wired-Hand, and sometimes reconverted television personalities with names like Uncle Wethbee, exuded their show-business charm through communications media to comfort, entertain, and tranquilize people.

But this time, previously effective bromides appeared to be unconvincing. Citizens' groups were formed and conservationist organizations brought suits to curtail the extension of power and pollution. Some utility management leaders began to concede in public that the old techniques were in need of review, that the new concern about nuclear plants (the "nukes," as critics called them), air and water pollution, rising electrical rates, and power failures could not be stilled anymore by circumventing fact and substance in favor of public relations packaging. A few managers in the power industry, along with an occasional engineer and administrator, began to sound like hard-core conservationists. Some even joined the Sierra Club and the Audubon Society.

Because the electric utilities, like automobiles, were so clearly visible, so perpetually and abundantly in evidence, with high-tension towers, belching stacks, poisonous fumes, and noise, they bore the brunt of the fury and frustration expressed by people and some of their legislators. But scarcely any sector of industry was guiltless—not the chemical companies, paper mills, food processors, steelmakers, oil and mining operations, cement producers, timber cutters, farmers and their pesticides, and air transport systems with their screaming jets' entrails discharging horizon-to-horizon graffiti across the sky.

No less culpable was a familiar figure once identified by the old *Saturday Evening Post* as *Swineus americanus,* that indigenous dispenser of waste and trash in all its forms: beer cans and pop bottles, hulks of automobiles, crumpled cigarette packs, foil and paper cups, disposable diapers, plastic and pressed aluminum discards, and similar residue. Not only on land but afloat, too. Garbage and human effluence were ejected in a mounting torrent from toiletless boats into harbors and waterways, there to join in turbid union with the coagulant contributions of commerce and industry.

After World War II, federal and state governments, and occasionally a local government, made generally unsuccessful forays into the field of pollution control. In a number of cities, notably St. Louis, Pittsburgh, and Los Angeles, organized efforts to prevent environmental disaster conditions had achieved interim success. But regulations and standards were not generally popular, and violations both of law and of civilized restraint were so widely practiced that, for all practical purposes, it was a lawless land insofar as environmental protection was concerned.

It had, in fact, always been a lawless land with respect to resources. For the better part of three centuries, little had been done to curtail even the most ruthless and predatory destroyers of human, animal, and vegetative life. Because the continent was so vast, settlers saw the resources, the breadth of the country, the forests, water, and grassy plains as a limitless bounty.

Except for staking out parks and wilderness areas now and then, no concept of preservation existed. In the presence of immeasurable treasure, restraint was scorned.

It was from this careless, often rapacious world that electric power companies emerged with the energy explosion set off by the multiple inventions of Thomas Alva Edison. The producers of electric energy simply joined those already engaged in exploiting oil, timber, agricultural, mining, water, and other resources.

The process was subjected to only minor and sporadic reforms until the era of Franklin D. Roosevelt, during which the Federal Power Commission was strengthened, holding companies were restricted, and the Securities and Exchange Commission was established. These legal mechanisms routed the marauding electric utilities for a time, but their wild proliferation seldom faltered nor did the dependence of American families and industry on them.

The pattern of expansion and dependence paralleled the doubling of the population in the United States. In the years from the end of World War I to the 1960s, the energy explosion and the population explosion were generally recognized as contributions to the growth and good of the nation; that, in fact, the country's future well-being depended upon them. It came as a shock for millions of people to have to learn that a popular assumption that seemed so righteous and true was ultimately false.

The dual assault on the country's resources by the energy and population explosions advanced in a vacuum of virtually no significant government countermeasures. Industry was unresponsive to the few scarcely audible cries for a measure of tender loving care for the environment. Industry and the largest sector of the citizenry were joined in a dependency on an expanding population providing markets for the polluting automobile, the basic end product of economic growth; on the enormous annual increase in electric power, which fueled the industrial system; and on an order of values that made the "good life" a bench mark of achievement. Reduced to simplistic terms, Americans were using up too much, consuming it too fast, and putting back nothing of value.

Considering the magnitude of the world resources problem, the failure of government to address itself firmly to the issue in the crucial years following World War II may very well stand as its most dangerous and inexcusable oversight in two centuries of national history. In the case of electric power, which energized every manufacturing process in the land, no agency or authority of importance noted that somewhere along the way, both the process and the products produced—and especially the internal combustion engine—were bringing the nation to a commitment to pollution. It was a commitment so vast, so institutionalized, that profound changes in the American economic and value systems and new behavioral patterns contrary to national tradition would be required for its abandonment.

The electric utilities industry was a primary polluter of water and air. The mining industry that supplied the hundreds of millions of tons of coal to feed the boilers laid waste to the land and waterways. But together, the measure of the damage they caused was a small percentage of the incalculable destruction perpetuated through the expanding grids and power-line networks that supplied electric current to the consuming, productive country. However, except for concentrations of smoke around metropolitan areas, where coal- and oil-burning generating plants produced complaints from residents who simultaneously demanded more and more electricity, the utilities did not evoke the full measure of mass fury over pollution until they started to build nuclear reactors.

The single event that began to put into focus and make comprehensible the deadly dimension of the ecological crisis was the publication in 1962 of *The Silent Spring* by Rachel Carson, a book that broke down the mythology that characterized the nation's previous response to ecological truth. Although *The Silent Spring* addressed itself largely to the effects of pesticides and herbicides on the food chain and lower forms of life, the publicity and dialogue that followed cracked open for millions of people a new and frightening view of a nation, if not a world, bent on its own ruin.

Even so, the suspicion lingered that conservationists were somehow eccentric, insensitive to economic tradition, committed to nostalgic and bucolic ways in contradiction to contemporary needs. Yet, the tide slowly began to turn, and a previously apathetic public, which had been so easily persuaded by government and industry that the benefits of progress outweighed the costs of dislocation and destroyed resources, bestirred itself. For the first time, ordinary citizens began to reflect on the doomsday perils of man-made poisons in the biosphere.

Since this turning point coincided with the emergence of atomic energy as a force to fuel power plants (thus giving promise of a vast, new nuclear power industry), it caught the electric utility corporations in its backlash. The power industry was under heavy pressure to increase production. In order to do so, utilities had begun to occupy large and highly visible sites along important waterways on which they planned to construct nuclear power facilities. They became a prime target for the newly released resentment of pollution and unrestrained expansion.

Suddenly, nearly all large industrial enterprises were under attack, warding off severe complaints, and forced at last to respond with dialogue if not with action. But it took some years for the government itself to respond, and even so, when it did react, it only halfheartedly confronted the dominant issue.

The Department of Justice directed some of its attention to General Motors Corporation and its three more or less allied auto makers—American Motors, Ford, and Chrysler—in the last year of the Lyndon Johnson administration. It had the industry indicted for criminal antitrust practices. It seemed, according to the indictments, that the automobile manufacturers had conspired among themselves, in an exercise antithetical to competitive free enterprise, to keep antipollution devices off all their vehicles until such time, perhaps, as all the competitors could produce models on which such installations would appear simultaneously. Nothing resembling so vile a charge had ever been directed against the electric utilities industry.

Good fortune rescued the motor makers from any punishment for their conspiratorial zeal. With the arrival of Richard Nixon in the White House and his new attorney general, John Mitchell, the indictments were set aside and a consent decree permitted. The auto industry and government spokesmen jointly promised the public that substantial progress would be made, beginning at once, in curtailing poisonous exhaust emissions from all combustion-engine vehicles. Motor manufacturers, who for years had, like the electric utilities, bothered little with the whole pollution challenge, pledged to undertake new research programs and comply with upgraded air-quality standards.

Meanwhile, Secretary of Transportation John A. Volpe—an exquisitely perfect choice for the job in President Nixon's cabinet, since he had been a contractor and highway builder—reported that 100 million vehicles were operating in the United States by 1970. A net gain of 5 million a year could be expected thereafter. Thus, much of that qualitative progress the industry was said to be making to reduce exhaust pollution was offset quantitatively by all those new cars on Mr. Volpe's highways.

In numerous instances, federal action against corporate lawbreakers was nullified, neutralized, or made palatable by compensating policy. Invoking a law on the books since 1899, the federal government in 1970 took action that resulted in fines for seven oil companies engaged in accelerated drilling operations made necessary to keep up with the needs of the electric utilities (which generate 40 percent of their capacity in plants fired by oil and gas) and, of course, of the automotive industry. The old law of 1899 had somehow escaped application and even notice over the years, but after a series of disastrous oil spills and offshore fires at Santa Barbara, California, in the Gulf of Mexico, and elsewhere, it was invoked to punish Chevron Oil Company with a fine of $1,000,000; Continental Oil, $242,000; Humble Oil, $300,000; Kerr-McGee Corporation, $20,000; Mobil Oil, $150,000; Tenneco Oil, $32,000; and Union Oil of California, $24,000. After its Gulf of Mexico platform and twenty-two wells exploded on December 2, 1970, Shell Oil faced a possible fine of $340,000.

When the Department of the Interior leased 539,000 new acres of offshore oil fields in the Gulf off Louisiana for $845 million, the largest venture of its kind on record, the successful bidders included Shell, some of whose wells were still burning at the time (January, 1971), Chevron, and each of the other oil companies fined for previous derelictions of one kind or another.

Because of a mounting shortage of fossil fuels intensified both by electric power expansion, with a huge new generating plant scheduled to go into operation every two or three weeks for the next twenty years,* and by a net gain of 5 or 6 million automobiles annually over the same period, the government announced that it had no choice except to permit the lawbreaking oil producers to increase drilling operations. Some of the same companies had been provided with further opportunities to help their country cope with the fuels shortage when they won the right to resume underwater drilling in the Santa Barbara Channel where, early in 1969, a half-million gallons of oil had disgorged upward from the ruptured sea bottom and stopped operations for a time. Far to the north, on Alaska's upper slope, perhaps the most extensive and remunerative oil deposits ever discovered await development when fears of ecological disaster can be reconciled with the necessity of keeping up with the energy production schedule.

Within a year of President Nixon's election, he found himself engulfed in a wave of national protest against pollution and ecological catastrophe. Although no one could remember his having mentioned the matter in twenty-five years of public life, Mr. Nixon reassessed the situation and made a moving speech about how awful things had become and how essential it was to clean up the American environment in the interests of survival. He proposed a modest legislative program to deal with the problem, and some of it was translated into law.

Nearly all the states established boards or commissions to implement federal standards or establish their own, but environmental cleanup operations in the states moved forward at an agonizingly slow pace because, it was reported, at least thirty-five of the state commissions had become populated with corporate and industrial personages whose companies were themselves recognized and even notorious polluters. Meanwhile, state regulatory commissions obliged to keep watch over the electric utilities and other franchised services were here and there reorganized to eliminate from public view a few of the kind of regulators who seemed

---

* Inconsistencies appear in nearly all documents and texts, including this one, with respect to the number of new power plants to be built by the end of the century. The number projected depends on their individual and collective generating capacities. The Atomic Energy Commission has predicted as many as 900 nuclear plants in the country by the year 2000—30 a year, on the average, beginning in 1970. If some of the nuclear plants reach a generating capacity of 10 or 15 million kilowatts, which is altogether possible, a single plant will be the equivalent of 10 or 15 generating 1 million kilowatts each. Some scientists have urged that new-plant size must be controlled by law, with capacity limited to 1 or 1.5 million kilowatts at each location.

excessively responsive to enterprises lacking enthusiasm to confront environmental problems. Mr. Nixon himself established a prestigious advisory board to convey counsel to the executive branch—and to deflect unwanted counsel, as well—on pollution and environmental policy. It was thought by some, notably a disappointed group of United States senators and congressmen, that Mr. Nixon might have selected a more appropriate person for his advisory commission than Mr. Birney Mason, board chairman and chief executive of Union Carbide Corporation. That giant of the American industrial hierarchy, major defense contractor, and operator for the government of enormous Atomic Energy Commission (AEC) facilities, had become, with its electric power plant and ferroalloy installations, the undisputed ranking air polluter in the region of Marietta, Ohio, and the river valleys of West Virginia, where it was the state's largest employer.

Mr. Mason had been personally involved in a prolonged conflict over his corporation's substantial contribution to the pollution of the air and water, to the distress of some of Union Carbide's stockholders, who objected to a good deal of unfavorable publicity about the case. The corporation had successfully avoided compliance with pollution-abatement orders for eleven years and had even barred lawful government inspectors from its plants without precipitating arrests or litigation. After Representative Ken Hechler of West Virginia made a report to a congressional subcommittee on his own unsuccessful efforts to get Union Carbide to comply with the law, Mr. Mason stepped down as chairman of the board in favor of a successor who went to work trying to improve the corporation's image.

Serving with Mr. Mason on the presidential advisory commission were twenty-five or so other high-ranking executives of nationally known polluting corporations. Thus, he was not exclusively entitled to the distinction that descended upon him as a result of publicity, although objections to his presence on the commission were quite vocal. It was not the first time nor the last, regardless of the critical significance of pollution issues, that those appointed to agencies obliged to implement official policy were unenthusiastic about or even hostile to such policy.

The chairman of the Federal Power Commission, John N. Nassikas, was a Nixon appointee whose legal career included working for electric utilities, which were subject to state and federal regulation, and for agencies doing the regulating. The Atomic Energy Commission, which promotes and licenses nuclear power plants, is heavily staffed with engineers and administrators moving alternately between the private sector of the nuclear industry, such as Union Carbide, and the public sector, which is the government. Another example would be the Justice Department, which harbors lawyers sworn to the duty of prosecuting antitrust actions against corporations for whom they subsequently work as defenders in litigation they helped prepare for prosecution. Thus, laws and policies intended to serve the larger public interest become extremely difficult to enforce when enforcement and regulatory bodies, or perhaps even the office of the president, prefer for one reason or another to exercise what is sometimes called "minimum zeal" (which is none at all) in favor of law enforcement.

Senator Lee Metcalf of Montana, among others, on occasion has become so incensed by presidential selections to advisory boards and regulatory commissions that he has pressed for legislation that would compel the appointment to such bodies as representatives of the public, members of conservation and environmentalist organizations, and student groups, noncorporate scientists, and private citizens, with no vested interests at all. Inevitably, such legislative proposals wither and die in the committees to which they have been referred for internment, and people with financial or other interests in the decisions of such commissions or agencies go on with their work more or less unmolested by outside or intervening forces. It is all quite legal, at least most of the time. It is the way power works.

3

The Beginning of Power:
The Emergence
of Edison

ELECTRICITY IS an eternal elemental and phenomenal force in nature emanating from the presence and movement of electrons. It can be induced chemically, observed and charted in the human brain, and made audible and visible in the lightning and thunder of the skies. It is the fiery hand of God, the thunderbolts of Zeus, the apocalyptic and abundant evidence of which has given soothsayers, saints, and theologians an ultimate vision of a planet consumed by fire, a terminal development that has become less improbable, since the capability of fulfilling that fateful prophecy seems to have passed from the realm of God into the province of his savage and unruly children. It is light and heat and power, and its origin lies in a negatively charged particle, the electron, so infinitesimally small that nearly 2,000 of them equal the mass of a single atom of hydrogen. If 1 ampere, or measure, of electricity may be imagined as roughly the current coursing through an ordinary household light bulb, the number of electrons passing any point in one second is 6,242,000,000,-000,000,000.

The generation and transmission of the interaction of these electrons is the work of the electric utilities industry that, as part of the vast enterprise of energy production, and except for providing food in all its forms and processes, is the most valuable service performed in the world. Although the phenomenon of electricity has been present since the universe emerged, it was recognized as little more than a strange vapor, a mystical force, and later a laboratory plaything for experiments that seemed to be leading nowhere, until an American free-lance professional inventor accomplished precisely what he announced he would do. Untutored in physics or mathematics, the basic sciences on which, it would seem, his work necessarily had to be supported, he assimilated the knowledge and studied the experience of all who had ever experimented with the unseen and unexplained force. And there had been many such men, some of whom came close to exercising control over electric energy, before the already renowned Thomas Alva Edison virtually invented and developed within a few years what was to become the electrical equipment and electric power generation industry.

The word itself, *electricity*, was coined in Elizabethan England when Sir William Gilbert, a court physician, became intrigued with magnetic materials. He found that by rubbing amber, a yellow fossil resin, a force was generated, much as it was when one vigorously ruffled the fur of a cat or combed one's own hair. The Latin word for force is *vis* and the Greek word for amber derives from *elektron*. Hence, he called the energy observed when friction was applied to amber *vis electricia*. Thus was the name born, although the magnetic force that could move particles of metal had been observed for 2,000 years.

Gilbert found that a buildup of friction could be discharged as a visible spark, which occurred when a charged object was brought to a critical juncture with an uncharged one. Sometimes the force was observed to repel, at other times to attract; such were the positive and negative characteristics of the induced energy.

When Benjamin Franklin, in 1752, flew his kite to demonstrate that lightning was the discharge of electricity leaping from a charged to an uncharged point, it was a wonder he wasn't killed. Human beings are notoriously vulnerable as conductors of electric current.

Alessandro Volta, an Italian physicist, was the first to collect electricity in a container. In 1792, after years of experimentation, he stacked alternate disks of silver and zinc atop one another, separated by pieces of flannel. When the multilayered sandwich was soaked in brine and the upper disk of zinc connected by wire to the bottom piece of silver, current flowed through the wire. The scientist's name lives in the word *voltage*.

Ten years later, a chemist in England, Sir Humphrey Davy, passed current through thin metal strips and watched them heat up until they glowed and nearly melted in the moment before they oxidized, thus sending across the years to Edison and others the dream of incandescent illumination. A Frenchman named André Marie Ampère led the way to the first electromagnet, and his name became a measure of current. A German, Georg Simon Ohm, by measuring the resistance of a conductor, turned *his* name into a noun that means a unit of resistance. But it was the incomparably original work of Michael Faraday, a protegé of Davy, that in nine years of effort converted magnetism into a continuous output of electric power. An obscure nobody who worked for a bookbinder, Faraday became a pupil of Davy's and met some of the celebrated scientists of the period. On August 29, 1831, Faraday made a discovery of unparalleled significance.

To an iron ring, he wound two coils of wire opposite one another, with insulation separating them from each other and from the ring itself. He discharged current from a battery that magnetized one of the coils while the second coil remained free of current. But at the moment of connecting and disconnecting the first magnetized coil and the battery, current was produced in the second coil. In changing the magnetic field of the first coil, he *induced* current in the second. Now he was on the very verge of controlling what were not known to exist: electrons. He spiraled copper wire around an eight-inch magnetic bar. When he stuck the magnet into the spiral of wire, current flowed through it. When he removed the magnet, current flowed in the opposite direction. When the magnet was held still in the coil, no current flowed. He could develop and sustain current by repeatedly severing "the lines of magnetic force." He was, in fact, making electrons behave according to his will in one of the great scientific discoveries. He said it was "power called into action." He did not know why this was so, but it was the beginning of man-made generation of electric energy.

He built a device in which a rotating copper disk turned between the poles of a horseshoe magnet, and as it moved, it cut the magnetic curve and dispatched current along an attached wire. He had invented the dynamo. Forty years old at the time, he lived another thirty-six years and never patented his invention.

Before and after Faraday, other men, often remotely located from one another, were at work fashioning the pieces of the mosaic that Edison fitted together less from theory than from practical application. Some of them made discoveries that, because of erratic communication among scientists and the disinterest of sources of capital, had to be rediscovered or appropriated many years later. Like the modern computer, which had to await development of high-tolerance hardware; and radio, which emerged only with the perfection of component technology, electricity could not emerge for use until cumulative experience over the years provided the foundation on which practical experiments could be conducted and the complex hardware, from generator to a bulb socket, could be designed and manufactured.

In 1870, in Belgium, a dynamo (to be known later in America as a *generator*) was devised to produce continuous current effectively. It was not yet evident, but with the development of the dynamo and the subsequent drum armature, the golden age of steam power was coming to an end. The centennial exposition of 1876 in Philadelphia was the last great show on earth in praise of steam.

While some visionaries and tinkerers were laboring to generate electricity, others were trying to make it do something useful. Edison was one of these. It was the incandescent lamp that illuminated Edison's name as the telephone rang for Bell. It was old when Edison invented it, and only with editing can it be said that he invented it all. But he made it function and kept it aglow.

In 1840, forty years before Edison's successful experiments, Sir William Grove made an incandescent lamp from a glass vessel partially filled with water and shielded from air to keep as much oxygen as possible from a coil of platinum wire that glowed from battery current. It worked, too, but only for moments at a time. The following year, another Englishman, Frederick de Moleyns, obtained the first patent on a lamp in which a bridge of charcoal glowed. And in 1847, a nineteen-year-old youth, Joseph Swan, who was a continuing threat to Edison, launched a twelve-year effort that produced lamps using paper carbon strips. But because he could not create a proper vacuum, he had to abandon the work until the mercury vacuum pump was invented in 1865. Ten years after that development, Sir William Crooks observed the presence of radiation when he directed current through an airless glass tube, and from this, in time, X-ray technology evolved.

When Swan learned of the experiment, he returned to work on incandescence, relying on the Herman Sprengel mercury vacuum pump and the Gramme dynamo to produce energy. Again, he produced a good lamp using carbon rods, but it burned out too fast for anything other than experimental usage. In America, Moses Farmer illuminated a room in his Salem, Massachusetts, home with lamps of platinum strips heated to a glow by batteries. And in 1874, two hundred lamps designed by a Russian scientist lighted the docks of St. Petersburg in what was then one of the wonders of the world, but they cost so much that they were abandoned. These bulbs filled with inert gas won for their inventor an award of $25,000 from the Russian Academy of Sciences. At the end of this primitively lighted trail came Edison to blaze a new one.

Thomas Edison's grandfather, John, was a loyal subject of colonial New Jersey when George Washington led a rebel civilian army against the king in 1776. A foe of the revolution, he was caught armed to fight against it, and was sentenced to be hanged by the New Jersey Council of Safety. With the acquiescence of his judges, he fled to Canada, lived out his life as a British loyalist, and sired a large family. One of his sons was Sam Edison, something of a reverse rebel, since he migrated back across the border to the family's abandoned country and settled in Milan, Ohio. There, his seventh son, Thomas, was born in 1847, the year Joseph Swan in England began work on the incandescent lamp. When young Thomas Edison took his fame and prospects to Menlo Park, New Jersey, in 1876, he was back at the place where his grandfather had been proscribed 100 years earlier.

A disheveled, slovenly boy, he was inattentive and preoccupied, a poor scholar reproached by his inferiors for being dull-witted. For an experiment in combustion thought to have been arson (he set his impoverished father's barn on fire), he was dragged to the village square and publicly thrashed. Unless the story was apocryphal, he was bloodily clawed by a pair of cats on whose furry backs he induced electricity by friction, having reduced their independent mobility by tying their tails together. His eccentricities moved his mother to channel misconduct and daydreaming into the study of classical literature and scientific texts, the works of philosophers, Shakespeare, Gibbon, and Newton, an extraordinary diet for a young boy. His education did not so much deflect his compulsion to experiment as intensify it.

Edison seemed driven to make use of knowledge as he acquired it. He set up a workshop laboratory in the family cellar with money obtained from peddling truck-garden produce, and built a crude neighborhood telegraph network that went out of action when a grazing cow tore down the lines.

At the age of twelve, in Port Huron, Michigan, to which his family had moved, he went to work as a hawker of newspapers and candy on the Grand Trunk Railway trains running between Port Huron and Detroit. After three years of riding the trains, he got a job for $25 a week as a night telegraph operator, a susbtantial salary notwithstanding Civil War inflation. The job followed five months of apprenticeship and training given him as a reward for rescuing the Port Huron station manager's toddling infant son from the path of an oncoming locomotive. By this time, at fifteen, Edison, whose hearing had been impaired by scarlet fever in childhood, was so deaf that he never, as he said pathetically, heard the birds sing again. It was a deficiency that seemed to increase his aptitude for telegraphy, in which the atonal clicking and irregular rhythmic sounds of dits, dots, and dashes were marvelously communicative.

As an itinerant telegrapher, he wandered from city to city, from New Orleans to Boston, an uncouth, supremely lonely, difficult youth, one of the nation's most accomplished telegraphers, experimenting with apparatus, getting fired, and building improvised devices for electrocuting cockroaches and rats. Along the way, he acquired a two-volume set of Faraday's *Experimental Researches in Electricity,* which served as his graduate study in transit. At twenty-one, in Boston, he had already developed a duplex telegraph for handling two messages simultaneously, doubling the capacity of Western Union transmission. Another inventor, J. B. Stearns, beat him to the patent, and Edison in 1869 sold his own dual transmitter for $400.

As an inventor-entrepreneur, he patented a device for counting and registering ballots, the forerunner of the voting machine, only to learn that an invention nobody wanted did not count for much. When the machine was demonstrated before a congressional committee, he learned that legislators preferred the delays and cumbersome inaccuracy of the old system under which manipulation of voting results and political chicanery could more easily thrive. Wiser, then, in the ways of the world, he went to New York, impoverished, homeless, and borrowing for meals until he discovered that although legislators disdained speed and accuracy in counting votes, financial operators were captivated by an efficient system of recording stock-market prices. In fact, it explicitly suited their practical purposes.

When Jay Gould and James Fisk were taking possession of the gold market in 1869 and all but sinking the United States Treasury, Edison was on hand to help them. As the gold raid progressed, the central stock ticker of the S. S. Laws Gold Indicator Company, which was indispensable to the Gould-Fisk high-speed operation, broke down. As dismayed brokers streamed into the street, Edison was on hand at the company's office, where he had been sleeping in the cellar. Franklin L. Pope, electrical engineer of the company, had befriended him. Edison fixed the ticker system, and within two hours the manipulators had their ambitious exercise in thievery under way again. He was hired at $300 a month and all that summer kept the ticker in operation. The United States government dumped its own reserves on the market, and the price of gold, which Fisk and Gould had engineered to sky-high levels, fell. The robbers then repudiated their purchase agreements in the spirit to which they were accustomed. They lost nothing, it was said later, but their honor.

Competition in the stock-ticker business was bought up by Gould, whose admiration for competition was proportionate to his ability to eliminate it. Thus, Gould had acquired power in Western Union, also in the stock-ticker field. Edison, who had no further enthusiasm for working for either Gould or Western Union, went into business with Franklin Pope at 78 Broadway. Theirs was a pioneer firm of consulting engineers. Edison turned out devices that Western Union sometimes bought to keep them out of the hands of incipient competitors. When he received $5,000 for a newly designed ticker using relay magnets, and Pope and a second partner split $10,000 for contributing nothing to the project, Edison quit and worked alone.

Making his own invention obsolete, he sold yet another design for $40,000 and won a contract to produce 1,200 of them for gross sales of half a million dollars. He learned for a time to stay out of the line of fire of Gould and Commodore Cornelius Vanderbilt as the latter sought to wrest control of Western Union from Gould. Even so, Gould ran him down.

Edison designed new machines and made a number of technological innovations for Automatic Telegraph Company, which constantly threatened the supremacy of Western Union's monopoly. Edison was somewhat delighted to be helping the smaller company take some of the business away from the giant. His delight turned to disgust when it became known that Gould, in absolute secrecy up to the time of disclosure, had been in full control of Automatic and monarch of the telegraph business all the time. Thus, Edison was tricked into making Gould richer with his inventions. And in the meantime, he was besieged by administrative and legal problems, especially litigation over patent infringements. He left the telegraph field altogether to develop the mimeograph, the phonograph, motion pictures, the vibrating diaphragm for the telephone, the electric light, and the system for generating and transmitting electricity, including the design and manufacture of components.

In 1876, at the age of twenty-nine, he established a laboratory and workshop at Menlo Park; and from it, there flowed what seemed to be an endless number of inventions. In one year, 1882, he filed 141 patent applications and by 1886 had more than 200 patents in his name. His shop in Menlo Park employed 250 men.

He devised an electrically powered pen for making stencils on paraffin-coated paper, which brought about the first production in quantity of a small battery-powered motor to run it, and then almost offhandedly invented the mimeograph.

Although Edison was disenchanted with Western Union, the company had persistently tried to persuade him to develop a "speaking telegraph," and he worked on the idea. Alexander Graham Bell, the progenitor of Ma Bell and the United States telephone system, beat him to it, however. At least Bell filed the first patent in 1876, but his telephone, which could receive sound fairly well, was an unsuccessful device for transmitting it over substantial distance. Edison's severe hearing impairment seemed to keep him compulsively interested in conveying sound clearly. He demonstrated almost to perfection his own vibrating diaphragm transmitter in a telephone connection bridging the 107 miles between Philadelphia and New York in March of 1878.

It is difficult to understand why he got virtually no credit for his contribution to the development of the telephone and Bell got all of it, largely for his work in the reception of sound. Edison was, however, in an important sense the coinventor of the telephone, for which he was paid $100,000 when Western Union sold its interests to Bell a year and a half later. In the interim, Edison and Bell poached on each other's patents, but the result produced a vastly improved and workable telephone. It also gave Western Union a rental income over the seventeen-year life of the patent of $3,500,000 from which Edison's $100,000 had to be deducted in what was a remarkable bargain for everybody but Edison.

The transmitting diaphragm could be redesigned to transmit sound for other purposes. Edison had in mind a device he thought might be commercially useful as a business office machine. In one thirty-hour work session at the Menlo Park laboratory, his little device of brass, iron, tin-foil, and a needle was successfully put together; and engineers spent half the night singing and declaiming into it, listening enraptured to the sound of their own voices over the first phonograph. No one had ever heard his own voice before except, perhaps, as an echo.

It was a new and absolutely original invention on which not even a related or supporting patent had been previously issued. Until demonstrations of voice recordings were offered in public, there were some doubts about Edison's accomplishment. The idea of preserving sound inside some device and summoning it forth on command defied credibility. Suggestions appeared in the press that perhaps the invention was an advanced form of ventriloquism. Even after it had been demonstrated, and before issuance of the patent on December 5, 1877, a skeptical clergyman, who had mastered the pronunciation of a long list of nearly unutterable names culled from the Bible, shouted the names at top speed as the recording cylinder turned, in a mighty effort to trip any ventriloquist, who would be so tongue-tied trying to match the performance that the suspected fraud would be exposed. Edison was unperturbed and emerged from the demonstration and the enormous publicity as a more renowned celebrity than he had been before.*

Edison never deluded himself; he knew he was not a scientist. Nevertheless, he began work on the project that had thwarted physicists and other scientists with a simple directive to himself to convert electricity into light. Encouraged by Grosvenor P. Lowrey, a patent lawyer and counsel for Western Union, whose interest in corporate income was at

---

* The literature on Edison is, of course, extensive, although earlier biographical material is overdosed with hyperbole and unlikely anecdotes. The latest biography, and a good one, is by Robert Silverberg, *Light for the World: Edison and the Power Industry* (New York: Van Nostrand Reinhold Company, 1967).

least equal to his scientific hopes, Edison picked the brains of the living experts and absorbed the literature of the past to give himself intellectual mastery of the field he would transform into the generation of energy, light, heat, and power.

When the inventor disclosed that he and his Edison Electric Company intended to develop a practical, long-burning incandescent lamp, he was at the pinnacle of fame. His stature was sufficient to depress the price of stocks in gas companies, some of which depended on lighting for 95 percent of their income. Edison predicted that gas would survive and prosper as energy for heating, not for illumination, and he was altogether prescient about that. Gas indeed became a significant form of heat energy, and in the next century, after World War II, it became, along with oil, the new fuel that generated electric power.

Edison, to fulfill his promise, had to conquer a problem his gifted and highly educated predecessors had been unable to solve. Electric current was simply too dangerous to be transmitted into households at the voltage levels dispatched from a generating plant. Low-resistance conductors were required to allow current to flow gently and safely without producing intense heat. Edison proposed, he said, to "subdivide" the current, parceling it out, so to speak. Experts scoffed, and one acknowledged authority in England, Sir William Preece, said that the proposal was beyond accomplishment.

Using a carbonized sewing thread as a filament, Edison got a lamp burning for forty hours, which was not long enough and too expensive anyway. He would, he said, make electric lighting so cheap that only the rich could afford to burn candles.

With the unpromising 40-hour lamp discarded, Edison sought a longer-lasting filament. He tried using hair from the beard of an assistant but could not make it work any better. Then, a carbonized strip of paper served well enough to burn for 170 hours. This had been used before, notably by Swan in England, and patent suits would have been inevitable if Edison had not bypassed them with the subsequent use of bamboo fibers. Concurrently, he developed a vastly improved dynamo, first scorned as a perpetual motion machine, that was three times more efficient than any previously used. Edison stock went to $500 a share and in time reached $5,000, making him worth, on paper at least, $10 million. He held open house and lighting demonstrations at Menlo Park, stimulating public interest and stock-market activity. In fact, there was in Edison more than a touch of the huckster.

When he discovered that bamboo fibers made the best filament for his incandescent lamp, he indulged in a publicity hoax that titillated newspaper readers for a year and a half. He dispatched scouts to faraway places in the world, presumably to locate the perfect bamboo supply.

One prospector, Frank McGovern, returned to New York after fifteen months with tales of adventure, battles with monstrous serpents, and extreme privation. He told of his unlikely exploits at a publicized dinner in a Manhattan restaurant, from which he departed late in the evening, walking toward the West Side docks, never to be seen or heard of again. Like the lost Judge Crater of a later day, he simply disappeared. Meanwhile, Edison's first and more quietly productive scout, William H. Moore, contracted in Japan for all the bamboo ever needed.

Edison was acclaimed anew when he installed dynamos and lamps in private yachts owned by conspicuous consumers of the era. The S.S. *Columbia,* owned by railroad magnate Henry Villard, was equipped with an electric power system, and its lights burned without a failure for 415 hours on a two-month voyage to San Francisco. Villard joined the board of the Edison Electric Company and advanced $40,000 in development funds. Despairing over expenses and perhaps irritated by the carnival quality of the publicity, rather than the electricity, that was generated, investors pressed the inventor to get an effective, land-bound power system in operation. He complied with a demonstration on Election Day at Menlo Park. When Edison's own choice for president, James Garfield, was elected, he illuminated the area in a dazzling display. It was, nevertheless, an extension of a laboratory demonstration, nothing that could be sold and serviced to the public for corporate income.

The Edison Electric Illuminating Company, an early ancestor of the giant Consolidated Edison of New York, was then organized to dig trenches in the streets and to build and operate the first city power system. Edison himself despised the overhead telegraph lines that disfigured the city and insisted that electric wires be placed underground. He would have endeared himself to twentieth-century conservationists and urban planners, repelled as he was by utility poles, towers, and overhead wires across the land.

With the help of a young administrative genius named Samuel Insull, imported from England to serve as his secretary, Edison sold his equity to raise capital withheld by his wary backers. He formed manufacturing companies to make switches, fuses, fixtures, dynamos, virtually everything needed to build a central power station and a transmission system. While Insull roamed the country tracking down capital, Edison, at thirty-four, found a plant site at 255–57 Pearl Street and began training technicians at his headquarters at 65 Fifth Avenue. He learned at once what electric utilities were seldom in the future allowed to forget: that graft in one form or another must be paid for the freedom to do business. He paid $5 a day to city inspectors who had nothing to inspect and whom he never saw.

By August, 1882, he had fifty buildings wired and lines leading into them. With new generators built in the Gardner C. Sims Rhode Island shops and a thousand lights tight in their sockets, Edison was ready. J. P. Morgan, who by then had the largest holdings of Edison stock, had 106 lamps ready for illumination at the offices of Drexel, Morgan and company at 23 Wall Street. Edison arrived at the office collarless; he had been working at the Pearl Street plant and forgot to put a collar on. Insull, Morgan, and entourage were waiting. John W. Lieb remained at the plant, standing on a bench, ready to throw the circuit breaker connecting the generating units to the system.

At Morgan's office, someone bet Edison $100 that the lights would not go on. Gravely, Edison covered the bet. It was 3:00 P.M., the moment John Lieb, whose watch was set to the second hand with Edison's, was to do his job. Edison's hand was on the master switch in Morgan's office. He moved it to the connecting position. The lights went on. Calmly, he said: "I have accomplished all I promised."

The age of electricity was under way. Soft, mellow lights "grateful to the eye," as the *New York Times* reported, would now make daylight out of the night.

Safe, odorless, nonflickering light powered by energy produced in a central power plant elevated Edison to perhaps the most renowned celebrity status in the world. Had he been an accumulator of wealth, like his contemporary in the energy business, John D. Rockefeller, or had he possessed more of the latter's business and administrative ability, Edison could surely have become, like Rockefeller, one of the wealthiest and most powerful of men. Interest in such rewards simply did not sustain him. Yet he liked to speak of modest opportunities to make money that were brought to his attention.

When a junction box at Ann and Nassau Streets began to leak current into the moist earth, such an opportunity presented itself. A ragman on a wagon hauled by a poor old horse passed over the electrified ground, and the shocked animal reared and thrashed in its traces. It was guided to safety beyond the range of current. The incident inspired a dealer to go to Edison with a proposal to electrify the ground of a paddock where he bought and auctioned horses. It was his plan to round up derelict animals and, by judicious applications of current, make them prance around like energetic thoroughbreds. Although promised a generous share of the profits for his contribution to the scheme, Edison declined this and other fanciful proposals.

J. P. Morgan, present on the first day of the world's most promising new industrial creation and an acquisitive investor in the Edison enterprise, wanted immediate and maximized profit for his act of faith and

capital commitment. He was, however, disinterested in central power
stations of the kind installed on Pearl Street. They were costly capital
investments and probably would be slow to pay short-range dividends.
He preferred the installation of on-site generators supplying single customers, as in the case of Henry Villard's yacht, commercial buildings,
public institutions, and the like. Each customer would thus purchase his
own coal, see to it that his own machinery was manned and maintained,
and of course pay for the installation at once, at which point profit could
be instantly realized. In this manner, the largest amount of income would
be returned most quickly at minimum capital outlay on the part of the
Edison companies. It would be a point-of-purchase product, delivered
and paid for and done with.

Edison saw the electrical industry's growth as dependent primarily
on central power stations, each generating and transmitting current to
hundreds or thousands of customers, all paying operating companies
year after year, all their lives. The chasm that separated the opposing
outlooks of Morgan and Edison was a wide one, and Edison tried to
bridge it by moving in both directions simultaneously. By the spring of
1883, his illuminating company had 334 single-purpose, on-site generating
systems in operation. But he put Insull in charge of the Edison construction department, which within eighteen months had contracts to build
central power stations in more than twenty cities and towns. The Edison
Illuminating Company, of which Morgan was the largest shareholder,
paid its first dividend of twenty-five cents a share in the summer of 1885.

Edison knew he was no Rockefeller and that the business needed
administrative talent. He hired a telephone company executive, Charles
E. Chinook, with a promise of a $10,000 bonus if he raised profits to a
level of 5 percent of a capitalization of $600,000. When Chinook accom-
plished this, the Morgan group declined to honor the commitment, and
Edison personally paid the bonus. Morgan said he was "sorry," but Edison called it "Wall Street sorry," and remained embittered by the
rapacious Morgan bankers. His independent companies began to make
money in 1884, and he acquired equity in the local power stations established through Insull's contracts. Then the Morgan group, eager to control what they had earlier disdained, tried to take over full control but
retreated in the wake of Edison's fierce opposition. By 1886, 500 of the
on-site plants that Morgan liked were in operation; but at the same
time, 58 central stations were generating power and transmitting it to
customers. Edison lighting companies had reached Italy, Russia, South
Africa, Germany, and a dozen other countries. He had grown rich on
dividends alone. Then electric streetcar companies began to expand, and
power output increased accordingly. After a conflict with his employees,

Edison moved his manufacturing operations to Schenectady, New York, only to relinquish control altogether to General Electric Company, the giant in the electrical and, in time, the nuclear power equipment field.

Henry Villard, after losing his railway empire, tried in 1888 to turn the electrical industry into a worldwide cartel controlled by German interests. Edison was offered $500,000 worth of stock in the proposed conglomerate, but Morgan, horrified at the prospect of a cartel he himself did not control, rebelled. A new company, Edison General Electric, was formed; and Edison surrendered control to it for $1,750,000 in cash and securities, glad, he said, to be rid of "the leaden collar" of Morgan. Insull got $75,000, and Edison Illuminating Company became an independent concern. General Electric dropped Edison's name entirely from its corporate masthead; Morgan remained banker of the operation; and Henry Villard was cast out entirely. Nine of eleven directors on the GE board in 1892 were Morgan men. Only Edison himself and one associate, Frank S. Hastings, remained. Insull departed for Chicago to start a utilities empire of his own.

Blackouts and power breakdowns plagued the central electric stations from time to time, and in 1890, eight years after it opened, the Pearl Street station burned down. The power was off for only one day; by that time, neighboring plants could absorb the load.

With the creation of GE, Edison had little or no further influence on the development of the great power industry. Grief-stricken over the death of his wife, he faltered, his judgment wavered, and although still a young man, he never again moved with the sure touch or sustained fertility of mind that characterized his earlier years.

Edison had adopted the direct-current technology. He was committed to low-amperage systems because they were safe and the current of 110 volts could not ordinarily kill anyone unless the victim was soaking wet. But low voltage meant that transmission was limited to a mile or so, thus necessitating more and more central power stations.

The development of the transformer allowed long-distance transmission, and at one point, Edison was sufficiently interested to take a $5,000 option on the idea before rejecting it. It was a foolish move, for he was rejecting, in fact, the pulsating, alternating-current system that revolutionized his own electrical empire.

Standing by in the wings of industrial history was George Westinghouse of Pittsburgh, who had made a fortune supplying air brakes to railroads, ready to snap up the opportunity Edison lost. With a consultant, William A. Stanley, Westinghouse patented a system for generating 500-volt power stepped up to 3,000 volts for transmission, then lowered by transformers for use in lighting. Westinghouse bought a little lighting company in Manhattan in order to build up his inventory of patents and conducted a full assault against the entrenched business.

The threat seemed to unhinge Edison. He began to sound like the old conservative experts who said he could not subdivide current. With Westinghouse talking about using power of 10,000 volts, stepped down for conveyance into households and offices, Edison retorted: "Westinghouse will kill a customer within six months."

Nikola Tesla, a former low-level employee of Edison's, had developed the alternating-current motor, but with only direct current available, it was useless. Tesla had worked with the French Edison Company in 1883, at the age of twenty-seven, and was sent by discerning advisers to the inventor, who directed him to perform menial tasks and would listen to no talk of alternating current. Tesla quit within a year, rounded up some financial support, and established the Tesla Electric Company as owner of his patents on the a.c. motor and distribution system. Westinghouse found him, gave him $1 million and royalties for his patents, and in his predatory fashion, all but ran him off the premises, retaining in his own possession the most advanced technology in electricity.

Edison, determined to prove that his own system was not passing into obsolescence, decided to demonstrate that alternating current was deadly and dangerous. He chose a gruesome method of doing so.

Having set up an alternating-current generator in West Orange, New Jersey, with 1,000 volts of current, Edison invited the press and witnesses to view the electrocution of a collection of stray cats and dogs. The animals met their death when the current was applied to metal sheets onto which they had been herded. He moved from that experiment into the realm of political lobbying and tried to get state laws passed limiting electric current to low voltage, and nearly succeeded in getting an 800-volt ceiling in Ohio and Virginia. Failing that, he promoted a demonstration in which a human being would be electrocuted with alternating current. That, he surmised, would prove conclusively how dangerous George Westinghouse's system was.

Harold P. Brown, of Edison's laboratory, was assigned to lobby for a bill in the New York legislature to develop an electric chair for the execution of criminals condemned to death. Brown bought Westinghouse generators and in highly publicized, and highly repulsive, demonstrations electrocuted a number of large dogs, four calves, and an aged horse. Eight hundred volts of alternating current (the maximum Edison thought allowable) killed the dogs in ten seconds. The young cattle, offering more resistance, died in fifteen seconds. The horse lingered for twenty-five seconds at 1,000 volts. Mr. Brown thought 2,000 volts would provide a painless, "humane" death for a human being. As it happened, one was available.

William Kemmler, having been convicted of murder, was sentenced to be electrocuted at New York's Auburn Prison on June 24, 1889.* He had been reprieved twice while Brown's experiments were in progress. Edison himself had testified at a legislative hearing on the matter of the electrical resistance of human beings. It seemed they varied a great deal. Of some 250 people measured, he testified, some had an average resistance of 1,000 ohms, one went as low as 600, and one as high as 1,800. One of the convicted killer's lawyers, W. Bourke Cockran, wondered whether Mr. Kemmler would be carbonized like the filament in one of Mr. Edison's lamps, in case it took him five or six minutes to die. Probably not, Edison deduced, since all the fluid in the man's body would evaporate or boil away under such a charge of current. The body would be only mummified, not carbonized.

On August 6, 1890, a Westinghouse generator capable of 1,500 volts, powered by a steam engine in the prison basement, administered a prolonged shock to Mr. Kemmler, who consumed more time dying than Edison had thought he would. Although invited to attend the affair, Edison stayed away.

In 1922, eighteen-thousand employees and guests of General Electric at Schenectady welcomed Edison at a ceremony celebrating the seventy-fifth anniversary of his birth. The great Charles Steinmetz, German-born engineer and inventor, was on hand to vaporize a bar of tungsten, which replaced bamboo in lamp filaments, with 120,000 volts of electricity.

Encouraged by his friend, Henry Ford, Edison labored in his laboratory on such projects as making rubber from goldenrod. He made a set of tires for his Ford touring car in 1929.

On the 50th anniversary of the successful demonstration of his incandescent lamp, President Herbert Hoover journeyed to the festive public relations ceremony, with Henry Ford as host, at Dearborn, Michigan, to praise the inventor for his contributions to humanity. The all-day program was arranged by Edward Bernays, a pioneer in engineered opinions and image building.

When Edison died on October 18, 1931, it was suggested that all the lights in the country be turned off for one minute. To cut off illumination everywhere at once would have required pulling the switches at every central power station in the country. The plan was abandoned on the grounds that electricity had become so vital that its loss even for sixty seconds could not be tolerated. No blackout involving 30 million people had yet confirmed the point.

---

* A fictionalized account of the electrocution of William Kemmler, the conflict between Westinghouse and Edison, and a good deal of other conflict as well, is given in an excellent novel by Christopher Davis, *A Peep into the Twentieth Century* (New York: Harper & Row, 1971).

Edison was always confident that electricity would provide the energy to power the motor cars which his friend Henry Ford had made in such volume and so cheaply that, even then, pollution, traffic congestion, and noise had begun to offend the nation that bought and enjoyed them. He was as wrong about that as he was about alternating current, but in his distaste for the internal combustion engine, as in his objection to above-ground transmission lines, he anticipated conditions that became a paramount issue of a later time.

At Edison's death, $15 billion had been invested in the United States power industry, which served 87 million people. Nearly 3,900 central plants were generating power. By 1960, investment had increased beyond $50 billion, and 10 percent of all capital investing was channeled into the industry. The total passed $104 billion by 1971 and is expected to exceed $200 billion before the end of the decade. Dollar values cannot be predicted for the year 2000, but with a little year-by-year inflation as a continuing character trait of the economy, and with power industry expansion more or less certified, at the end of the twentieth century it could very well be producing 10 trillion kilowatt-hours of electricity with its capital investment of $1 trillion. When one considers that the gross national product reached $1 trillion in 1971 and that in twenty-nine years the electric power industry alone might equal that figure, the outlines and imagery of the growth picture become increasingly clear.

The electric utilities have flourished beyond any measure that could have been predicted or imagined at the time of Edison's death. Yet, it has scarcely begun its explosive course. Edison's associate Samuel Insull had already built a power empire holding company of gigantic and profitable proportions, and it, too, even after its financial collapse, could only grow. The industrial cities of America lay under interminable deposits of fly ash and soot that fall from skies darkened by the disgorgement of smoke from unfiltered, wide-open stacks over coal-burning power plants.

Yet, in eighty-five years of electric power expansion, little thought was given either by government or by the utilities—or by the great industries they energize—to the conditions they were causing. Ruin of environment has gone all but unnoted except among a somewhat-suspect group of people known as conservationists, bird watchers, and naturalists. Sporadic complaints on the part of health officials were held to be of little significance as the nation praised and congratulated itself on its prosperity, ingenuity, peaceful intentions and competitive free enterprise. Cumulative knowledge and technology and the development of responsive political mechanisms, in the forty years since Edison's death, should have made, one might suppose, a basic contribution toward planning for the future. It does not appear to be the case.

The utilities have looked to the future in 1971–1972 for the most part as they did in 1931. They have assumed that continuing industrial expansion and consumption of resources is, with adjustments to problems posed by pollution and congestion, more or less beyond challenge. Nothing basic in the growth projection scale will change. More and better technology can—indeed, it has to—resolve any problems of future years. So it has been proclaimed.

The only questions, by and large, are how to produce the staggering loads of increased power, by what means and what fuels, by what technology, and how, if possible, to reconcile the loss of land and water to plant sites and the damage done by pollution. Unasked and unheard in the upper echelons of economic, political, and electric power is a haunting question that sometimes disturbs individual men and women at lower levels of the power hierarchy: Is so much power serving essential human purposes? Or, more simply stated: Who needs it?

4

The Marketing
of
Convenience

ON THE DAY that Samuel Insull, at the age of twenty-one, came into Edison's life, the inventor became, by any comparison with the past, an organized man. Selfless, tireless, imbued with relentless self-discipline, Insull quietly and competently helped the thirty-four-year-old slipshod genius become the managerial personage he was otherwise incapable of becoming. Insull accomplished it virtually without Edison noticing it, which was probably why the touchy, often-temperamental Edison tolerated it. Strong, overtly ambitious men withered or became resentful around Edison, or they were driven off.

Edison was Insull's hero long before the two met. As a gifted administrator with the deceptive detachment of a professional diplomat and a capacity for invisibility, Insull nevertheless possessed a computerized, Machiavellian mind. He was one of the most perfect subordinates in American industry and had no equal until the arrival of Thomas J. Watson, the puritanical peddler who contributed his formative years to John Henry Patterson and the National Cash Register Company in Dayton, Ohio, before he went onward and upward to International Business Machines and industrial immortality.

Something in the dualistic nature of men who worked long and effectively in the ego-bruising subordinate positions seemed, in the Victorian era of capitalism's explosive growth, to develop in them the discipline, the single-mindedness of purpose that drove them, and sometimes compelled them, toward dominance and success. To Edison, Insull had the value of a dozen staffmen. He was as undemanding as a contented slave, thriving solely on the freedom to serve his master in work.

Insull was born into a family of lower-class, radical British prohibitionists. He was a defender of, and personally assimilated, the stuffy style, the pompous virtue and conduct of the mercantile era. Forest McDonald, who was associate professor of history at Brown University when the University of Chicago Press published his biography of Insull in 1962, wrote that the young bluenose Samuel imbibed the "prejudices, values, and platitudes" of the Victorian age. He even responded constructively to the cruel thrashings administered by a clerk who was teaching him shorthand. The clerk, an inheritor of British cultural and educational traditions, birched him periodically to stimulate the learning process.

Samuel's parents were temperance crusaders, and the father's job as secretary of a British prohibition league had taken the family to Oxford, where the two Insull boys attended a school staffed by Oxford students. After a menial post with a firm of London auctioneers, he was hired by Thomas G. Bowles, founder of *Vanity Fair* and a celebrated figure in England and on the Continent. He found that he could commit nearly everything he read to memory and call forth stored knowledge on command. These natural aptitudes, combined with his capability in shorthand, made him a human computer, quite able to store data, classify it, recall it, and print it out. His rapid accumulation of encyclopedic knowledge in international business, real estate, publishing, finance, and the pecking order of European society compounded his value.

When Colonel George E. Gouroud, European representative for the Edison interests, met the youth, he was so impressed that he hired him away from Bowles to accompany him to conferences with bankers, government officials, and businessmen. His high-speed shorthand and a photoplate memory gave Insull more retained information about Edison's operations than Gouroud or anyone else possessed. All this was noted at their first meeting by Edward Johnson, who, in 1879, as Edison's chief engineer, decided to try to get the young man into the United States and into the office of Edison himself. Johnson knew by intuition and experience that the disorganized Edison and the emergent but not fully developed Insull, with his quick, sure grasp of knowledge and subserviently unobtrusive nature, belonged together. The meeting of Insull and Edison was the industrial equivalent of wind against sail, of converging forces creating together what was beyond accomplishment alone.

It took Johnson two years to get them together, but early in 1881, he cabled Insull to go to New York. Arriving at the great man's office at 65 Fifth Avenue, Insull looked for all the world like a neat but callow teen-ager. Edison, looking a good deal older than his disheveled thirty-four years, was reported a bit dismayed by the improbably boyish Insull but nevertheless addressed him with cool dignity. He explained that Morgan and his backers had put half a million dollars into Edison's electric light company but would advance not a dollar more. Thus, there was virtually no money for manufacturing equipment and components or for constructing an absolutely essential central power station.

Moreover, Edison went on, capital not available through Morgan was equally unavailable elsewhere in the United States. With $78,000 cash on hand, only Edison's own telephone securities in Europe offered any chance of financing an electrical-system development.

Morgan and the bankers would, it appeared, have allowed the promise of electric power to diminish and, for a time, die. It was Edison who took the larger risks with his own resources, fulfilled the promise, and enriched Morgan and the bankers.

Moved by Edison's tribulations, Insull developed an unrelenting loathing of Morgan and the eastern Establishment bankers. He crossed the Atlantic again and, with discreet skill improbable for one so young and physically unimpressive, disposed of Edison's shares on the European continent. He returned to New York and began guiding Edison and his chaotic enterprises toward an orderly big business.

He gentled the impetuous, often tyrannical Edison and made the system function without ever having a clear line of authority or even a title. Insull always said they never made a dollar until Edison and his companies were separated by the distance between Manhattan and Schenectady, where Edison's principal manufacturing operations were finally located.

Insull worked with Edison for twelve years, galled but undeterred by the Morgan investors who wanted, not central stations for developing long-range power service, but fast-dollar, on-site systems paid for in cash. Insull grew to despise the investment bankers more intensely for forcing Edison to pay them for the right to use his own resources— his own patents and inventions—to finance manufacturing operations that made fortunes for those who opposed them. His Victorian morality, which he later adjusted to comply with the harsh realities of combat and corruption in Chicago, was then outraged. He had not yet come into contact with the institutionalized larceny of the cities or the well-ordered felonious dilution of security values that electric utilities and freewheeling holding companies converted to common practice.

Eight companies made up the Edison complex, with the Morgan-dominated holding company the beneficiary of much of the profits while generally free of liabilities. Insull traveled around the United States selling power plants, and the Edison companies built them, from generator to transmission lines to the lights in the sockets.

A business slump in the mid-1880s and the death of Mary Stillwell Edison, whom Edison had married when she was sixteen, seemed to stun the inventor. Insull recognized that after the electric lighting business was started and after Mary's death, Edison was never the same vital man again. He worked around the vague, often apathetic Edison. Other associates, among them Johnson, the chief engineer, teamed up with outsiders and made fortunes in the electric streetcar business. Insull himself found a partner and went into business as the Bates Manufacturing Company. But by then an authority in the banking and electrical businesses in the United States and Europe, he ran the Edison enterprises with a skill bordering on magic, particularly in view of the fact that Morgan's financial policy seldom allowed more than $10,000 cash on hand in the Edison treasury. Insull developed and refined the practice of expanding credit, almost never paying cash for anything when he could sign a note.

Morgan's tight-money policy made his education in the art of credit essential, but Insull was induced, in any case, to do what his whole nature preferred. He took to loans and credit and later to floating bonds and stock issues with the fervor of an aroused maiden hungry to widen the range of experience. But unlike the maiden in the metaphor, he was immune to disenchantment or satiation.

With the formation of General Electric after Edison surrendered control of the company that no longer bore his own name, Insull was in the market for a new job. The best electrical industry executive in the world, he rejected a $36,000-a-year managerial job with what to him were the unscrupulous "cowbird" companies that made up GE. Nor did he care to associate with the rival Westinghouse. In the summer of 1892, he turned his back on the $50-million corporation that GE had become and for $12,000 a year took a job as president of the Chicago Edison Company. It was scarcely one-sixtieth the size of GE, but at a departure dinner in New York, Insull said he would make it bigger than the new giant. He fulfilled his threat by making it the greatest utility monopoly of all time.

What Morgan had forced Insull to do in New York—grow and operate on borrowed money—he did on a larger scale, not incautiously most of the time, but with a good deal of daring as the system was expanding and, eventually, with ruinous results as he tried to pay off old creditors by courting new ones. First, he borrowed $250,000 from Marshall Field to buy Chicago Edison stock, the ownership of which neutralized opposition to his bold administrative decisions. He hired Frederick Sargent, a great engineer, who designed a new generating plant with advanced water-cooled condensers, and cut costs with an efficient system that used less coal. Reduced kilowatt-hour costs followed what proponents of enormous nuclear-fueled plants now call *economies of scale*: the larger the plant, the lower the unit cost.

In the panic of 1893, as the stock of hybrid General Electric fell from $114 to $30 a share, Insull bought out his two largest Chicago competitors. Insull suspected that General Electric's contracts and credit practices with central power station customers militated against freedom of action on their part in raising new capital. Not one of GE's own utility customers was able to produce the money (a legacy of the Morgan style) to buy two of the largest generators then in existence, which had been on exhibit at the Chicago World's Fair. It was sweet joy to Insull to give GE an interest-free note for $50,000, install the equipment in his Harrison Street plant, and turn it into the greatest power station in the world for the next forty years.

With prescience and in secrecy, he acquired purchase rights to GE's and other American-manufactured power plant equipment and to that of the only German firm, Siemens and Halske, likely to export it. By 1895, six more small power stations in Chicago sold out to Insull, and before long, he had them all. Only Insull could then generate and sell power in an area of a million people, unless a competitor wanted to use power plants, manufactured by Westinghouse, the only major producer he did not have tied up. GE had the resources to invade the Insull domain, but it could scarcely be expected to do so with Westinghouse equipment; and Insull, not GE, had the exclusive right to GE generators. Insull had a clear field. Westinghouse did manage to get one small plant started in the suburb of Evanston, but Insull had it surrounded and soon bought it.

Even so, with a monopoly among 1 million, he had only 5,000 customers. Notwithstanding reduced costs, the kilowatt-hour rate was still too high at twelve cents, and electricity was not yet a service the low-paid could buy. The problem was that plants had to operate around the clock and that electricity was used largly for nighttime lighting, leaving the daylight hours a profitless wasteland. A second problem was competition from gas lighting, which, with vastly improved mantles, remained quite effective and which cost less.

Insull started to sell electricity at whatever price he had to take to get the business, and in three years, his revenues tripled. He developed a metering system and rate schedules that reflected lower charges for volume consumption and brought an English municipal power plant manager, Arthur Wright, to Chicago to educate his plant operators. He sold bonds in the London financial market and raised capital with open-end mortgages, without resorting to the despised New York bankers for a dime. More importantly, he learned to operative effectively and profitably under the advanced system of graft and corruption that had been fashioned into a political art form in Chicago.

Insull had not sold Edison's power plants in towns and cities without encountering outstretched hands. Much of the American system of utility and transit monopolies grew in response to the purchased privilege of doing business. It was in part the means by which the democratic system financed the political parties. The system was so pervasive, and even effective, that it produced the beautiful irony of graft-paying monopolists seeking liberal reforms through legislation in order to stabilize corrupt conditions within workable limits. It was intolerable to have to buy an ordinance or a franchise to operate a trolley line or a power plant and then to have to pay again and again to keep the laws from being repealed or from giving a competing company a more inclusive franchise. Whimsical and unpredictable conditions were then, and remain, inimical to any business in which substantial capital investment is required. Bribery, to guarantee the right to do business, had to produce mutually desired ends, value received for value given, if anarchy and volatility were to be avoided. All this Insull knew and understood, and he could deplore it, but he worked within it with Victorian rectitude.

He and other practitioners of what in Chicago was called "ethical corruption," failed to get the system reformed, out in the open, with stabilized regulation. Their failure rested on a credibility gap, and there were times when reforms sought were rejected by popular protest on the grounds that anything desired publicly by suspect corporations and political figures had, of necessity, to be corrupt. Thus, even when they sought to achieve objectives clearly in the public interest, it was necessary to manipulate and negotiate dishonestly in order to keep the process traditional, familiar, and palatable.

In the years during which Insull was expanding his utilities empire and creating new consumer markets for electric energy, the principal source of money for Illinois lawmakers and party leaders was Charles Tyson Yerkes, the traction magnate, whose life and times have been reviewed in the novels of Theodore Dreiser. Yerkes disbursed vast sums to avoid litigation that would have altered or deprived him of his purchased rights to run his streetcars around Chicago. His traction system had been developed by buying one regional franchise after another, and every couple of years, one or the other of them would be up for renewal. It was a conditional kind of monopoly, some fragment of which was continually vulnerable.

Roger Sullivan, a Chicago ward heeler who achieved statesman status through his talent for remaining in power, brought a system of order to the Chicago style of seasonal larceny; but he could not prevent entirely the council and ward bosses from launching out-of-season extortion expeditions against Yerkes.

The maximum franchise period for any Chicago utility was twenty years, and Yerkes thought that if it was lengthened to fifty years, it would give him a breather between raids on his bank accounts. Yerkes established a fund of a half-million dollars to buy the votes for utility regulation and reform, under which he hoped to bribe everybody satisfactorily, once and for all. The Yerkes plan called for a progressive public-utilities law along the lines of those adopted years later in Wisconsin and New York. It would have extended franchises, paid the government a mileage fee for transit tracks, a percentage of gross revenues, established a regulatory commission independent of corrupt officials, and exercised jurisdiction over rates and schedules. It was the kind of state reform Insull himself subsequently proposed for the electric utility industry, not because he particularly courted state regulation, but because he loathed the prospects of federal regulation, which might be less vulnerable to his own persuasion.

The *Chicago Tribune* got word of the Yerkes fund and exposed the details of the plan to the citizenry, who had elected to the city and state government those malefactors standing by to accept their bribes. Little of it was news to the banking and financial elite, and none of it to the political community, since they had ratified the scheme in the first place. But with the press in full cry, the abundance of enemies Yerkes had made when he was responding defensively to extortion on a piecemeal basis joined in the assault against the perfectly reasonable regulatory proposals. But because bribe money was involved, the proposals were widely interpreted as brazen criminality to extend, rather than terminate, previous conditions.

Although the Yerkes program to purchase stabilizing legislation was, in the political context of the moment, one of reform, the assault against it preempted the cause of righteousness. Thus, the ward bosses and bribetakers gleefully presided over the death watch of legislation they might not otherwise have been able to stop.

Delighted at their good fortune in a victory that came to them without cost or effort, the confident corrupters took out after Insull, the next-best source of income, as they computed it, among the monopolists. Insull was ready for them. He had at times an instinct for analyzing his enemy's intent as though it were his own. He watched the Yerkes drama play itself out and was insulated against the next development.

Now sure that Insull would pay heavily, perhaps $1 million or so, to prevent authorization of a franchise for another electric power company, the city council created a dummy corporation called the Commonwealth Electric Company and conferred upon it the right to do business for fifty years, the franchise period rejected by the virtuous reformers. But Insull had long ago learned that an electric company with a franchise was worth little if it could not buy light bulbs and equipment. Since he had quietly bought the rights of purchase to everything any new company needed, the council's new company could not very well function for purposes of extortion if there was no possibility of it functioning as a electric utility.

Insull played along with the itchy-fingered publicans by buying the company for the penny-ante price of $50,000 and thus obtained the only asset the dummy corporation possessed: its fifty-year franchise. It was one of the greatest bargains since the Russians sold Alaska, and Insull had the only fifty-year claim on electric power service in the state. His revenge was sweet and his company held the franchise until 1947 without paying another dollar. Commonwealth became the city's alternating-current company, with Chicago Edison generating direct current. They were interconnected at every key point to give the area unified service. Robert Todd Lincoln, son of slain President Abraham Lincoln, was the president of the law firm that guided Commonwealth's affairs.

With the Chicago metropolitan area sealed and delivered to Insull, he began extending outward in the Midwest, solidifying his positions in the process. He saw electric power development as an industrial-consumer ecology, its interconnected parts balanced within a system. The utility supplied power, which ran industry, which grew, produced urban development, and attracted inhabitants, who consumed electricity, made industry expand, and demand more electricity. His concept was not wholly original, of course, since electric power companies in New England, New York, on the Pacific coast, and elsewhere beyond the range of Insull's operations were simultaneously developing the strategy and tactics that Insull raised to a standard approaching perfection. Many operational and expansionist innovations that have characterized the power industry began in the Insull domain.

He bought mines to supply his plants with coal, bought a railroad to diminish his dependence on rail carriers, lobbied for mine-safety laws in Illinois to win the favor of unions whose members dug his coal, shut his eyes to the ways in which politicians got their money, and established mutual assistance pacts with authorities whose interests could be allied to his own. John L. Lewis, a young firebrand organizer in the United Mine Workers, wanted his union recognized, and Insull obliged him. He made concessions to the International Brotherhood of Electrical Workers, run by the fist-swinging "Umbrella Mike" Boyle, who returned the favor by allowing Insull's operating personnel to work in a union-free environment.

Insull became a dominant figure in the Association of Edison Illuminating Companies and the National Electric Light Association (NELA), powerful trade and lobbying organizations in which Insull was identified as something of a liberal because he favored state regulation. It was liberalism restricted to industrial interest, since he hoped state regulation might help head off public ownership of power plants and federal influence over electric utilities. Public ownership was, indeed, increasing—from 400 systems in 1896 to more than 1,200 in 1907. He organized the National Civic Federation, with representation in cities and towns, and guided it into expressing a neutral position on public ownership of electric power. The federation pressed for local option, with each community deciding for itself the issue of private versus public power, a position that allowed private utilities free rein in equating public ownership with bolshevism and anti-American ideology.

By 1910, Insull was paying an 8 percent dividend, and electrical rates to his 200,000 customers had gone down as power output, most of it by then supplying daytime electric transportation, expanded. His electric output was more than the total generated in Boston, Manhattan, and Brooklyn. Rates in New York, Boston, Philadelphia, and elsewhere were 40 percent to 300 percent above his own. His counsel was sought by other companies, and he bought stock in, and became a director of, power systems in Wisconsin, Indiana, Kentucky, Pennsylvania, Louisiana, and California. Borrowing, expanding, extending his empire, he had assets in 1917 of more than $400 million and was operating in thirteen states, with visions of encompassing the whole country in his embrace. He acquired the Central Illinois Light Company system, covering fifty-six communities. His own holding company, Middle West Utilities, fenced in an electric power kingdom never again equaled, and it continued to grow for another twenty years.

At the outbreak of World War I, his holding company owned its biggest customer, the Chicago Elevated Railways; and he had become chairman of the board of the Peoples Gas Company, formerly his competitor in the lighting field. He led a campaign to persuade America to enter the war on the side of his native England, creating a communications and propaganda organization to promote patriotism, later subverted to promote his monopoly and sell stock, which he thought was an extension of patriotism anyway. He was something of a national hero for selling, through his war propaganda campaign, $1 billion worth of government war bonds.

He was fifty-nine years old in 1918, when, the war over, he resumed his drive to bring the nation's electric utilities under his own management. He had tasted the energizing blood that poisons some men who see themselves in the false image created by their public relations machines. Having generated an enormous volume of favorable publicity about his activities and himself, he believed his own propaganda—a common fault of the demagogue and the accumulators of power.

He organized the Illinois Committee on Public Utility Information and directed his associate, Bernard J. Mullaney, to expand its operations. Within five years, regional committees encompassing thirty-six states were functioning as a superpatriotic public relations industry extolling the private utilities as the ideal of the free-enterprise system, the epitome of public service, honor, and human concern.

In becoming the most celebrated spokesman of the electric utilities and industry in general, Insull was extraordinarily successful in imposing his exaggerated views on the nation. As an industrialist and gifted management executive, he was held in high regard. Save for one company he apparently tried to save from disaster in an effort that brought him profitless grief, his electric companies neither cut dividends nor raised rates in the postwar inflation. His company was the only large utility of such distinction. But his zeal, egotism, and compulsion to keep his empire expanding led him into heady departures from clear judgment and critical self-analysis.

He formed the Utility Securities Company to sell stock and compelled his employees to go out as teams and peddle it among their neighbors. He pushed and cajoled them into various forms of unpaid community service in order to widen their range of acquaintanceships, bedeviled them, instructed them on how to "be a credit to the company," instructed them on questions of what was right and wrong in politics, and expected them to subscribe to the militant, flag-waving form of patriotism defined in his "Americanization program." He equated religious virtues and patriotic citizenship with Insull stock and bond sales promotion.

If he could sell war bonds with hoopla and heavy-handed appeals to patriotism, he decided he could sell stock by the same techniques of mass marketing and strident public relations. With a multitude of stockholders, he concluded, he would not be at the mercy of his investors, as he feared was possible with a comparative few. He was changing the complexion of capitalism, breaking the stranglehold of the hated New York bankers, and developing an industry owned by its customers—or so he said. His public relations chief coined a word to fit the new image: the *Insullization* program. His investment house, Halsey, Stuart and Company, sold $200 million worth of bonds in one year. Power corrupted his outlook to the extent that he arranged to have the county treasurer *forget* to send the faltering Peoples Gas Company a bill for taxes after the war. Subsequently, the stock of this broken company rose from $29 to $400—a tribute to the manipulation of mass psychology—before it collapsed in the depression.

In the decade after World War I, Insull put the stamp of his presence and gigantic energy on the nation. He met Andrew Mellon, later to become Secretary of the Treasury, and persuaded the boss of Koppers Company, Gulf Oil, and the Aluminum Company of America to finance a power plant for him. With advanced technology developed in Italy, he increased the transmission voltage in his power lines from 23,000 to 138,000 and extended Middle West's electric service into thirty-two states.

When the Morgan interests tried again in 1927 to bring all the utility-financing business under their own control, Insull stepped in and bought two holding companies operating in fourteen eastern states. In Pennsylvania, the scandalously corrupt Republican machine of William S. Vare, supported by Insull and the utilities, defeated the progressive conservationist, Gifford Pinchot, in a senatorial election riddled by fraud. Vare was excluded from the United States Senate. Insull admitted contributing $125,000 to the senate campaign of Frank L. Smith, head of the Illinois Commerce Commission, but was silent to such questions as those asked by the public power advocate, Senator George Norris: "How many senatorial campaigns has Mr. Insull financed? . . . Are we going to turn the [Muscle Shoals] plant over to these interests?" Another senator publicly denounced the "power trust."

At Muscle Shoals, on the Tennessee River, where the government had built a wartime nitrate plant, a skirmish in the battle between public and private power interests was shaping up. Henry Ford wanted to lease the plant for a hundred years. George Norris, among others, wanted the federal government to keep the plant and use it as an industrial nucleus around which to develop a vast public power operation. The Alabama Power Company wanted to lease it and might have done so had not Senator Norris appeared before a special committee investigating frauds in the Pinchot-Vare election with evidence damaging to electric utility interests. Norris several times steered bills through Congress that would have put the government into the power business at Muscle Shoals, but Presidents Calvin Coolidge and Herbert Hoover vetoed them and the power trust, for the time being, was victorious.

Throughout the 1920s, electric utilities, in company with investment banking houses, courted outrage and investigation until both developed. On a resolution offered by Senators Norris and Walsh, the Federal Trade Commission was authorized to conduct an inquiry into the electric utility business. Some of the utility leadership actually wanted an open inquiry for the ultimate health of the industry, but jealous state regulatory commissions and investment bankers protested and balked. Banking interests, especially, wanted no inquiry into profits on utility bonds that were often equal to the face value of the issues. The investigation went on for seven years, disclosing almost incredible patterns of greed and corporate plunder.

Insull himself sought money less for personal wealth than to feed his passion for operating electric utilities. He became obsessed with power but probably never had a net worth of more than $5 or $6 million. He wanted to possess the total power market. He had $3 billion worth of properties, and his companies had 600,000 stockholders, nearly as many bond holders, and more than 1 million customers in the mid-1920s. When his fortune was estimated at the time of the stock-speculation madness in 1929 at $150 million, it was neither real nor liquid, nor were the fortunes of thousands of others as computed on paper.

In the midst of speculation, national economic frenzy, and investigation of the industry, Insull remained always the manager, desiring rather to control his empire than to exploit it for riches. His madness for capital, for money through stock and bond issues, his conspiracies to get sympathetic or obligated friends into offices of political power, were relentless, but were directed to the protection of his fortress, to his compulsive desire to rule and pay dividends.

When stock-market gambling on margin accounts had become a form of national insanity in 1929, Insull built a lasting monument to himself: the Chicago Civic Opera House, which opened with a performance on November 4, 1929, four days after the Black Friday crash. Before and during this period, Insull found time to go to England to advise the British government on the planning of its unified grid system, which later was studied as a model. Elements of it were copied in the Tennessee Valley Authority (TVA) public power network.

He had to take the time, too, to fight off Cyrus S. Eaton, the Cleveland industrialist, who for twenty years had been buying his way into utility operations. Eaton frightened Insull, who created before the crash a company called Insull Utility Investments, the purpose of which was to perpetuate his own management, whatever might happen to Insull himself. The New York bankers began closing in on Chicago in the riptide of the market collapse. Chicago banks were overextended, in default to Wall Street; and Insull's collateral, so vast on paper, required shoring up with resources that, by 1931, were wholly in the hands of creditors. He transferred money from one place to another, inevitably (in the wake of diminishing values) overstating his holdings to the point where it could easily be said that his loans were unsecured. He was a fraud, it was said, an embezzler, whose depredations had impoverished all those superpatriotic citizens in the neighborhoods who had invested in the American dream. With Chicago banks failing to supply credit and unable to stand up against Wall Street, Morgan at last had Insull caged.

It appeared, in part because he had made it seem so, that Insull was the only utility tycoon in the land. The Hearst press caricatured him as the embodiment of avarice, the fat plutocrat of capitalism defiled, who had ruined the innocent and smeared the image of holy free enterprise. Even Gifford Pinchot resorted to hyperbole with a public accusation that the utilities had overcharged the people by $750,000,000; to which Martin Insull, son of Samuel, retorted that since the whole industry's total bill to residential customers was $650,000,000, the utilities would have had to pay the people $100,000,000 prior to taking from them the amount computed by Pinchot. Martin went on to attack the Democratic candidate for president, Franklin D. Roosevelt, who had denounced utility holding companies. Roosevelt could hardly have passed up the campaign opportunity presented by Insull's troubles, and in overreacting, Martin fanned the flames. FDR easily capitalized on the outrage against Insull and the utilities to become the champion of the frightened and dispossessed, a man with a program and a cure for the terrible ills of a decaying nation.

Insull had a $10,000,000 note falling due on his eastern companies on June 1, 1932. It was a time of soup kitchens and breadlines, of fist-fights before the doors of employment offices that might have advertised a half-dozen job openings at fifty cents an hour, only to be confronted with hundreds of applicants; of bank failures, factory closings, bank-ruptcies, evictions, and despair.

Insull, with commitments to cover his note obtained in England, Canada, and from the Rockefellers' Chase National Bank in New York, was summoned to a meeting at the Manhattan offices of Owen D. Young, chairman of the board of General Electric. According to family records made accessible by Martin Insull, five Morgan bankers entered Young's office, and the seventy-two-year-old Samuel Insull was asked to leave the room. An hour or so passed; then Young, the "neutral" mediator of the discussion, appeared to inform Insull that nobody anywhere was going to cover the $10,000,000 note. The empire was going into receivership. In the wreckage of the national economy, there stood Morgan with the power.

An Insull associate wanted him to rent the Chicago Stadium for a mass meeting to tell the public that the bankers preferred to pillage his industry rather than preserve it. Insull declined, resigned from sixty corporations and went with his wife to Paris. He was broke, owing many millions of dollars more than any remaining assets he possessed, but he had his pension payments that the bankers had promised not to take away. His son, Samuel, remained to help the new management run three operating companies.

In 1933, Roosevelt summoned Norman Thomas, the country's frequent Socialist candidate for the presidency, to assist with an investigation and suggest regulatory procedures that could be written into law. Thomas's concept of regulatory powers became textbook study for an oncoming generation of political science students, and his ideas intended to compel electric utilities to improve their behavior became law in a number of states and a part of the procedures of the Federal Power Commission.

The United States Department of Justice and the state's attorney for Cook County, Illinois, also opened investigations on Insull. John Swanson, who faced a battle for reelection as state's attorney in Chicago, captured the headlines as a belated defender of the public interest when he produced a "secret list"—which was not difficult to find in the well-kept company records—of government officials and well-placed business leaders who had been permitted to buy Middle West Utilities stock at half the 1929 market price. To the dismay of the New York bankers who had arranged the meeting from which Insull had been expelled while his fate was being determined, the names of Owen D. Young, chairman of General Electric, and Anton Cermak, the mayor of Chicago who was later killed by an assassin's bullet aimed at Franklin D. Roosevelt, were on the preferred list. But outrage was directed exclusively at Insull, who fled from Paris to Greece, from which he could not, in the absence of a treaty, be extradited. The bankers cut off his pension then, and apparently his sons, Martin and Samuel, and friends supplied the funds he required.

The Cook County Grand Jury, a month before the November elections of 1932, indicted Insull and Martin, who was in Canada, along with Harold L. Stuart, the broker, on a charge of using the mails to defraud the public, which had been urged in printed material and letters to buy utility stock. When an extradition treaty between the United States and Greece was ratified, a Greek board of judges twice dismissed an extradition case for lack of evidence. Insull balked at returning to the United States voluntarily on the grounds that what had been prepared for him was a political trial, not a court case. He planned to stay in Greece and become minister of electric power, but the candidate with whom he had made the arrangement was defeated in the Greek elections. When the United States threatened to stop Greeks from sending dollars back to their families in their old homeland, the government there capitulated. Insull was not extradited but simply ordered to leave the country, which he did in a chartered ship.

Congress quickly passed a bill authorizing the seizure of Insull in any country that would allow it, and Insull sailed around the Mediterranean trying to decide what to do. When his vessel anchored off Istanbul to take on supplies, he was, in spite of the fact that no extradition treaty existed between the two countries, hauled off the ship, questioned, and delivered to the American embassy.

Bail of $100,000 was set for him when he was returned to Chicago, where he spent a night in jail with a collection of less-celebrated culprits. The bail was doubled as soon as the $100,000 had been raised. From the spring of 1934, when he was released on bond, until the following October, he dictated his memoirs while defense and prosecution prepared for the trial.

It was a memorable exhibition, in which the American industrial and banking system was presented as innocent of wrongdoing; only such rare creatures as old Sam Insull gave it an undeserved bad name. The evils of the utility business were the evils of Insull and certainly not of the highly placed banking institutions like Morgan or corporations like General Electric and Westinghouse. (When those corporations were caught in criminal price rigging a generation later, no one like careless old Sam Insull was around to absorb the shocks and the companies had to endure their own blame.) Even the holding companies were exalted as good, honest instruments of corporate organization, except for those Insull alone had sullied.

Voluminous and meticulous records from Insull's company files were produced to show the depth and measure of his intention to defraud hapless investors of their small savings. Not germane to the issue, of course, were all the losses of savings and deposits put into banks that had not been invested but might with no less risk have gone into Insull companies. The trial revealed that Halsey, Stuart and Company had not exactly panicked and dumped worthless securities on the market but had in fact made heavy purchases at offered prices and taken large losses. One of the jurors wondered why, if Insull was such a crook, every fact and figure of his operations had been recorded and filed for handy availability to the prosecution. The defense put Insull's whole life into the record, beginning with his first job with Thomas Edison. The jury was reported to have reached a decision in a few minutes. The old order went free, and so did Insull. All the defendants were adjudged innocent.

In March, 1935, the Insull sons, Martin and Samuel, Jr., were tried on state charges of embezzling $66,000. They were acquitted and pending charges dismissed. In June, on another charge, the jury was instructed to return a verdict of not guilty. The show was over, although the depression, for which Insull was blamed by Thomas Lamont, a Morgan partner, in a *Collier's* magazine article, lingered on. Lamont happened to be on the board of directors of *Collier's* at the time his exercise in journalism was published.

The New Deal administration passed the Public Utility Holding Company Act, set up the Securities and Exchange Commission, passed the Rural Electrification Act, and brought the bankers under regulation in two outbreaks of legislation in 1933 and 1935. In the latter year, the Wheeler-Rayburn "death sentence" bill against holding companies became law, but the holding companies were back in business, nevertheless, when the era of nuclear power began. Not only electric utilities but banks, insurance companies, transportation companies, and the whole range of corporate enterprises often owned, or were owned by, conglomerates. Collectives of unrelated businesses had sprung up like roadside fried-chicken stands.

Passage of the "death sentence" legislation gave the investment bankers, who had inherited Insull's far-ranging publicity and propaganda mill, their first chance to make full use of it in a campaign to defuse the Federal Power Commission. When Insull used the mails and his vast propaganda organization to promote patriotism and utility stocks, he was charged with using the mails to "defraud"; when the banking and finance lobby used the same organization and the same techniques of flooding the press, schools, and air waves with propaganda to try to prevent Federal Power Commission regulation, it was not challenged. This time, however, the public supported federal proposals for power regulation, and President Roosevelt got his reforms.

David Lilienthal, a celebrated administrator on the Roosevelt New Deal team, was chosen to be the first director of the Tennessee Valley Authority (TVA), the nation's most extensive commitment to public power and regional development, for which Senator George Norris had labored so long and futilely until FDR was elected. Mr. Lilienthal and members of his technical staff went to England to study the British power-grid system, which had been developed in consultation with Insull. Government spending and war preparations rescued the United States from its devastating and prolonged economic depression, and the electric utilities prospered under the reform measures and in spite of TVA, which power industry leaders had bitterly declared together constituted socialism and a threat to destroy the American concept of free enterprise.

Throughout the depression years, about 40 percent of the securities of all corporations were lost to their owners. Of the securities held by the public in Insull companies, according to the most sympathetic computation, about 20 percent were forfeited, which was bad enough, to be sure. Twenty years after Insull's death, his utilities were generating 12 percent of all the electric power in the United States. Ernest Gruening, who became a United States senator from Alaska, wrote that "to measure what the investing public, as distinguished from the speculators, lost in these [utility] issues is impossible but it is not overstating to say that the losses were . . . in the billions."

Insull fell dead of a heart attack in a Paris Métro station on July 16, 1938. He had eight francs in his pocket but no wallet or identification. It was altogether possible that his pockets were picked as he lay dead, a fallen king in exile. But his kingdom of power remained, albeit in other hands. Edison's edifice, pyramided and extended to two-thirds of the nation's states by Samuel Insull, had come chastened but only temporarily ashamed into a new era.

5

Persuasion, Propaganda, and Power

DISPOSING OF Insull was seen as exorcising the evil wizard, leaving the world from which he had been banished purified. The power industry was restored and cleansed, free of the stain of Insull, again the bright star of the free-enterprise economic system. Or so the public was asked to believe, and so, for the most part, it did. But the utilities and Insull had been together so long and had achieved so much growth and profit together that resolve to pursue the paths of purity was difficult to sustain.

The New Deal years and the prolonged Federal Trade Commission investigation into the utilities industry, which produced a shelf of volumes of testimony pretty well documenting years of iniquity and swindling in the industry, brought about some banking and securities reforms. But the utilities continued with astonishing effectiveness to develop the transparent propaganda methods that had characterized the Insull years. That they continued to be so successful was an index of the extent to which the public responded to institutionalized persuasion in day-to-day life.

The investor-owned utilities (the IOUs), through repetitive and well-organized communications programs that Insull devised and extended across the continent, presented themselves before the public as an embattled, unorganized minority of power producers, harassed in their patriotic endeavors by a couple of thousand publicly owned and subsidized power systems that disdained the high-minded principles of capitalism by which the nation endured.

From the reform of the 1930s until the age of nuclear-powered energy was under way, the investor-owned utilities at times appeared to lose their collective reason in response to the development of publicly owned power. Yet all the while, even years after the Tennessee Valley Authority demonstrated that public power could not deter growth of the IOUs, the deeper truth was that many small electric utilities were in danger of absorption into larger and better-funded private networks. With the arrival of nuclear power, the danger to public systems became more immediate, since very few public systems could expect to raise the kind of capital required to build and operate reactors. Many of them were saved from absorption or elimination by some new legislation that went into effect by 1970 and by a landmark Supreme Court decision in September, 1971, that affirmed the right of municipal systems to purchase generating and transmission services from private utilities.

The danger of publicly owned systems intruding on private investor utilities was nonexistent in proportion to the extent that it was needlessly feared. The danger that did exist, however, was the inverse one, and power policy that failed to provide safeguards for small municipal systems would have delivered the business of generating and transmitting energy (except for TVA and larger federal and metropolitan districts) to the private sector altogether.

Although Insull had originated and expanded the organized propaganda movement throughout his own empire, it had in a short time encompassed nearly all electric utilities in the country. In terms of distribution and intensity, it enjoyed its highest level of effectiveness in the decade preceding Insull's acquittal. Anyone who worked on a newspaper or magazine, served in a legislature, or worked in a library; who planned programs for civic and service clubs; the teachers and preachers, editors of house organs, publishers—all were courted, persuaded, and often paid to exalt the private utilities as the epitome of public service, honor, and human concern. The effort was so extensive and relentless that rarely was there any rebuttal, analysis, or objection.

A news service regularly provided 900 newspapers with news copy and editorials, much of it so heavy-handed and luridly gushy that it deserved, on its merit, to be dispatched to wastebaskets—and some of it was. But editors in general were not always independent, and sometimes they were lazy, overworked, or uncaring and welcomed printable material that seemed to support the familiar verities, the bromides, and the simply defined principles on which good Americanism and competitive industry was said to thrive.

In hundreds of cities and towns, the stuff was printed and its source attributed to local spokesmen and authorities, if identified at all. Bureaus prepared speeches and arranged engagements for spokesmen before civic and service clubs, school organizations, adult education courses, church groups, and the like. In Illinois alone, 800 high schools were supplied with lessons and classroom literature for debating-club use. One official of the National Electric Light Association cheerfully reported in 1922 that 8,500 column inches of such material were printed in the newspapers of six states, or something more than "500 pages of reading matter every month." In an era when the newspaper was the sole source of communication and education with which most people came in contact once they were out of school, this was good saturation for any propaganda program masquerading as enlightenment. And as for youngsters in the schools, newspaper reading and classroom instruction confirmed one another.

Bernard J. ("Barney") Mullaney, who had sharpened his public relations expertise as proconsul for Insull, warned the industry that "a proper state of public mind" was essential to the prosperity of the electric power business. How the utilities could have avoided prosperity regardless of the manipulated condition of public mentality was difficult to discern, but Mullaney was chiefly concerned, as was Insull, with eliciting money from individual citizens in the promotion of securities. Without appropriate conditioning of the public, said Mullaney, "we do not get the money with which to build plants, and we do not get the favorable reaction from the public mind that enables us to sell our product. . . ." He described the conditioning process as "purely educational."

In 1924, P. H. Gadsen, vice-president of the United Gas Improvement Association, whose member companies had branched out into electric power, recounted the growth of the information program that began with twelve men meeting in one room and "now it takes a theater to take care of us. What a tremendous growth has come about in that time! Five years only has this great movement, which is now sweeping over this country, been in existence." The industry, Mr. Gadsen thought, ought to "take stock, consolidate our positions, and mop up." In those rosy days, the industry was doing just that, taking stock and mopping up.*

The managing director of the National Electric Light Association, M. H. Aylesworth, issued an exuberant advisory directive to member utilities in a 1923 speech that became part of Federal Trade Commission

---

* Quotations are taken from transcripts of hearings conducted by the Federal Trade Commission. Reference works containing documented accounts of the power industry's forty-year venture into propaganda and public relations include: Ernest Gruening, *The Public Pays: A Study of Power Propaganda* (New York: Vanguard Press, 1931; reissued in 1959 and 1964); and Lee Metcalf (United States senator from Montana) and Vic Reinemer (Senator Metcalf's executive secretary), *Overcharge* (New York: David McKay Co., Inc., 1967).

investigation records. What it lacked in subtlety, it possessed in explicit counsel on how to buy an educator.

> I would advise any manager who lives in a community where there is a college to get the professor of economics—the engineering professor will be interested anyway—interested in our problems. Have him lecture on your subject to his classes. Once in a while it will pay you to take such men and give them a retainer of one or two hundred dollars per year for the privilege of letting you study and consult with them. For how in heaven's name can we do anything in the schools of this country with the young people growing up, if we have not first sold the idea of education to the college professor?

John C. Parker, of the Brooklyn Edison Company, was chairman of the Committee on Cooperation with Educational Institutions. He told a NELA convention that the committee's work

> must be properly to relate the professors to the sources of information. . . . It is desired that coming generations of bankers, lawyers, journalists, legislators, public officials, and the plain ordinary men in the streets shall have an intelligent and sympathetic understanding of the peculiar conditions under which utilities operate.

The conditions were getting more peculiar all the time.

Mr. Parker and his committee were "persuaded that there is a very real opportunity to serve American education and incidentally strongly to benefit our industry." That opportunity was seen more clearly by the Reverend Dr. Charles Aubrey Eaton, a New Jersey congressman, who happened concurrently to be manager of the industrial relations department of the General Electric Company. With an insider's view of "one of the three starveling professions," as he termed the school, the church, and the press, he saw merit in the electric companies attaching themselves to "the three institutions that we persist in starving to death."
He said:

> Here is a professor in a college, who gets $2,500 a year and has to spend $3,000 to keep from starving to death, who walks up to his classroom in an old pair of shoes and some idiot of a boy drives up and parks a $5,000 automobile outside and comes in and gets plucked. Then because that professor teaches that boy that there is something wrong with the social system, we call him a Bolshevik and throw him out.

The compassionate clergyman–congressman–GE manager had a plan for correcting the evils of the social system.

What I would like to suggest to you intelligent gentlemen is that while you are dealing with the pupils, give a thought to the teachers and when their vacation comes, pay them a salary to come into your plants and into your factories and learn the public utility business at first hand, and then they will go back, and you needn't fuss—they can teach better than you can.

The idea of enlisting the educated mind in their cause captivated quite a few power executives. Insull quickly approved the employment by the Commonwealth Edison Company of four engineering professors for the summer, but one of his vice-presidents thought the company should look around for someone other than engineers, "someone in other departments whose society we are particularly anxious to enjoy." A sub-committee of the NELA, which included four university professors, developed the education-subsidy plan more fully in a formal report. One of them was Dean C. O. Ruggles of Ohio State University, who was engaged for $15,000 to devote a sabbatical year to directing the Committee on Cooperation with Educational Institutions.

"Our friend Ruggles," as one state information committee director called him, "is one of the most diligent little letter writers you ever came across . . . his ideas coincide with our own." Dean Ruggles was diligent in his job, too, but not all the college professors he tried to recruit had ideas that coincided with those of the propaganda directors. In Iowa, for example, some of the educators balked at the idea of getting together for a planning session in Kansas City. The Iowa director of the Public Utility Information Committee, Joe Carmichael, had some trouble "rounding them up." He explained, "Some of the college authorities were a little cagey about the matter. . . ."

With their expenses paid, however, the professors met as arranged and discussed "cooperation." Their ruffled feelings were assuaged by the delicate foresight of Thorne Browne, an official of NELA, who decided not to expose the educators to too much reality. Power company executives were simply forbidden to attend the meeting, "my idea being," said Mr. Browne, "that better results would be obtained if utility men were not conspicuous when Dean Ruggles presented his very wonderful plan to the educators." A meeting "with these educators, many of whom have tendencies toward suspicion, should not be particularly loaded with public utility men," said the sensitive Mr. Browne.

Such discretion, however, became less necessary by the end of the 1920s, as college administrators, warming up to the program, assumed more responsibility for the utilities' public relations accounts. The segregation of educators from power executives gave way to full integration. At one meeting, five college presidents, ten deans, and eleven professors mingled freely and cooperatively with executives who, together, represented the power industry and higher education in Mississippi, Louisiana, Arkansas, Oklahoma, and Texas. This session was organized by Dr. Hugh M. Blain, head of the Department of Journalism at Tulane University, the president of which, Dr. A. B. Dinwiddie, welcomed the assembly with an interesting new concept of college education that later became alarmingly commonplace.

Dr. Dinwiddie disapproved of colleges "monopolizing education." A college that clung to this idea, insisting on exclusive control over "material for education, is a college that is not in touch with modern life." He said he was "heart and soul with your purpose" and invited industrial and commercial enterprises to share with colleges the "common problem" of education.

Seldom had a university president's idea of education coincided more explicitly with that of power company executives. Thus, in pursuit of their own monopoly, the electric utilities were ready, with the help of Dean Ruggles's wonderful plan, to protect the colleges from *their* educational monopoly. They would provide instructional material and guidelines for the professors, all adapted to the new cooperative concept of higher learning.

For organizing the memorable conference, the head of the Tulane journalism department received high praise, especially from his colleagues on the Louisiana-Mississippi Committee on Public Utility Information, of which he was chairman at a salary equal to the one paid him by the university. Dr. Blain's colleagues in education were as fervent in their commendation as his associates in the power business were. In congratulatory letters that enclosed their expense accounts, the educators also lauded "the masterly way" in which Dean Ruggles made his presentation of common concerns affecting academic and industrial society. Checks for $100 were sent to each college president and professor who had been exempted from itemizing his expenses.

The utility industry moved solidly and expansively into American education, prorating the cost of the project and the supplemental salaries of the academicians among their customers. In Colorado, "every college and university in the state" joined the movement, it was reported by George E. Lewis, director of information committee programs in the Rocky Mountain region. Dr. Charles A. Lory, of the Colorado Agricultural College, in a speech before a gathering of educators and utility executives, only seemed to be indulging in irony when he said:

I thought I'd never live to see the day when the utilities would be providing educational material for our universities. Plainly, a new day for the utility industry has arrived. I am certainly impressed with the progress you are making.

If anything, you are too modest in presenting the story of the utility business. Don't be afraid—tell us even more of your problems, hopes and ambitions. We believe you are truthful and sincere.

Colorado was warmheartedly friendly, to the extent that J. G. Crabbe, president of the state teachers college, promised the information committee he would deliver captive audiences of 3,000 or more "starveling" school superintendents, principals, teachers, and administrators to lecture courses prepared by the utilities. They were "required to not only listen to your speakers but in addition to study subjects presented outside of class. . . . We want this thing to go over big, real big! Let's not limit it to a few hit and miss lectures. We should have regular courses in public utilities."

Not surprisingly, the Rocky Mountain area leader, George Lewis, was able to report in due course that "we now have twenty-four public utility executives as members of the University [of Colorado] faculty."

Now and then, grousing emerged from the euphoric collegiate atmosphere. A chemistry professor at the University of Denver suggested that "propaganda" had crept into the courses and educational work there. The utilities had become overconfident, too arrogant, and again had to exercise their concept of restraint. It was thought prudent to allow the initiative to appear to come from the universities rather than from the industry. In a communication from the Colorado committee giving advice to the Georgia Utilities Committee, W. C. Sterne, a utility executive, explained that "while the idea originated in the committee, it reached the colleges and universities through a man high in educational circles who broached the subject without mentioning the public utilities as being interested."

When a fellowship was set up by Mr. Lewis and his colleagues, half the cost of the endowment was "derived from affiliated companies, chiefly in Colorado," the other half presumably borne by the university. The first fellowship was conferred on Hubert P. Wolfe, a graduate of Northwestern University, whose selection was left to the university after the information committee "scrutinized his credentials and his intellectual leanings." The committee committed itself to pay $1,000 for the first year of the fellowship, $1,100 for the second, and $1,200 for the third. Mr. Wolfe's duties consisted of preparing material for lectures by the twenty-four utility executive faculty men, a correspondence course in public utility economics, and screening textbooks in search of criticism of utility policies. After a time, the committee increased his salary, and Mr. Lewis suggested: "By the way, tell me again, what your salary is at the university, so I can make proper arrangements for the future."

Agitation for extension of electric service into rural areas and the lower rates charged by a few municipally owned power systems, particularly the publicly owned system in Seattle, Washington, unnerved the leadership of the college-administered propaganda mill. Mr. Wolfe and other holders of fellowships were expected to provide intellectual, authoritative counterassaults against these outbreaks of bolshevism. In 1928, the Puget Sound Power and Light Company was so exercised about "the claim of successful results" for the Seattle municipal power operation that it authorized an expenditure of $150,000 "for giving proper publicity to the facts" it planned and expected to expose against the public system. A special report prepared by the utilities acknowledged that Seattle rates were "continually cited as lower than those charged by privately owned plants." With proposals being made here and there in the United States for public ownership of power systems, the report found the Seattle situation "dangerous and [it] requires reform."

University correspondence courses, for which the utilities recruited students by advertising in local newspapers, helped explain the anti-American dangers of the government going into the power business. At Pennsylvania State College, one of the courses was taught by Prof. N. C. Miller, under the supervision of C. E. Reinicker, an engineer for the United Gas Improvement Company of Philadelphia. Mr. Reinicker felt called upon to point out to the professor, in a fifteen-page critical evaluation of his work, the inadvisability of using the word *profit* too frequently in the course, "since in the utility business, in a sense, there are no profits." He also frowned on the professor's use of sentences "referring to bribery and corruption" and required that they be "entirely eliminated." Professor Miller, it was found on further checking, complied.

In Nebraska, a utility committee "went through the motions of setting up an actual joint committee on the relations of electricity to agriculture." The committee was staffed by people from agricultural societies, the Farm Bureau Federation, the Farmers Union, the Grange, women's clubs, "a banker or two . . . twenty-one in all, and but two men from our industry." Thus, the Nebraska Agricultural College took the leadership in the fight against rural electrification, persuading farmers that they could not afford it.

The College of Agriculture at the University of Missouri was counseled to "step softly on the electrification of farms in a wholesale way unless you have the approval of the local power companies affected." J. B. Sheridan, director of the Missouri committee, reminded the college that "there is always the danger that if farmers cannot get power from the companies, they may try to form power districts of their own, as is being tried in Nebraska, etc. It is tricky business."

Northwestern University in Chicago received $25,000 a year from the

National Electric Light Association for giving courses on the utilities, but the nearby University of Chicago declined to cooperate. A few universities rejected all overtures, Princeton and Columbia among them. Dean F. R. Robinson, of the School of Business at the City College of New York, brushed off the propaganda raiders with a note: "We find no difficulty in getting very competent instructors in the city of New York, and we have adequate material for the successful conduct of our courses."

Northwestern and Harvard, the latter having been guaranteed $30,000 in utility subsidies for three years, caused some anguish when they failed to respond to "the generous financial support of the association [NELA] of research work in public utility management." Disquieting reports of articles in economics journals that "stirred up some of the members of the association," suggested that not all the university research was laundered to the satisfaction of the subsidizers.

An embarrassing development caught utility spokesmen in an outright lie. Prof. E. A. Stewart, of the University of Minnesota, had made a supposedly impartial and scholarly survey of rural electrification in Ontario, which was widely publicized in New England and throughout the utilities industry. He found that the Canadian farmers served by a publicly managed rural electric system were considerably worse off than they would have been had they bought power from private utilities. American utilities looked on the Ontario Hydro-Electric system, then perhaps the best publicly owned utility in the world, with a good deal of apprehension. Professor Stewart's published report, considered authoritative and founded on Ontario Hydro records, was valuable support for the private utilities and highly damaging to public power advocates. The NELA promoted the report as gospel well into the early 1930s.

C. A. McGrath, chairman of Ontario Hydro, revealed that Professor Stewart's data were false and that the report had not been (as had been indicated) checked by Mr. McGrath himself. Moreover, it developed that the professor was on the payroll of the Minnesota utilities, and the Federal Power Commission had copies of checks and expense vouchers to prove it. Professor Stewart departed from the university to find a more suitable career as president of a Minnesota power company. But his "impartial and scholarly" report on public power in Ontario circulated for a long time.

Dr. James Mavor, professor emeritus of political economy at the University of Toronto, wrote and published *Niagara in Politics,* a book that denounced government power plants as destructive and dangerous. In particular, Dr. Mavor cited the Ontario Hydro system as a failure brought about by "the insidious methods of politicians." Until the Toronto professor noted the matter, it had not been thought that the

hydroelectric system was a "failure" at all. It had been universally regarded as a notable and successful public power development in a
country that had a critical need for electric energy. Dr. Mavor's judgment lost some of its validity when it was disclosed that he, too, had been
touched by the wand of private power. It seemed that NELA, channeling
money through a mutual friend, had paid him $1,000 to help him along.

Thus, another educational document that had enlightened students
and general readers alike turned out to be largely an extension of official
NELA doctrine. During this period of utility dominance in public education, it was possible for a student to go through high school and a university and never hear a word or read a line of criticism about electric
utilities that, as subsequent events disclosed beyond dispute, suborned
educators, swindled the public in stock promotions, rigged rate bases,
corrupted regulatory bodies, and engaged as a matter of common practice in bribery and purchase to secure monopoly franchises from approving public authorities.

The public information committees of the private utilities served all
but a few states in the country, in which a more or less uniform pattern
of operation developed along lines of a wholesale-retail system, with
the utilities devoting their efforts to the wholesale distribution and
management of propaganda, which was then funneled outward and downward to the consumer. In the process, the general public was seldom
aware that the creative and financial source of "public information" was
not the university or periodical delivering it but the power industry.

It was not possible, as a Brooklyn Edison Company executive conceded to the NELA, to make utility public relations work so inclusive
that it would "stretch from the cradle to the grave, but we can at least
begin early enough with it. . . ." Mr. S. L. Sloan was chairman of a group
that had "analyzed" some school books and found them deplorably
warped. The books studied had presented, not one, but two or more sides
of public utility questions, which was enough to warp any book as a
utility man saw it. Textbooks were regarded as more important than
teachers because the contents of a book remained unchanging during its
life, whereas a teacher could grow weary of responding with enthusiasm
to the flow of propaganda.

The NELA was urged to get "honest" books into the schools to replace "valueless, and in many instances poisonous" texts of the type
turned up, for instance, in Missouri by that state's public information
committee secretary. Too many of them, it was felt, were prepared
by Socialists or by advocates of public power, which amounted to the
same thing. A poisonous book was one that contained a paragraph such
as this one taken from a civics book in general use:

Franchises were valuable and were frequently secured by cor-
rupting the city council. Attempts to limit the privileges of public
utility corporations often have been resisted by similar methods.
Privately managed public utilities have, therefore, been a very
potent cause of municipal corruption.

The electric utilities prepared an Index of proscribed books and
evaluated others as "good," "fair," "unfair," "bad," "very bad," and so
forth. Committees then set to work recruiting writers and publishers
to direct history on a straight, narrow, one-way path.

One of the books cited as "bad" contained a few sentences that offended the utilities without so much as mentioning them by company
or generic name. The work was written by two professors, John Albert
Woodburn, of Indiana University, and Thomas Francis Moran, of Purdue
University, who cited several causes of municipal corruption, including:

> private contributions by rich men and corporations who are inter-
> ested in securing certain laws and policies enacted by the success-
> ful party. Corporations have been known to give generously to
> both party funds so as to stand in well and get what they want
> whatever party is successful. Large campaign funds coming from
> hidden sources have led to serious corruption in the elections.

Other textbooks, summarizing equally commonplace practices in
similar primer style, were viewed as undermining American principles,
or at least needlessly calling attention to times when the application of
laudable principles had fallen short of perfection. At best, said Mr. John
B. Sheridan of the Missouri committee, such books were "out of date."
Following the survey and analysis of textbooks, two courses of action
were proposed to the utilities by a director of the study.

One approach was to start

> getting at the thing locally right away and stopping it in the local
> schools, and the other was reaching the authors and publishers
> and taking such steps as would prevent publication in the future
> of textbooks containing misinformation. The latter is a very slow
> process, but has to be gone through with. The other . . . gets action
> in the form of immediate removal of books from the schools.

John Sheridan thought the problem called for extraordinarily delicate
handling

> by tactful personal contact . . . we should get direct to the text-
> book writers, tell them that their books were all right for the period
> for which they were written, but that changes in the past ten
> years make a new textbook necessary. This will give the boys a

chance to write new textbooks and make some more money, and
we can show them individually just wherein the old textbooks
are obsolete.

Martin G. Glaeser, economics professor at Wisconsin State University,
had written a book called *The Outlines of Public Utility Economics,*
only to find that the Institute for Land Research and Public Utility
Economics at Northwestern University, which paid part of his salary,
had been receiving contributions from many utility corporations. He had
thought, as he testified before the Federal Trade Commission, that only
the NELA and a Milwaukee light company had put up money. Professor
Glaeser, in some indignation, had rejected a suggestion of Dr. Richard
T. Ely, director of the institute, that authorship be shared with a public-
utility official, which under the circumstances was a reasonable idea. He
fought for his integrity further by turning down a guaranteed purchase
order from the NELA of as many as 40,000 copies, with proceeds to go
to the institute.

With the book in galleys at the Macmillan Company in New York,
Professor Glaeser was distressed to receive, in advance of publication,
criticism of his work from the NELA Educational Committee. In fact, the
association's publicity director, of all people, asked that parts of the
introduction be eliminated, it was disclosed at the FTC hearings. Although piqued that proofs had somehow reached alien hands, Professor
Glaeser agreed to drop one paragraph, written by Dr. Ely, because he
said he never liked that section of the introduction anyway. He said he
made other amendments, too, as requested by utility officials, but only
those he thought valid. The utilities liked the revised book very much
and launched a movement to get it distributed to all the high school
principals in Missouri, for a start.

Another work in general circulation for some years that electric
power leaders thought should be revised was *Community Life and
Civic Problems,* by Howard Copeland Hill. Barney Mullaney himself,
Insull's public relations man, and Fred R. Jenkins, chairman of the
NELA Educational Committee, took over the work of the "revision
committee" for the book, which was published by Ginn and Company.
Mr. Jenkins was enthusiastic about the prospects, feeling that "we have
made a good start in getting the largest school-book publishing house,
who printed over 12,000,000 books last year." He was confident that
"after the larger publishers are straightened out and are working with
us, the small publishers will naturally fall into line."

The Jenkins-Mullaney revision of 1928, which Ernest Gruening
thought should have entitled them to billing as coauthors with Mr. Hill,
did not alter the text of the important classroom book to the extent

desired by the utilities. Someone at the publishing house balked at admitting all the verbiage sought by the revisionists.

Although the utilities' committees had what they thought was an understanding with leading publishers, who were expected to submit texts to the National Electric Light Association, "people connected with the higher institutions of education were very touchy on that subject . . . and reports . . . were not such as to encourage a very high-handed attempt to directly control what should go into any textbook." Thus wrote Carl D. Jackson, chairman of the utilities' Committee on Cooperation with Educational Institutions. For the most part, the utilities' pressure groups worked through chambers of commerce and community organizations to keep objectionable textbooks out of local libraries and classrooms. They were not very successful in trying to keep them from being published. They did better at keeping the books out of the schools.

The subversion of education to the narrow vested interests of private utilities was national in scope and so successful for many years that two generations came to believe the foolish hyperbole equating public power with communism and private power interests with the idealism of democracy.

It is said by some observers of the industry that the utilities, both technologically and from the standpoint of the character of much of their leadership, are getting better. As retirement and "more funerals," as one critic has inelegantly put it, occur, improved management and public relations, reflecting merit and true public service, will most certainly develop. In the meantime, however, some of the old techniques remain in force.

The techniques still work, too, although in the private councils where utility executives assemble, there is occasionally an expression of regret over the fact that they are used. Attempts on the part of large investor-owned power networks to pounce upon some municipal operation trying to float a bond issue to replace an aging power plant are not as uniformly welcomed as they once were. The feeling is growing that the big power companies need all the friends they can get and that municipally owned systems should perhaps be allowed to exist, especially when problems of raising large sums of capital by private power companies, opposition on environmental matters, and the like are getting more serious all the time.

Nevertheless, assaults do continue regularly against municipal systems by private corporations, often resorting to heavy-handed evocations of free enterprise reminiscent of the Insullization period. A typical case occurred in Danville, Virginia, in 1969. In a concentrated attack, Appalachian Power Company, one of the subsidiaries of Donald Cook's American Electric Power holding company, came close to consuming the municipal power system, which needed a bond issue passed in a referendum in order to maintain and expand its power plant equipment. As it developed, what was thought to be a citizens' committee trying to defeat the bond issue and get the city out of the power business turned out to be an extension of the private power company. The town system managed to save itself when the IOU sabotage was exposed, but it was a close call.

The government of Danville tried to get the United States Congress to intervene in its behalf and in behalf of other municipal systems vulnerable to takeover by power companies commanding a good deal more capital, management specialists, legal staffs, and freedom of action than a local government could call upon. Unable to arouse response in Congress, Danville appealed to the Federal Power Commission, charging that, among other things, Appalachian was discriminating against the city in its contract to supply bulk power. In September, 1971, the FPC dismissed the Danville claim that it was entitled to the same power-exchange agreement that Appalachian had with other suppliers. The commission noted that Danville in 1968 was generating no more power than it had been in 1958 when it negotiated a "partial requirements" contract with Appalachian. If Danville wanted relief from the 1958 restrictive contract, it would have to expand its generating capacity, thus providing a warrant for the FPC to intercede. In order to rewrite the contract providing for an exchange of power between the city and the private utility, some "mutuality of benefits" was called for. Danville was not producing enough power of its own to support the mutual benefits factor.

Yet, when Danville sought to float a bond issue to fund the expansion of its generating capacity, the private power company, with its greater resources and strong motivation to take over the municipal system in order to eliminate the competition, was charged with organizing enough electoral support against the bond issue to kill it. It was an old political formula that had worked many times in other parts of the country. When citizens are asked to vote for a bond issue, the timing is generally right for the private utility to urge its defeat and the transfer of the municipal system to the IOU, thus making a public bond issue unnecessary. Of course, the utility, once it has acquired the publicly owned system, establishes power rates without the restraining influence of the competition that previously existed.

The old National Electric Light Association, fearing investigation and possible indictment, ran for cover when Franklin D. Roosevelt was elected president. Before he was inaugurated, the organization simply dissolved itself. A successor organization was the Edison Electric Institute (EEI), a trade association whose stated purpose was to provide a forum for the exchange of technical information relating to the electric power business and for the compilation of accurate statistics to help government, industry, banks, and investors in making judgments. Institute members who cringed at the old tactics hoped that the industry's propaganda adventures were over and that the policies of distorting facts and of subversion by pressure were discarded. As far as the Edison Electric Institute itself was concerned, some behavioral improvement was noted. But the industry as a whole still did not permit high hopes for internal reform. The fact was that the old days, the old conduct, the old style had been effective enough to justify their survival, regardless of new hopes for lowered voices, high morals, and good corporate manners.

Between 1935 and 1941, the private utilities were at it again with some of their old verve and a few refinements. Five power companies in the northwestern region of the country were found by the Federal Power Commission to have channeled more than $1 million into propaganda activities. The objective was to influence legislation and political opinion. Although the money had nothing to do with the interests of consumers, half of it was charged to operating costs and was paid by the public.

Reforms instituted by the Roosevelt and Truman administrations were circumvented; propaganda budgets reached several million dollars a year by the time Dwight D. Eisenhower became president. With the help of White House aide Sherman Adams, who doubtless took his cue from General Eisenhower's statement that the Tennessee Valley Authority and public power generally were examples of "creeping socialism," Congress turned over valuable hydroelectric resources to the private utilities. The Idaho Power Company moved in on Hell's Canyon on the Snake River and built three dams.

The party line of the utilities in the 1960s was in important respects unchanged from the days of Insull and the subversion of the education system. In every state and in the nation's capital, the utilities, until they altered their posture toward the end of the decade, made the endless and groundless charge that the country was drifting to "socialized" power, meaning power not generated by private corporations. It was a charge that was contradicted by the continuing capture of municipal systems by the private utilities. Federal power supplied only 20 percent of the electricity that reached the public, but it did not collect the meter fees nor did it transmit energy to the people. It was, and remains, a wholesaler of power to utilities, both public and private, which in turn transmit and sell it to the public.

After 1970, the private utilities had all but quit calling themselves an "unorganized majority" of taxpaying companies threatened with extinction by "organized minorities . . . socialized power groups." Self-pity had become passé.

In the spring of 1963, Federal Power Commissioner Howard Morgan told a special subcommittee in Congress that the utilities were "siphoning off hundreds of millions of dollars a year of consumers' money" by computing their federal taxes on a basis of accelerated depreciation while reporting tax payments to the FPC

> on the basis of the full taxes they would have paid without accelerated depreciation. This means that the consumers are being charged huge amounts representing phantom taxes which are not paid. . . .
>
> Worse still, these funds are reinvested in the corporations with the result that the ratepayer must pay a return on capital involuntarily extracted from him by the utilities. As a result, equivalent amounts are paid out to stockholders, in many cases, as dividends which are in part or in whole tax free . . . the ratepayer is charged for taxes which never go to the Treasury, and stockholders receive income on which they pay no or little taxes.

In that same year, 1963, the National Rural Electric Cooperative Association published an analysis covering a five-year period showing that thirty-eight electric utilities had added $1,259,043,000 to their customers' bills by passing on costs that were either phantom in nature or that should have been paid by investors. Disclosure of this overcharge enraged the utilities, which had for many years conducted a bitter assault on rural electric cooperatives, through which farmers and small communities generate and pay for the power they themselves consume. The cooperatives were formed in the first place when private utilities declined to extend service into low-yield areas where profits were insufficient to interest them. As franchised corporations, they might have been obliged to provide the service at cost or even at a loss, much as railroads were expected to run trains in low-traffic hours, not because the trains were guaranteed to fill up with paying customers, but because the privilege of possessing a guaranteed monopoly carried with it the corresponding mandate to provide service on a modified around-the-clock basis. In due time, of course, railroads tended to adapt to the exclusionary style of the electric utilities by terminating passenger service.

The REA report of $1.25 billion in overcharges and Howard Morgan's testimony disclosing how the utilities collected from their customers for taxes they did not pay came at a time when the power companies were engaged in one of their more memorably spurious national advertising campaigns. It is still recalled at committee hearings in Washington and elsewhere as the apogee of the electric companies' orbit around truth.

The campaign was a by-product of the overconfidence that prevailed in the Eisenhower administration. The full-page ads appeared in most of the nation's leading magazines over a period of several years. Students of advertising and public relations remember them as extraordinary examples of their genre.

The campaign was the work of the Electric Companies Advertising Program (ECAP), which engaged advertising agencies and bought the space to enlighten the public on the threat to freedom inherent in any cooperative or voluntary association that provides electricity—any except, of course, a conventional corporation with investors and stockholders. The program could serve as a classic, if horrendous, example of the evocation of visceral fear by propaganda. Seldom has the chasm been more vast between dreadful conclusions and false premises. A study of these advertisements, which repeatedly reached most of the American reading public, raised the question of how educated people could in conscience authorize, write, design, publish, and collect payment for them.

The first in the series was illustrated with a somber photograph of a worried and worn old couple being taken back toward the Berlin Wall, after nearly reaching the barbed wire across which they might have escaped from East Berlin. Armed guards were shown thwarting the pair's pathetic quest for freedom. The stark headline above the text of the ad was: "Freedom Is Not Lost by Guns Alone."

The text drew a parallel between the Communist capture of the aged couple at the Berlin Wall and the generation of electric power by publicly owned systems. "When government owns business," said the text, "it can control both goods and jobs. It adds economic powers to its vast political powers. . . . Then freedom has slipped quietly away. A quiet threat can be the deadliest. You may not know it's there until too late." The sponsor signature was "Investor-Owned Electric Light and Power Companies."

President Kennedy called this advertisement an example of "a particularly ugly advertising campaign" in a speech at Muscle Shoals, Alabama, on May 18, 1963, marking the thirtieth anniversary of TVA. He deplored the implication that TVA and public power "were comparable to the Berlin Wall and the East Berlin police as threats to our freedom . . . the tremendous economic growth of this region, its private income, make it clear to all that TVA is a fitting answer to socialism—and it certainly has not been creeping."

Another ad in the series asked: "Do You Know YOUR Family Is Taxed to Pay for Public Power?" It went on to say that Americans had been taxed $5.5 billion to put the federal government into the electric light and power business, neglecting to mention that such funds were repayable as loans.

> Now the lobbyists and pressure groups for this so-called "public power" are pressing for another $10 billion more—to put the government still farther into that business. This additional tax spending would be completely unnecessary. The hundreds of independent electric light and power companies are ready and able to provide all the low-price electricity people will need—*without* depending on your taxes. These are the companies that have doubled the supply of electricity in the past ten years, and will double the present supply in the next ten. . . . So spread the word among your friends and neighbors. As soon as enough people understand, they'll stop the unnecessary spending of everybody's money. . . . When "Public Power" Wins—YOU Lose!

Senator Ernest Gruening wondered how the "independent" companies, as they were called in this advertisement, could find themselves in peril when they could double and redouble power output in twenty years. Among the companies achieving this notable record of growth were the independent utilities competing with, and buying their power wholesale from, the Tennessee Valley Authority.

Still another ad showed an appealing baby boy, his face gooey from a rambunctious and playful refusal to eat tidily the spoonfuls of food being ladled out by his mother. It was a "Picture of a Man Who Owns the Electric Companies" and was intended to illustrate an important facet of utility company economics. The year-old boy was said to be a new stockholder of America's electric light and power companies, one of 94 million such threatened participants in the capitalistic system. His father had bought him seven shares of stock in a Dayton utility, which made him one of 4 million direct owners of United States power companies, and his grandfather had opened a savings account for the child, which made him one of 90 million indirect owners through bank savings, insurance premiums, and pension funds.

From this capsule report, the text took off into space with: "Some people would have the federal government take over all of the power companies. But isn't there a real danger in a single monopoly—rather than in 400 independent electric power companies owned by more than 94 million people?"

The strange need to conjure the presence of the insidious nonexistent enemy seemed to go on forever.

It is no longer the fashion to send checks to university department heads. Nor is it common to expend large advertising budgets to persuade people that the Tennessee Valley Authority, the farmers electric cooperative, or the public power plant in Burlington, Vermont, are somehow extensions of bolshevism designed to pervert the American system of free enterprise. It simply would not be considered believable, after the winters and summers of power brownouts, voltage failures, and generator breakdowns from 1965 to 1972, for the utilities to spend advertising money advising the public of the dangers of publicly owned power. The old, much advertised slogan, "When 'Public Power' Wins—YOU Lose," lost its meaning to people convinced by the facts of daily life that all the utilities together, public and private, were unable to transmit sufficient power to meet the requirements of a hot summer day.

But in much of the country served by small-town daily newspapers, chain-owned in many cases, and by weekly publications, the same old falsehoods have continued to be published. The source of editorial material is never identified. Thus, it has appeared to be the considered judgment of the editorial writers of the publications.

These editorials, which promote what Senator Lee Metcalf has called "prehistoric political thought," are prepared by E. Hofer and Sons, a publicity and propaganda mill in Hillsboro, Oregon, that for a fee writes and sends material each week to most of the newspapers in the country outside metropolitan and urban areas. Twelve to fifteen editorials, each 200 to 300 words or so in length, are contained in a packet, and each constitutes approved copy paid for by industrial and trade association clients. The privately owned utilities have been customers of Hofer and Sons for years. Publishers of Hofer material range from lazy editors glad to get free material to fill space to owners delighted to print old-fashioned trash in which they personally believe, or think their readers believe. Here is an example of one 1970 editorial from the *Daily Times* of Glasgow, Kentucky.*

Miniaturized Socialism

Quite frequently, in an attempt to escape economic reality, people will vote for public ownership of a taxpaying private enterprise. In this way, the taxpayers of local communities are saddled with the burden of running school buses, transit systems and other utilities including electric power.

The pitfalls of this kind of miniaturized socialism were brought to light with dramatic clarity recently when the analysis was made in San Diego, California, of how much it would cost the city to take over the local electric company's power distribution system. A nationally known engineering firm came up with figures that

---

* Glasgow, Kentucky, is not exactly "saddled with" ownership of a publicly owned power system. It is one of 2,000 communities that own their own generating or transmission facilities. The rate in Glasgow for 1,000 kilowatt-hours of electricity is $10.93. In San Diego, the same quantity of power costs $16.07.

should be an eyeopener to taxpayers of San Diego or any other
community contemplating a similar step.

The engineering firm's study showed that in the case of San
Diego the residents would be burdened with between $4.5 million
and $8.3 million a year in higher electric rates and additional taxes
as a consequence of city operation of the power system. Some of
the costs of such a move were detailed in the study. Not only
would a bond issue be required in excess of $200 million to take
over the company but once the city removed company property
from the tax rolls, local taxpayers would be forced to assume a
number of new burdens. Among these would be the cost of under-
grounding power lines which will run to the tune of more than a
million dollars a year. In addition, the power company now pays
more than $2.63 million annually in school taxes to the city.
A municipally-operated power system is tax exempt so the taxpayers would have to make up this loss.

There is no magic in the operation of any commercial enterprise by a public agency. The arithmetic of economics remains unchanged, irrespective of who owns and runs the business. The only
difference is that usually public ownership is less efficient than taxpaying private ownership.

The idea that there was something inherently evil about a community
owning its own transmission lines or a power plant, whether in San
Diego or Glasgow, has historically produced recurrent attacks of para-
noia among private utilities. Their response to publicly owned power and
their prolonged expensive campaigns to equate it with ideological origins
have been so ludicrous that reporting them and citing the tactics and
language they use seems to approximate defamation of the utilities industry. The leadership and spokesmen for the electric utilities over the
years lost their credibility, and in view of the reckless risks they took
with reason and veracity, perhaps the loss was both understandable and
deserved. But in the emergent, and in the forthcoming flourishing, era
of nuclear power, such corporations need to regain their credibility—
assuming they ever possessed it—and demonstrate a candor, an integrity,
and a responsibility that have never been characteristic of most corporate
conduct.

The electric utilities were the corporate pioneers in the application of
public relations and propaganda, heavily laced with patriotism and
idealism, to win and sustain public support for practices and policies
that were often odious. They refined the techniques for presenting
avarice and mendacity so attractively attired that they were socially and
educationally desirable.

Now, vast sums of money flow into universities and colleges from
government and industry, money offered with public fanfare and money

concealed beneath arrangements that hide secret goals, sometimes secret because disclosure would bring on a public outcry. Money and contracts come from the armed services, espionage projects, and research and power promotion agencies like the Atomic Energy Commission. A substantial body of researchers and permanent students move from industry to government to educational institutions, often (as in the old days) drawing income from two or more sources at the same time. The difference is that the process has become legitimatized and institutionalized at the highest levels. Educators serve on boards of corporations, and many more industrial executives serve on the boards of trustees of private and state universities. Federal agencies train legal and technical experts to regulate and prosecute corporate transgressions, then observe the departure of the experts to the corporations, there to defend what they formerly prosecuted. Propaganda and the manipulation of opinion is a major business of the executive branch of the government, and the policies and the product it promotes are the administration's and the president's.

Authorities with a recognized cachet in a given field serve as consultants to industry by the thousands, on a scale that Insull could not have imagined. What was once considered subversive because of its blatancy and directness has become, with refinement and upgrading, common professional practice; and the utilities can scarcely compete successfully for the attention and educational services they once dominated.

6

Power in the Tourist
Trap
Kingdom

THOSE WHO plan the dimensions of electric power foresee in the generation closing out the twentieth century, and seek to impose upon it, a continuation of the staggering consumption statistics of the past. They see a per capita increase of 200 percent in the 1980s alone. It is a projection based on national experience and past accomplishment. Rarely in the inner councils of power is the necessity for such enormous growth questioned. The future presents opportunities that must be grasped and developed. Nothing in past experience suggests that a tapering-off of power expansion is useful or socially necessary.

All planning is based on a projected growth in which a doubled population and expanding industry will consume more and more power every year beyond the millennium. It is not an assumption; rather, it is considered to be a mathematical certainty.

How can people be expected to consume 10 trillion (10,000,000,000,-000) kilowatt-hours of electric energy annually by the year 2000 when the power industry was stumbling along trying to produce a little more than 1½ trillion kilowatt-hours back in 1971? They cannot, it seems, avoid it; and no one of stature in the world of energy expects people to want to avoid it, anyway. President Nixon, in 1970, saw no inconsistency between continued existing industrial growth patterns and the advancement of the good life for Americans. Nor did the Edison Electric Institute, the electric utilities trade association made up of 180 operating companies in the United States, 11 holding companies, and 26 affiliated members from countries and islands of North, Central, and South America.

For twelve years, until his retirement in 1969, the managing director of the institute was Edwin Vennard, a familiar and persevering personage repeatedly recognized for his clear, uncomplicated interpretation of the American industrial system and his uncompromising opposition to public ownership of power. An advocate of aggressive marketing and hard selling in the utilities field, Mr. Vennard sold his ideas on capitalistic enterprise and American liberty so persuasively and assiduously that he won seven awards from the Freedoms Foundation, a conservative institution supporting fundamentalist concepts of competition not necessarily applicable to the electric utilities. He was succeeded in the EEI by W. Donham Crawford, administrative vice-president of the Consolidated Edison Company, a nuclear specialist, and a graduate of the United States Naval Academy, who had served with the Atomic Energy Commission at its Savannah River operations in Aiken, South Carolina.

Mr. Vennard left on the EEI the stamp of his durable philosophy, which he developed on his upward course through electric utilities companies in Louisiana and the Middle West. He had become, upon his retirement, respected by some as a relic of the industry and by others as a monument to it.

Vennard's measure of a successful electric utility was its return on money. He thought aggressive marketing had proved itself by expanding profits at relatively low investment cost. He found in television some of the promise for the future that atomic power held out to the newer breed of nuclear engineers. He said:

> The first pattern [in marketing] was house-to-house canvassing to show that new appliances would work. Then still in the residential area, the idea was to sell the whole electric kitchen or laundry. Then from that the idea was for total electric living, for homes, offices, and industry. Now, of course, just over the horizon you see the electric city coming.
>
> Certainly you see more mass selling than house-to-house. Dealers are selling the units, the utility is selling the concept. Television now is one of the strongest media with which to sell. It's more economical and more effective to reach local customers through national media. Keep in mind that during the evening hours, 65 percent of the people to whom the utilities want to sell the benefits of electric living are watching one of the three major TV networks. And the only way to get those customers is to use one of those major networks. You can't do that on a local station basis. More and more you've got to use the national media to tell your story . . . and the electric living concept is common to all.

Always, the best opportunity open to electric utilities, in Vennard's view, was to sell more and more electric lighting. It offered the highest profit for the lowest cost. "I happen to believe in a strong, prosperous, aggressive, efficient sales organization, complete and full, selling everything we have across the board . . . provided that you measure the cost of getting the business against the value of the business you're getting. You *can* measure that." Lighting was the first service Edison's companies sold and it "still offers the biggest market, with the biggest return. Increase the wattage of every lamp in a territory by thirty watts and you'd realize more net revenues than from all the electric heating."

The trouble with marketing heating had been that promotional costs failed to return as much income and profit as lighting sales, largely because the cost per kilowatt-hour went down as the volume of electricity went up. But in household lighting, a company was not required by competitive factors or rate procedures to cut back hourly charges. Hence, there was more money in increased lighting for the elementary reason that it did not cost anything more to provide the current, and therefore the company got back a lot more on the dollar. The return on increased lighting ranged from 12 to 18 percent on marketing investments; whereas other forms of promotion offered perhaps one fourth of that.

Why households needed 30 more watts in every light bulb when 65 percent of the people spent their after-dark hours pinned down in front of television sets, Mr. Vennard never made clear. But it was a marketing policy that characterized the power industry. Power sales were exploited less because they filled an existing need than because the public seemed always ready to be persuaded that it could consume more and more electricity if it tried. Even though residential use of power seldom exceeded 32 percent of the total national power sold, it produced 42.5 percent of total revenues. Heavy industry, which consumed 42.6 percent of all electric energy, produced 25 percent of the revenues. The more a customer used, the less he paid.

Mr. Vennard saw nothing to be concerned about with regard to occasional threats of more federal regulation or investigations into utility practices. It was a confidence based on forty years of experience. Regulatory bodies could be counted on to keep conditions stable in the industry by allowing rate fixing that made the promotion of increased household usage highly profitable. In the fifteen or twenty years after World War II, electrical rates in many areas were reduced; but with people using 8 or 9 percent more current each year, everything worked out to the industry's benefit. If Mr. Vennard differed with his colleagues on basic points, it was on the question of how to make the most money expanding the use of power, not on whether to keep promoting its expansion.

Rate decreases after World War II produced heady predictions from industry spokesmen that the unit, or wattage, cost of electric power would continue to go down—down to "next to nothing at all," one optimistic leader declared—over the years as per capita consumption increased. Such optimism proved unwarranted, alas, when, after the mid-1960s, the rates all over the country began to climb, alarmingly in some areas. By 1970, with a few oil companies largely in control of the oil, gas, coal, and uranium fuels markets, the upward thrust of electric power rates completely routed the old promises of cheaper rates with expanded consumption.

However, Robert H. Gerdes, who retired as president of the Edison Electric Institute a year or so after Edwin Vennard, was easily persuaded by his experience that the history and prospects for the future of the electric utilities offered little cause for anything other than joy. In a study published by the institute, entitled *The Year 2000*, Mr. Gerdes found solace in the increase in capital investment from $90 billion in the private electric utility industry (in 1969) to a modest $550 billion at the end of the century. This would be necessary, he thought, to feed the public all that power they were going to need, or were going to be persuaded that they needed. It was true, of course, that social problems were being encountered along the way, that "high on the list are the problems of minorities," but the industry is "helping train and find rewarding employment for them." Another problem was the communications gap between the industry and "the younger generation—and other groups as well—and we are helping build bridges to better understanding."

Mr. Gerdes found no other industry

doing more than ours in these areas of human concern. Our efforts are notable in fields ranging from environmental controls and recreation to conservation and esthetics. . . . We are also in the forefront of industrial statesmanship, in aid to education, community betterment, and on-the-job training for hard-core unemployed.

Unfortunately, gifted young people did not seem very interested in careers in the utility business "because they say they want to serve humanity . . . they seem to disdain higher income opportunities in the business world."

The challenge of the future, as Mr. Gerdes saw it, was to maintain "our free form of government—and no less important, our free form of business enterprise. . . . We are anticipating the needs of the future and actively helping to shape it."

Whether or not Mr. Gerdes and his associates in the power business were correctly assessing the needs of the future, it could not be denied that he spoke for an industry that was "actively helping to shape it," and the prospect gave some people the shivers.

According to the Edison Institute's vision, the more fortunate of the 300 million (or maybe 360 million, depending on the birth rate) expected to be on hand by the time the utility industry has its $550 billion invested, will be the beneficiaries of life in electrical dream cities. An artist's rendering of one planned city, with its history rooted firmly in the playland fantasies of Walt Disney, shows an urban complex of multiple levels, antiseptic, unlittered, as orderly as a stage set.

"Note the grouping of major facilities around an electric rail terminal," the student of *The Year 2000* is advised. It is worth noting, too, that almost none of the 360 million people of the country are visible in the planned electrified city. The streets are gleaming white and noiseless; the air is unpolluted; and a panorama discloses one bus, nine vehicles in motion, thirty-five others parked in capacious, unfilled lots, and a few pedestrians making their way between a dispersed cluster of buildings, each of which resembles an air terminal. The structures are identified as sites for clearly compartmentalized activities: The Arts, Engineering, Vocational Studies, Family Education, Commerce and Industry, Education Center (presumably nonfamily), Nuclear Research, and Museum.

"Convenience," the text asserts, "will be a prime consideration" in the development of this large, if somewhat unpeopled, city. The staff of the Edison Electric Institute, in consultation with designers, scientists, city planners, and power company ecologists, assisted with the study. (The employment classification "power company ecologist" was itself relatively new, wedged into the planning structure by the necessity of public relations response to the rising outrage against environmental ruin by power plants, industry, and people. Some of these new experts have been influential in their companies and have tried to serve as emissaries of the public in intracompany dialogue.) The electric-city planners projected the following developments within a generation:

Half of all energy used in the United States will be used to generate electricity.

Half of *that* energy will be produced by nuclear fuels.

All electrical service will be more reliable and lower in cost than it is today, despite continuing inflation.

Use of computers and a broadened use of credit will mean that society will be almost "cashless." Thus, with currency virtually invisible, people will be called upon to devote an increased portion of their money to conduct computerized transactions to disburse and dispose of their own money.

Computers will make greater product variety possible through the control of production and scheduling.

Computers and copying machines will make publishing and printing radically different, particularly in the mass-information media.

Individual electric cars will be widely used both for short- and long-haul travel, a projection that overlooks the reincarnation of a steam-powered vehicle, possibly because it would not relate to electric energy expansion. (Authorities less committed to electric energy than utilities specialists thought the steam car offered better prospects for long-haul transport than electric cars. In 1970, a Japanese auto manufacturer was reported readying a Freon-powered steam car for the market and in the United States, industrialist William Lear, after an earlier failure, announced that design and engineering problems had been solved, leading the way to production of a vapor turbine engine and a pollution-free automobile.)

Mass transportation will combine the use of rapid transit systems with individual electric automobiles. A new type of mass transportation would be a "people mover," such as one planned for downtown New York City. Longer-range transportation projections involve dispatching interurban travelers through conduits by the use of compressed air.

Large-scale enclosures of advanced design, reminiscent of those built by Buckminster Fuller and similar to those that have put baseball parks under roofs, will envelop recreation, farming, and shopping activities. They are technically capable of containing whole residential areas.

Climate control will be in general use. Purification of air and odor control will be available to some.

Mind-expanding and mind-affecting drugs, for possession of which people were imprisoned in 1972, will be available and, it must be assumed, made legal. Included among such drugs may be one to "increase" human memory.

Where land is scarce, multistory farms and food factories will be in use, although oceans and lakes will supply a large part of human food.

Aircraft will carry 900 or more passengers, as many as an ocean liner, at supersonic speed from New York to Los Angeles in two hours. "The difficulty," as seen by the electric industry's projections, is that it will create noise and airport-siting problems. "But there seems general agreement in the aircraft industry that the problems will be met." Not necessarily solved, perhaps, but "met," or tolerated. Instead of in-flight movies being viewed under more or less "improvised" conditions aboard the plane, showings may take place in "real theaters." Magazine racks will be replaced by libraries. Such advances will improve "travel comfort and conveniences." *

Nine out of ten Americans will live in urban centers.

Every one of them will have a home computer.

Electric lighting will be so abundant that the city will be designed for "viewing at night as well as day," with illuminated curb lines, mailboxes, bus shelters, bulletin boards, traffic signs, and street names. Floral window boxes and both private and public gardens are to be wired to provide low-level "accent" lighting, enormously increasing all year round the profitable consumption of wattage previously familiar to the Christmas season.

The Edison Institute study acknowledged that some of the psychologists, sociologists, and ecologists had warned against dependence on domes covering large areas and enclosing many different kinds of activity:

> Questions of economic and engineering feasibility aside, these people argue that the general population will not want to live in domed communities. Of course, as people become used to more climate control in limited areas they may find it more desirable than the social scientists predict.

On this point, utility company engineers and Mr. Vennard's aggressive marketing organizations had considerably more experience in what the public would tolerate than the sociologists. The persuasive power of television could only increase once wall-high living room pictures for life-sized reception in the home became available. The larger the television reception screen, the more color, the more authentic the sound, the more perfectly the presentation could simulate real life, the more impact communications would have in inducing people to adjust and respond with favor to the kind of life the electric utilities and industrial society had in mind for them.

Engineers and marketing specialists were confident that air-purification and odor-control facilities offered in domed communities would easily neutralize latent disdain people might feel for the well-managed life under plastic skies.

After a few preliminary years of subjection to life-sized, full-dimension television in maximum-energized households in which people could move from room to room without ever being out of range of sight or sound, it is felt that emotional objections to efficiency and progress would give way (as they always had in the past) to the collective desire for accep-

---

* This vision of supersonic aircraft crossing the country in two hours received a setback late in March, 1971, when the Congress defeated the Nixon administration's prolonged fight to build the SST, after spending $850 million on it. By a close final Senate vote of 51 to 46, funding on the SST project was stopped.

tance and status. Holdouts in all probability would be limited to that culturally deprived 10 percent of the population beyond the megalopolis limits. The utilities were prepared "to use every resource of technology to the full to make power so cheap, so abundant, and so available that it ceases to be a limiting factor in man's designs."

That was the plan for the future. In the meantime, the threat of power failures and *brownouts* (as voltage cutbacks were called) have characterized the peak-load operations of power companies in the early years of the generation that is to bring to the people the miracle of the harmonious, well-ordered life of inexpensive, abundant power. Even more embarrassing has been the nagging necessity on the part of power companies to apply time after time to regulatory commissions for permission to raise their rates to tide them over tax bills and operational problems that plague them on the way to the promised land.

It is a promised land of supercomputers to select the most economical power for varying load requirements. They will be in uninterrupted communication with each other, controlling and conveying power through integrated systems. "Negative" nuclear fuels, as they are called, which produce more fissionable material than they consume, will be generating electricity in such boundless volume that the waste of 60 percent of the energy consumed in making it will not matter. The fissionable material produced by this advanced form of nuclear power is plutonium, the most dangerously toxic substance now on earth.

Yet, it will—at least the world is assured it will—drive down the kilowatt-hour cost to the point where, in a few years, it will be more expensive to meter and collect the charge than to produce it. In fact, the highest cost factor will be the price of money (financing and credit) itself, for the banks and investment houses that, with securities buyers, must supply money in some ratio to the supply of electric power, have their commodity to market, too.

Electric utilities have committed, they say, $150 million a year to "our future . . . today's research and development." This is quite modest, of course, compared with the $536 million spent in a single year by the Atomic Energy Commission for reactor development, plus another $237 million for research in nuclear physics, which with a few other odds and ends, adds up to $1 billion. Since Atomic Energy Commission funds come from the taxpayers and company money comes largely from utility customers who thus contribute twice, and since the utilities and other corporations by law must get the benefits of AEC resources anyway, few obstacles militate against the corporate vision of the future.

Yet, it was asked in the Edison Electric study, was $1 billion a year enough? Alas, it was not. It was, perhaps, enough to shape a *great* future, but surely not sufficient for the "greatest future." Not when one considers "the operation of all kinds of marvelous devices, some we can imagine and some we cannot now have any gleaning of."

The prevention of air pollution in cities was not deeply examined by the utilities industry, but the prospects of marketing power in urban centers "now plagued by polluted air" held great promise. Electricity makes possible the air conditioning of entire cities and makes prevention of pollution less necessary, if not less interesting. Abatement of pollution, of course, is restrictive and enormously costly. Air conditioning of whole cities to shield the populace from the thermal and toxic pollution that surrounds them can create billions of dollars worth of new markets, thus expanding the economy.

The 85 billion discarded tin cans and bottles that seem to breed like plutonium along highways, in vacant lots, and in public places and that will grow in number and variety will be converted into usable materials in electrically and chemically devised recycling processes. In the electric dream city, civilization will become "junkless," for junk itself will be a profitable harvest.

As for fresh water, "there is all the sea to desalinate and all the sewage to salvage." The sea, of course, is seen as "inexhaustible." Dependence on inexhaustibility remains largely a condition of dreams for making deserts bloom, installing warm and covered cities in Arctic region, producing costless electric power, and creating an acquisitive society, where, as seen by the Edison Institute, consumerism and utopia go hand in hand: "Food, clothing, and the creature comforts for the hungry peoples of the world would be within our reach . . . and perhaps peace, too."

But, the electric power industry warned,

Let's not get carried away with specifics, because this age awaiting us is incalculable. There will still be problems and still work to do. But this we can be sure of: this unrestrictive power supply can unbind our present civilization to release us into a much higher one. The burden of responsibility for bringing this about lies in great part on the electric utility industry. It is even now engaged in prodigious undertakings . . . the surge to nuclear generation [has] surpassed the wildest expectations.

Whether such expectations were wild or not, they were, and remain, real, modified by the fact that unenlightened and often obstinate people failed to appreciate the values defined and enumerated by the helpful electric power industry. It should "not expect, in the interest of the socially important task before it, to be heavily handicapped." On the contrary, "we would look to an informed public to understand the virtual impossibility of burying very high voltage lines underground at this stage of transmission technology. We would hope that the big new nuclear plants receive the cordial public acceptance that their great benefits warrant."

It did not seem altogether fair to the Edison Institute that so many people, rather than accepting cordially the great nuclear centers, were in fact questioning the sanity of their promoters, at worst, or the wisdom of their plans, at best. Power plant management, with the initiative and support of the nuclear fuels and equipment industry, always made it absolutely clear that the most pressing reason for larger generating plants was rooted in economies of scale, meaning, the larger the power plant, the more economically every kilowatt could be produced. With nuclear plants, even though the waste in lost energy was enormous and the dangers to the environment threatening, the kilowatt-hour cost could be held in check, perhaps kept from rising under the pressure of inflation. With electricity costs favorable, in comparison with other production and consumer costs, power would remain both abundant and a bargain. More customers would buy more and more power, increasing gross income to the utilities, amortizing the staggering capital outlays required to build the nuclear generating plants in the first place.

All this is mandatory "to build the heavy loads necessary for the full realization of the possibilities of the new technologies." The disclosure of such goals and the pride expressed by utilities leadership in them had an unintended, sometimes chilling effect on people. What public relations spokesmen defined as *beautility*—a word reminiscent of *Insullization* in the 1930s, intended in this instance to make power plant installations less objectionable—was not uniformly accepted as the essence of beauty and utility.*

In its projections of plans for the future, the Edison Institute outlined in sometimes imaginative, frequently grotesque detail the kind of model or experimental cities intended to encompass total electric living. These cities were an extension of the electric kitchen and the complete electric home for which Mr. Vennard campaigned—the electric city on which the industry relied for increased consumption in the next generation when people will buy four times more electric energy than they bought in 1970.

The first city designed evolved from the vision of that master of make-believe, the creator and producer of real-life fairy tales that entertained millions of people for many years: the late Walt Disney and the

---

* Pretty words to mask unpleasant truth are the cosmetic creations of public relations, commonplace in the power industry. The Atomic Energy Commission in June, 1970, selected an abandoned salt mine near Lyons, Kansas, as the nation's first underground radioactive-waste repository. The 1,000-acre site could handle all commercial atomic waste to the end of the century, the AEC said. The new name for the place was also announced: Kansas Nuclear Park.

corporate empire he left as a legacy to eternal childhood and its profitable markets.

The second is an experimental city, which began in 1968 with a
planning grant of $248,000 to the University of Minnesota, and which,
although scarcely beyond the level of a Disney fantasy in terms of development, nevertheless suggested that the complicated, even horrifying
problems of urban rot stimulated specialists both in science and fiction
to plan at times along separate, sometimes parallel lines.

Construction of the experimental Machine City "could begin right
now," according to one of its designers, Dr. Athelstan Spilhaus, dean of
the University of Minnesota Institute of Technology when the planning
project was undertaken and later president of Franklin Institute in Philadelphia. Dr. Spilhaus had achieved popularity by turning out for some
years an instructive daily cartoon dealing with science, planning, and
ecology for a syndicate of newspapers. He was also known through his
teaching, writing, and social criticism directed at man's reprehensible
assault on his environment. He saw the future city as a machine, and
he and two colleagues designed one to function at a specified capacity.
"When demand exceeds a machine's capacity, you do not tack new parts
onto the machine or feed it more work while it breaks down. You build
another machine." The experimental city was designed more or less explicitly for 250,000 people, and it could not be expanded into the chaos
typical of conventional cities. "You will build another city." Thus, Machine City, on which construction could indeed begin at once if there
was any money to be made by doing so, was intended as a prototype
for the mass-produced city. No engineer would dream of mass-producing
anything, said Dr. Spilhaus, without first building and testing an experimental prototype.

Machine City would offer a haven for a single month's supply of the
3 million new citizens being added to existing cities that, as Dr. Spilhaus
said, are "already overburdened by problems no present solution can
remedy." In Machine City, people would be set down in an environment
providing economic sufficiency and "the least amount of private harassment and public regulation" at a minimum expenditure of money and
energy.

At the center of Machine City, which was intended not as a laboratory model but as a real city with "real people" living in it, as Dr. Spilhaus has said, will be a nuclear power plant. Before the city comes to
life, the power-generating and transmissions system will be capable of
providing limitless energy for completely operational factories, residential
areas, public and private transportation, municipal and business buildings, and all utility, educational, and supporting facilities. Only then
would 250,000 volunteers move in to occupy their own homes "as indi-

viduals," appropriately dispersed around town to support a neighborhood social and cultural life.

This "chosen population," selected for qualifications and temperament characteristics that remain to be determined, would be linked to one another and to shopping centers, homes, factories, information and data processing centers, banks, and so forth through multipurpose computers. Their city would be centrally heated and probably fully air conditioned by abundant electric power.

No external water supply will be needed once a basic quantity is furnished as standard equipment at the outset. Thereafter, water will be recycled and reused through a "closed system." Grades of water will be separated, drawn from the original bulk supply, with reserve tanks to be topped off from time to time to correct the loss from evaporation. No water will be thrown away, nor, presumably, collected from rainfall or snow, if there is any. Only water of the best purity will flow through the system used for drinking, cooking, and bathing. A second grade will be bacteriologically acceptable for washing, laundry, street cleaning, and the like. Effluent will be treated and used for cooling and industrial purposes, with solids and chemicals removed for cycling back into industrial use. A municipal greenhouse, fertilized by wastes and irrigated by recovered evaporation, will supplement the city's food supply. Refuse that cannot be reused will be sent away on deadheading freight vehicles.

All materials must be designed for decomposition into nutrients or for recomposition into something useful, thus eliminating garbage disposal and trash heaps. Packages and containers that fail to meet the requirements would have to be taxed so heavily at the manufacturing level that they would have to be replaced by others suitable for recycling.

Fuel-burning automobiles and industrial plants will be outlawed in Machine City. All vehicles will be powered by electricity. There will be no superhighways, no rush-hour traffic, no slums or ghettos, no garbage or junk, and no urban decay. It will be a quiet, clean, comfortable, gracious, and "if these qualities make for human happiness—a happy city." Dr. Spilhaus thought things could stay that way because the city is designed as a machine, to be repaired and readjusted to conditions as they develop or are planned.

Construction methods will make it unnecessary for a business or industry to work a factory to death to get its money back. A structure that fails to function as planned, and does not make its contribution to the entity, will be dismantled and rebuilt in some configuration more related to the community operation. Obsolescence will be caught as, or before, it develops, and a cure will be built into the system before the disease of decay advances beyond the point of toleration. Slums, "another form of obsolescence, would lose their economic excuse for existing."

Because men can design a machine to do what it is intended to do, they can do the same thing to a city. Yet, it would be "repugnant" to think of imposing preplanned conditions on individual human beings that would compel them to behave according to prescription, Dr. Spilhaus cautioned. No force should dragoon hordes of human guinea pigs into Machine City or compel them to conform to certain patterns. The experimental city is not a practice run for some manipulated social order. It is

> an attempt to find out what kind of city can be built that will best guarantee a decent life for those who live in it. I would like to see the citizen be master of his own living space, rather than the present situation in which ant hill crowding and multiple abuses of common rights make the city a blind, headless master of its people.

Everyone in the city must be a "volunteer," and the planners are confident that applications for admission will exceed capacity. All volunteers will be "screened carefully," there being no good reason to admit persons whose skills are unneeded or who perhaps have no skills at all. Appropriate vocational categories will be filled through computerized studies to determine the precise services needed to back up the worker population. Banks, shops, beauty parlors, hot dog stands, theaters, and "every other need, comfort, or convenience" will be provided.

Yet, with all this, it is supposed that some people, notwithstanding the screening process, will not like such a city. Every flexibility will be provided to change things that people dislike. If they still do not like it, "we will have learned much of value from it, as happens with most experiments that failed."

Although Dr. Spilhaus conceded the possibility of failure in a manufactured city, owing to the variable response factor of individual human beings, the Walt Disney corporation entertained no such doubts. Disney World's electric and computerized city promised, in addition to economic rewards charted by the utilities, both happiness and investment returns. Of course, the Disney populace is also to be selected in a controlled screening process to rule out drifters, malcontents, and agitprop types so that what will be left will be happy people, content to be on display for tourists with the enterprises employing them and with the material things they produce. Free of stress and conflict, in a technological-age extension of the cheerful and industrious artisans of a Disney fairy tale, they will, no doubt, whistle while they work.

Nothing is to be left to chance in Disney World. Whereas Dr. Spilhaus reasoned that unpredictable factors might make Machine City an imperfect world, possibly even a stultifying one, and yet one that would provide experience and data for further planning, the perennial optimism and precisely controlled order of a Disney World were clearly in conjunction with the bright future planned by the electric utilities.

Moving along on schedule, the $400-million Disney World, built on 27,400 acres southwest of Orlando, Florida, opened for business in October, 1971, with 7,000 employees ready to greet 80,000 visitors a day. Each of them spent the expected seven or eight dollars daily on rides and concessions, in addition to meals and motel lodgings. Far from complete, the new Mecca was the result, said the master planners (using one of those *beautility* words) of five years of "imagineering."

The electric dream city of Disney World would sound like an outrageous parody if it were not for its growth from a design to a reality in five years. A full year before it opened, it had 2,500 employees on its payroll. Its impact on the state of Florida and the Deep South, on energy consumption, on the annual movement of perhaps 10 to 20 million visitors coming and going in automobiles and campers, on land and water resources will take some years to measure.

To a management fraternity familiar with computerized planning applied to real estate development, and confident that twenty-odd years of television had both created and conditioned their market, a whole new city created for the express purpose of making money is the ultimate business investment. This is Disney World, prototype of the community of tomorrow, a work-and-play land with audiences, participants, and customers combined. It is a show that could run day and night.

Residents of Disney World and visitors on tour will be equally, if separately, significant to its commercial success. A world's fair atmosphere offers ready-made opportunities for marketing teams and business developers. It is adjusted to the reflexes, pleasures, materialism, and cultural limitations of families who trace their heritage through Mary Poppins, Snow White, Donald Duck, the Seven Dwarfs, and all the rodents and mammals that escaped barnyard and jungle to cavort with and captivate cartoon human figures.

Nowhere in America have demands for increased electric power equaled those in Florida. In fifteen years, from 1957 to the projected usage of 1972, kilowatt capacity will increase 600 percent, to 7 million. In the decade between 1957 and 1967, when the country's population increased by 16 percent, Florida's grew by 43 percent. Tourism, development, and the aerospace industry produced so much expansion that money, it was said, ran down the gutters. The Florida Power and Light Company, serving the southern wing of the state, received a construction permit from the Atomic Energy Commission in April, 1967, to build an atomic power plant in the Turkey Point area of Biscayne Bay, which reaches southward twenty miles or so beyond Miami.*

Prospects of a nuclear reactor heating up the subtropical shallows of Biscayne Bay, where summer water temperatures rise to 90 degrees or more, horrified much of the populace and conservationists throughout the country. McGregor Smith, board chairman of the power company, a man given to cracker-barrel puns (he said Florida had "grewsome") and genuinely concerned about wildlife preservation in Florida, asked the aid of the Walt Disney organization to help him make his power plants acceptable to the public while concurrently protecting the animal life and flora of the mangrove swamps adjacent to the bay.

Mr. Smith wanted Walt Disney to establish a "Disney jungle," beginning a few hundred yards away from a nuclear plant and encompassing much of an 1,800-acre site. The wildlife refuge would surround a Seminole Indian village, recreated as a tourist attraction, to make the place look like Florida must have been "many, many years ago."

When Senator Edmund S. Muskie, chairman of the Senate subcommittee on air and water pollution, was presiding over hearings in Miami in April, 1968, to assess thermal pollution of Biscayne Bay by the new nuclear plant, it was disclosed that Walt Disney had turned down "for a number of reasons" Mr. Smith's hopeful plan for an organized jungle next door to a nuclear reactor. It was not revealed whether the Seminoles would have gone along with the idea, but as for Mr. Disney, he would not. At the time Mr. Smith asked him to "think up" some good jungle ideas, Disney was already committed to building the model electrified city of the future near Orlando. His brother Roy and other associates then felt that one big project in Florida was enough.

The management and marketing experience and the confidence developed by making Disney enterprises and entertainment projects famous and profitable around the globe are all to be focused on this city of the future, of power and energy, of eternal delight, where, like Las Vegas, the night cannot be distinguished from the day in the centers of business and play. Since Disney World, or EPCOT (Experimental Prototype of the City of Tomorrow), will address itself to the "endless task" of depicting life out there in the yet-to-come land, it "will never be completed." It will always go on introducing, testing, and demonstrating new ideas and technologies created by American innovation and industry. It will also market-test new products.

* The Justice Department invoked the 1899 Refuse Act against Florida Power and Light in March, 1970, in response to a public uproar over thermal pollution of the shallow Biscayne Bay. The case was settled in the fall of 1971, when the company, in a consent decree, agreed to build an "expensive" cooling system, independent of the use of water from the bay. It was the first such suit ever filed by the Justice Department against a private electric utility.

Sponsorship of sorts by the Edison Electric Institute of the EPCOT venture is a measure of the degree to which Walt Disney and his corporate heirs have extended the corruption of art and nature into the present and, it now seems, the future. Beyond that, it reflects the depth of confidence that exists in the capacity of well-organized and well-funded promoters to make kitsch widespread and economically profitable on the American scene.

Where the recreation area around Disneyland in California "grew by chance in response to public demand," according to the oddly contradictory explanation copyrighted by Walt Disney Productions in *The Year 2000* and published by the Edison Institute, Disney World in Florida will grow according to plan. It will expand from a master plan "that links tourist and permanent resident, yet recognizes and prepares for the needs and interests of both." The needs and interests of willingly captive workers in Disney World, as well as those travelers from afar who thrill to planned entertainment, have been analyzed, dissected, cataloged, and satisfied in computer simulations over a considerable range of experience, some of it related to real life and some of it to fantasy just assumed to be real in Disneyland.

Some of the facts supporting Disney World and neutralizing negative risks include construction of interchanges and roadways providing automobile access to the site by all major highway systems; one of the largest concentrations of motel rooms in America (eventually about 5,000 of them, built by three roadside chains and hotel corporations); and the presence, an hour's drive away, of the most wonderful tourist attraction ever built at public expense: Cape Kennedy.

The Disney version of the electrified future attracted investment from quite a few large American corporate enterprises, whose managements saw nothing nonsensical or frivolous about a daily drama of "One nation under God . . . operated by one management." They seemed as responsive in some instances as Disney folks themselves to the vacation kingdom, a journey into six exciting realms called Main Street, Adventureland, Frontierland, Liberty Square, Fantasyland, and Tomorrowland.

They were impressed by planned parking lots for 14,000 cars, from which an annual horde of 10 million tourists would emerge to watch the screened and industrious inhabitants at work. Tourist travel to Florida was running double that of California. And 82 percent of all visitors moved by automobile, many hauling trailers and campers, in search of what the late Roy Disney exalted as simple, clean, family-type mass entertainment.

At the heart of the mass-entertainment center is the Magic Kingdom theme park, which has an "interrelationship" with nearby resort hotels—five of them owned by Disney—called "theme resorts because everything from interior decor to employees' costumes and dining room menus will be an expression of the same overall theme." They will be Persian, Polynesian, Venetian, Asian, and so on—hence, the *theme*. Designed and built by giants of free enterprise—United States Steel, for example, will build two theme hotels—they will nevertheless be leased to the Disney corporation, which will operate them.

Through the marvel of something called Audio-Animatronics and with the help of Hollywood wardrobe skills, thirty-seven presidents of the United States will be recreated in sculpted effigy. On stage, the presidents will move and speak, their most familiar facial expressions carefully matched and animated to reflect the solemnity or wisdom of their words, the passages chosen to recall all that was best and memorable of other times. The good and the true America is to be brought to life, not some stirred-up radical version of it. Everything is to look and sound *right*.

After "processing," the visitors will be directed to proceed to a transportation pavilion and board a high-speed transit system spanning the length of the property, on which 20,000 or so EPCOT volunteer residents may be viewed at work and play. This imaginative concept "alone," said Disney spokesmen, would make the project an extraordinarily ambitious one; yet it is far more significant to the future than the ordinary mind might suspect. Conceived as a model after which other communities "one day may be patterned," its impact on the quality of urban life may be measured for generations to come. Its goals, it is said, are that high. It is to be "the first accident-free, noise-free, pollution-free city in America." People will "actually live a life they can't find anywhere else in the world today," it was reported in the Edison Electric Institute magazine.

It was all planned to draw investment capital to Disney World, said Roy Disney: "The amusement park is just a catalyst. This is a real estate venture for us."

Dedication to the future will not, however, exclude heavy emphasis on the happiness of the people who live and work there or those who travel across the country or the world to visit the place. No community yet in existence in 1970 could serve as a guide for the "city of tomorrow" because EPCOT is to be a balanced, dynamic city offering *a complete line of services* to satisfy the social, cultural, commercial, recreational, and administrative needs of the people—as the promoters measure those needs.

Fifty acres of city streets and buildings will be enclosed for climate control, protected from rain, heat, cold, or humidity by the magic of electric energy. A thirty-story hotel at the very center of the hub will accommodate conventions, corporate offices, and display space. A seven-acre outdoor recreation deck, with planted trees, waterfalls, and swimming pools, will provide pleasure and relaxation for happy hotel guests. "Reaching skyward through EPCOT's roof" will be other structures serving as headquarters for participating industries. Block after block of the shopping area will create the character, flavor, and adventure of exotic foreign places: a British square, an Asian market, a Scandinavian shop, a South American plaza, and none of it altogether make-believe, since real money (currency or credit cards) will be used in transactions for real material things. Foreign cuisine, dinner shows, and roving entertainers "will make the international shopping areas a must-see for residents and tourists alike."

In Disney World, pedestrians will find no traffic lights to remind them of the 14,000 cars they parked in the vast paved lots outside the gates. Nothing will be permitted to suggest those times and places where human beings and automobiles occupied the same space, consuming and exhausting the same atmosphere. Trucks will be out of sight, three levels below ground, where they will discharge and pick up cargo. Vehicles occupied by passengers who, inconceivable as it may seem, do not care to pause in paradise, will be expedited through the city at the second level. Only hotel guests and apartment residents may stop or park their cars beneath this world of pleasure. Tourists arriving in campers and trailers and those checking into motels will, after processing and computerized registration, find that a WEDway people mover (named after the Disney company that manufactures it), and a monorail make them all equally mobile. For those who care for it, walking will be permitted.

The electric-powered WEDway is a "never-ending service of cars" moving along an overhead track. It was designed for EPCOT and used successfully at Disneyland. Bicycles and electric cars will abound, traveling on paths that will be separated from pedestrians. Only when people depart from Disney World to confront unscreened and unprocessed people beyond the acreage will they again need their automobiles.

The city will provide the place where, as Disney people have said, *"new product demand can be created."* In this respect, nothing from the old world will be changed—nothing, that is, but appearances. Investigations will be made into nuclear power, fuel cells, and solar energy.

The industrial park will provide employment, of course, but "it will mean much, much more" as a showcase for industry at work. It will be especially suitable for the production of television commercials and public relations films promoting products and companies, with Disney World dominant in every theme.

Corporations are slyly reminded that they "will want to utilize Disney World's personnel center," the first step in a process to keep the snakes out of Eden. Applicants will be interviewed "before being referred to specific employers." Employees are not only to be engaged for jobs in Cinderella's castle; they are to be chosen as the cast for a new universe, for they are role players in the continuing drama, a fake city that is truly real, the capital of a magic tourist trap kingdom that is the ultimate, needless, managed corporate state. For all this the nation must produce more and more electric power, consume more and more natural resources, provide highways over which a million or more people a month can converge on forty-three square miles of developed land worth $1 billion a few years after Disney bought it.

The first day of creation for the new real estate development arrived in the autumn of 1971, and anyone who chose and had the price of admission could be present. The wiser travelers, of course, prepared for traffic jams, their credit cards at the ready, reservations confirmed, their spirits attuned to the American dream of a future newly arrived. The new world would be years abuilding, perhaps eight or nine years before all its occupants would be fully employed and housed, fitted with uniforms, and put on display. Meanwhile, the fiberglass turrets on fair castles summoned the wayfarer, and the concessions were open.

Whether the energized new Eden develops as promised only time will tell. Like the original, residents of the new odor-free climate-controlled garden doubtless will be vulnerable to temptations. Will war break out between the synthetic ethnics? Will the inhabitants of Venice be moved to attack idolatrous Polynesians in their theme park? Down along the WEDway, under the monorail, will some equivalent of Sodom and Gomorrah develop to short-circuit this computer-programmed, sixty-cycle paradise?

There is no precedent for Disney World, only a future in an all-electric community where happiness, energy, business, pleasure, family entertainment, redeemable Green Stamps, and complete parking facilities merge into a grand, supervised, unending design.

7

The Great Government
Power
Failure

THE AFFINITY between the private utilities and the electrified dream city reaches beyond mutual profit interest. A philosophical attachment also characterizes their affair. When Mr. Gerdes and Roy Disney and his Hollywood publicists either cited the deplorable departure of America from the paths of true greatness or evoked visions of a future in which happy folks would alternate between profitable work and organized play, not quite strumming heavenly, possibly electrified, harps, they tended to sound alike. They were, as were their counterparts in other fields promoting mass-market concepts of present and future consumption, victims of a mythology that cannot be expected to survive the realities of the growing environmental crisis.

Who can doubt that the promotion of electric power and Disney World family-oriented, GP-rated pleasure is the all-American, imaginative, sanitized kind of future environment that will be good for people? Clever entrepreneurs promoted the sizzle and charged for the steak, as advertising people of a generation past expressed it. In an age of impending environmental crisis, one promotes a dream and a theme and markets motel rooms, tourist attractions, industrial parks, and real estate. Now that the demand has been created, the need is being filled. The future is a vast shopping center, an infinite supermarket.

But at precisely the same time, the utilities have been caught with insufficient kilowatt capacity to meet existing demands. For several years prior to 1972, power breakdowns, voltage reductions, and brownouts were (and in all likelihood will continue to be for some years to follow) a condition of life. The utilities are, in fact, unprepared for the present, let alone the future they have dreamed of and invested in.

State and federal government was little or no help in the years after World War II, when critical aspects of the environmental problems developed. But by the late 1960s, a good many years late as measured by hindsight, the federal government responded ponderously. The administration considered a number of highly publicized proposals and adopted two or three potentially important policy changes, but new legislation provoked little, if any, change in the country's direction, although admittedly causing a few large construction and development projects to be delayed or stopped.

A man named William D. Ruckelshaus took command of the new Environmental Protection Agency, an umbrella agency supposed to coordinate antipollution activity previously dispersed throughout the government and especially empowered to pass judgment on and initiate action against environmental polluters of all kinds. With access to channels of publicity and exposure of polluting culprits and in possession of certain enforcement powers, Mr. Ruckelshaus has nevertheless been deterred to a considerable extent in his good intentions. No reorganization in government or realignment of political power has altered the influence of industry in national affairs, and it remains unclear how much independence of action will be permitted him by the White House. The wealthy oil and real estate man Walter J. Hickel had turned into an ardent conservationist as Secretary of the Interior. For exercising more independence and zeal than was permissible, Mr. Nixon personally fired him in a manner so pointed that the message to move with caution on pollution prosecutions was made quite clear throughout the administration. Nevertheless, Mr. Ruckelshaus has persisted within limitations. He has little power over the electric utilities, the Atomic Energy Commission, the automobile industry, and other traditional polluters and none at all over the issue of comprehensive national energy policy. Even so, and apparently with White House acquiescence, Mr. Ruckelshaus and a former Maryland congressman and Republican National Committee chairman, Rogers C. B. Morton, who was elevated to Walter Hickel's old job, united to delay construction of the North Slope oil pipeline across the Alaskan wilderness.

A barge canal across Florida, long regarded with horror by conservationists, was likewise stopped. A vote in the United States Senate, in contradiction to an array of power marshaled by President Nixon and the military-industrial establishment, dismantled the billion-dollar supersonic transport project, an unprecedented response to fears of excessive and environmentally ruinous technology. A few corporations, notably

Union Carbide and a group of oil companies, were either fined or given final warnings to clean up and quit treating the air and water as though they were corporate, rather than public, resources. Such developments have convinced the more easily persuaded segment of the public that the government means business and that a revolutionary concept of resources management and preservation is under way. Such is not the case, at least not yet. Skeptics, although welcoming both real and symbolic evidence that governmental passivity to pollution is diminishing, are not convinced that an outpouring of publicity and rhetoric, combined with an enforcement policy of making examples out of a few offenders, constitutes a revolutionary change in policy.

The United States Army Corps of Engineers, after seventy years of failure to invoke legal restraints that would have protected waterway systems from industrial and sewage pollution, has continued its uninterrupted course of planning huge projects, delayed or modified on occasion because of outbursts of local opposition. The $5 billion devoted each year to federal highway expansion evokes questions, as usual, but no action of significance to moderate dependence on gasoline-powered automobiles. The Federal Power Commission, almost as a backlash against the courts, which had instructed it to pay some attention to scenic and environmental matters, authorized Consolidated Edison Company in New York City to build the world's largest pumped storage hydroelectric plant at Storm King Mountain on the Hudson River. Citizens and private organizations had fought the case for seven years, won a review in the federal courts on the grounds of needless destruction of scenic resources, then lost to a regulatory agency that at the height of the furor over environmental issues, reiterated its earlier position, all the new laws and public concern notwithstanding.

A babel of television shows, press accounts, special editions of magazines, college seminars, millions of dollars worth of advertising, and the like has produced little alteration in the course of events. Although a few states—Minnesota, especially—have sought dominance over passive federal policy, the United States government itself has been, save in instances where it has responded to highly organized protests, largely devoid of demonstrated intention to enforce reform. In the meantime, it became clear to the electric power industry that business could proceed more or less as usual, deterred now and then by citizens' organizations. Such organized action shows prospects of becoming more formidable, as in the case of seven nuclear and coal generating plants bordering on Lake Michigan that, when faced with litigation and public uproar, were compelled to build cooling towers and yield to upgraded standards regulating discharges.

The power companies were running into more than the usual bureau-

cratic and delaying actions with the government, but in the AEC
they had an ally and advocate of extraordinary strength; but in the
general public, they confronted an angry, contradictory, not always
rational adversary. Both the regulatory agencies, which included the
Federal Power Commission and some state regulators, and the utilities
faced as they never had before a steady barrage of questions, intervention proceedings, and denunciations from previously impassive but now
unruly citizens.

Although no more, and in fact no differently, insensitive than industry
in general to public accusations of arrogance and failure to meet commitments to public safety, responsibility, and resources management, the
utilities nevertheless have endured an outsized share of the newly released aggression launched by an aggrieved public. The power industry
was standing there in the line of fire when the people—gulled into burning up twice as much electricity as an Englishman, three times more
than a Frenchman or a Japanese, nearly four times more than an
Italian, and one hundred twenty-five times more than a Chinese—
looked around for a vulnerable enemy to which to address their disap-
proval. The power industry is naturally endowed for this purpose. Like
the public, it had for many years helped cause conditions from which it
now sought escape.

Like many other service industries, privately and publicly owned,
the electric utilities cannot in all cases provide and sustain the ordinary
services required of them. The telephone monopoly has done little
better, to be sure. The United States postal system, the vast household-
moving business, automobile insurance, federal and local efforts at
crime control, taxpayer-financed educational systems, air and rail transport, and the housing industry in both urban and rural areas have
operated close to the border of chaos time and time again. The Penn
Central holding company complex went into bankruptcy under the noses
of half a dozen or more regulatory agencies. A brand-new federal corporation established to run the railroads responded to its obligation, not
by restoring and improving train service on a national scale, but by
obliterating half the passenger trains still operating in the United States.
Measured against the others, the electric utilities, for all their shortcomings and planning failures and monopolistic arrogance, have no
special cause for apology or shame.

The utilities have a proud record of having inspired and provoked
industrial expansion while, for most of their years of development, keeping apace with it and serving their constituencies extremely well.

But as with other industries, the utilities have not been able to maintain a standard of excellence under conditions that curtail their previously unrestricted limits of action and simultaneously demand of them

more service than their capabilities allow. If they fail to extend their systems, their performance can only deteriorate. They cannot pack up their power plants and transmission lines and disappear into the Establishment, nor can they alone raise the money, build the systems, and perform with the perfection required of them in the face of opposition from a public whose well-being seems to require more of what it loathes. The utilities are called upon to do more and more—and to do it better—when they are incapable of doing well what they are already doing.

In peak-demand periods (hot summer days in the North, unseasonal cold in the South) when use of electricity has exceeded the capacity to generate and transmit it, companies have reduced voltage, suffered power failures, and scrambled to bring in current from other areas— buy or borrow it, in effect. They have had to build plants to provide peak-load power never needed save in emergency periods.

Over the years, they have promoted and sold the use of more electricity than they could provide or transmit, and because they have successfully resisted the installation of a national grid system that might have largely saved them from the worst of their transgressions, they are reaping the whirlwind. A national grid system, linking every generating plant to transmission lines capable of carrying power anywhere at any time, could dispatch to any area short of power that reserve or unused capacity always dormant in most systems, at least some of the time. But in a national grid system, a power company would sacrifice some of its sovereignty, some of its independence; and with its independence would go some of the validity of the reasons for building its own generating and transmitting systems. Like birds in an orchard or animals in a preserve, power companies see their franchised monopolies as a territorial imperative, to be intruded upon solely by invitation or under conditions that guarantee mutuality of independence, however needless or inimical to the public interest that misguided independence may be.

With power failures commonplace, with kilowatt-hour costs rising while volume usage of power mounted, with utilities polluting the water and air of the nation, every conservationist in the country began to protest new plant construction, especially nuclear plants. The utilities were stalled by litigation, court orders, harassment, and public intervention, in addition to equipment delays and breakdowns.

Accustomed to winning in regulatory agencies and legislatures the battles that went against them in confrontations with the public, the utilities scarcely knew what hit them. The old arguments that a privately owned utility could always provide all the power ever needed and that it was somehow unpatriotic or un-American to doubt it could no longer be believed or even mentioned. The myth that competition,

free enterprise, and technology could inevitably accommodate all demands and conditions by motivating and challenging management dis-
sipated in a deluge of rhetoric, power failures, pollution, and operational
shortcomings.

Although public opposition focused on nuclear plants, to the dismay
of the AEC and utility managers, it was now and then directed at any
or all new power installations. In the Southwest's Four Corners region,
where Utah, Colorado, Arizona, and New Mexico meet at one boundary
marker, large coal-burning plants were beginning to foul the air and
darken the vast open space. Six coal-powered plants were operating or
under construction by 1972, with twelve more in the planning stage, in an
area that contains six national parks, nineteen Indian reservations, and a
widely dispersed population of 5 million. Most of the power, unneeded
by so few people, was to be provided by strip-mined coal and transmitted
beyond the area in which it was produced to consumers in the urban
West.

In five regional hearings conducted in the spring of 1970 by the
Senate Committee on Interior and Insular Affairs, people from every
stratum of life, including dissident Navaho and Hopi Indians, swarmed
into the hearings to express anxiety and resentment over power development that clearly threatened to pollute the clear air of America's West
and erode the land with strip-mining operations spreading across a
half-dozen states. What would happen, people asked at the hearings, to
the tourist business drawn to scenic land doomed to be crisscrossed by
transmission lines and coal-carrying railroads, with long vistas punctu-
ated by belching smokestacks, by ugly power plants more visible than
national monuments? Time after time, the visiting senators were asked
to curtail power expansion, to stop the doubling and redoubling of output. The Senate committee chairman, Henry M. Jackson of Washington,
listened to 200 witnesses. Utility spokesmen, in response, simply explained that the power was necessary, that industry, growth, and the
people themselves, in spite of their objections to the consequences, required it. They cited power failures and outrages as evidence of the
need for expanded production and conceded that they had perhaps
overpromoted electrical service in the past to the point where they could
not construct enough generating plants even if they could commandeer
all the sites and condemn all the land they desired. They had failed in
the past to keep up with the demand, said utility spokesmen, and they
did not intend to continue to do so.

In spite of all their troubles, with few exceptions, the otherwise-
harassed corporations had all but wallowed in earnings throughout
most of the country. In a good many instances, the IOUs wallowed to
the extent that state regulatory agencies dedicated to limiting such

earnings to 6 or 7 or 8 percent seemed to have fallen asleep. But then state regulatory agencies in general—barring a few, like those in Vermont, Wisconsin, and sometimes California—had developed justifiable reputations over the years for yielding their favors complaisantly to the courting utility corporations, especially when the question of money was at issue. In defense of the utilities, however, it had to be agreed that many state commissions were so incompetent, so poorly funded, or so subordinate to partisan and industrial leadership that they served little positive purpose whatsoever, either in behalf of the public or the utilities, except for providing patronage jobs to the prevailing party.

Even where state commissions fended off demands for rate increases thought to be premature or unwarranted, utility profits ranged from pretty good to truly splendid. Tax-free dividends, commonplace in utility securities, have always provided a lure for private utility investors. But the whole range of cost increases—wages, equipment, credit, land acquisition (much of it for real estate speculation), taxes, new technology, some costly management failures—made high utility profits worth a good deal less when they poured in than they seemed to be worth in prospect.

An electric utility had very much the same problem as the household of an overpaid nine-dollar-an-hour union elitist enjoying the benefits of a segregated craft monopoly. Regardless of one's individual or corporate condition, it was inevitably the same repetitive question: Is the total amount of income after taxes, whether or not it was fairly earned or wisely spent, enough to meet the needs? The utilities needed the high profits to attract the capital necessary to finance plants costing $200 to $500 million each. Beginning in 1970, the industry believed that it required one new plant a month for twenty years, each capable of generating 1 to 3 million kilowatts. Trying to find $9 or $10 billion a year at unparalleled interest rates would tarnish the shining profit picture, said cheerless utility executives.

Even so, their profits seemed remarkable. With "dozens" of utilities asking for rate increases in the summer of 1970, based on performance the preceding year, Senator Lee Metcalf of Montana complained in the United States Senate that "the Nixonomists at the White House" were carelessly overlooking one of the causes of inflation. He said that even if the president and his advisers could not routinely get from the Federal Power Commission, which does not publish the data, a compilation of utility company net profits, the information could be obtained with minimal digging. He himself had gotten the profit data by requesting the FPC to prepare it. The report was an unusual bit of economic news, distinguished by the fact that it proved to be of little interest to the press and wholly without interest to television newscasters. In fact, anyone dependent on television for basic news and information would never know that one company, the Citizens Utilities Company of Arizona, made a net profit in 1968 of 50.7 percent.

A special case, perhaps, Senator Metcalf conceded, since the next-highest profit reported on a list of 206 private utilities was the 31.9 percent, after all taxes, expenses, and interest, collected by the Kentucky Power Company. Sixteen utilities showed a net profit of 20 percent or more, among them the Montana Power Company in the senator's home state, a fact that nettled him as much as any other in the report. Others showing profits of 20 percent or more in 1968 were:

Idaho Power Company	22.4 percent
Central Telephone and Utilities Corporation	24.9 percent
Potomac Edison Company	22.9 percent
Montana Power Company	22.7 percent
Jersey Central Power and Light Company	20.0 percent
Ohio Edison Company	22.9 percent
Duquesne Light Company	21.4 precent
Pennsylvania Electric Company	21.7 percent
Safe Harbor Water Power Corporation	20.0 percent
El Paso Electric Company	21.8 percent
Texas Electric Service	20.3 percent
Texas Power and Light Company	22.7 percent
West Texas Utilities Company	20.9 percent
Wisconsin River Power Company	23.7 percent

Altogether, 70 percent of the 206 companies made a profit of sixteen cents or more out of each dollar of revenue collected, Mr. Metcalf reported. The utilities *averaged* a profit of 15.4 percent.

Thus, in mid-1970, when requests for rate increases, based on the preceding year's performance, added up to $2 billion, Senator Metcalf thought the requests should not be granted until their latest profits were made known. The senator tried to make it clear that rate requests are always being filed for a given year before a utility's customers know what profits are in the current or preceding year.

The Montana senator is a watchdog on utilities affairs, in much the same way as the more autocratic Representative Wright Patman for years has been disclosing the arcane, astronomically profitable, and interlocking power of the banking industry over the American public. Both men perform unduplicated and sometimes tedious service to the Congress and the public, most of which is seldom acknowledged and less often considered when suggestions arise for the reform of abuses common to the utilities and the sacrosanct money industry.

The banking, or money, business is probably farther beyond comprehension than any other sector of economic life. Within it is concealed the knowledge of who owns what and what combinations of financial interests exercise the power to extend or withhold credit. Private electric utilities sometimes concede to being intimidated by large oil and money interests that have taken command of the market for fuels. So dependent are the utilities on fuels that criticism of oil companies, which might normally be expressed by a utility well aware that it is being over-charged and subjected to high-handed treatment, is silenced. No power company is sufficiently moved to seek martyrdom, which might happen if it stood alone as a complainant; and no collective of utilities would unite for such an anti-Establishment purpose. Against both the money business and the oil business, electric utilities have legitimate complaints that are never publicly expressed.

With their insatiable appetite for capital, the utilities are prime cus-tomers in the money market but hold little influence over it, as in the case of the fuel-energy market. To be sure, they have neglected to exercise what influence they once did possess in a constructive fashion. Concentration and interlocked ownership in both markets developed over the years to militate against the electric power industry and, by extension, the public interest. Money remains the commodity with power over power.

All the regulatory agencies in the country, including the Federal Power Commission, which was fifty years old in 1970, have failed to pre-vent the cumulative conditions leading to a power crisis that remains to be experienced in its worst form. It is a crisis characterized by an enor-mously inefficient transmission system, which more responsible govern-ment intervention and regulation could quite readily have prevented, and by a shortage in too many places of power itself. The shortage was caused by the overpromotion of electric energy and the failure of power producers to prepare for the high-consumption market they created. In their accelerated haste to catch up, replace old plants and equipment. double their output, and prepare for the future while coping with the present, they have aggravated the crisis they are dealing with, for the generation of enough power may very well be worse than not enough.

Not, of course, that some progress has not been made since the blackout in the Northeast in the fall of 1965. The establishment of re-gional power groups, pooling of current with interconnections to speed reserves to areas caught unprepared by sudden demands, made many utilities capable of stamping out brush fires that otherwise might have flared into a cascade. Wherever small troubles can be prevented from developing into large troubles, progress in making electricity reliable can be reported.

If one read carefully the little two-paragraph items appearing from time to time in the newspapers near the stock-market listings, it was possible to be reassured that electric utilities 100 or 200 miles apart were prepared to switch power reserves directly to one's own community. The items could be read in Baltimore, in New York, in Pittsburgh, in Miami, in southern cities, in Williamsport, Pennsylvania, and in Wilmington, Delaware. If the news items were collected and compared, it was easy to conclude that all the citizens in all these distant cities, along with everybody in between, were depending on exactly the same power plants. Altoona could dispatch some power to Johnstown, or a switch could be thrown at the Peach Bottom nuclear station to bolster the voltage in Hagerstown if reserve supplies were not needed at the moment of emergency.

But a single sweltering heat wave, which often engulfs vaster areas than those served by a power pool, could tax the reserves of each city in the regional grid, leaving each one of the electric utilities vulnerable. Reliability was unquestionably improved for normal, or mildly abnormal, situations; and in an electricity network, every corner that can be cut, every capability of moving even a fraction of a percent of a total reserve pool to a threatened area, can sometimes keep burning lights that would otherwise go out. However, an extended emergency spreading across large regions would not be contained by the system, which was patched together by voluntary cooperation among utilities, cooperation they were somewhat goaded into exercising by a periodic threat of federal legislation. It was the kind of cooperation reminiscent of a very old shipboard joke about sailors doing one another's laundry. The utilities organized an interesting form of mutual self-help, but the net gain in terms of guaranteeing uninterrupted power was not very substantial.

Yet, the flexibility of the interconnected grid system devised by the utilities, with the Federal Power Commission looking over their shoulders, redounded to their immediate advantage. Although the system could not cope with unpredictable phenomena producing power outages on a vast scale, it could respond to a foreseeable regional crisis. When New York's Consolidated Edison Company was on the brink of disaster in the summer of 1970, Tennessee Valley Authority generating plants serving the country's atomic energy plants in Tennessee, Ohio, and Kentucky were able to swing onto the transmission lines to cover a portion of New York's losses.

Consolidated Edison's star-crossed and costly nuclear power plant at Indian Point on the Hudson River had to be shut down for the summer, which was bad enough. But when its million-kilowatt generator at the city's Ravenswood plant burned out, reducing reserves to the very edge of disaster, the TVA plants were in a position, in a peculiar and incorrectly reported fashion, to deploy a marginal supply of current from the southern hill country to the stricken metropolis.

The country was told that TVA power was dispatched across the transmission system of the PJM (Pennsylvania–New Jersey–Maryland) pool network, which was directly interconnected with Consolidated Edison's own overtaxed grid. A cutback in uranium production and processing had left TVA plants with more power than they needed, or so it was widely reported. TVA had never supplied power to New York before, an accomplishment that was possible because carefully devised transmission plans could be developed quickly. It was not a feat that could be accomplished in a hurry, as in the case of a sudden cascade.

Private utility managements were nettled by several days of high-impact publicity in the multiple-channel New York area. It was felt that Consolidated Edison and its problems were giving the power industry a bad image, which, considering the facts of the matter, needed none of the trumped-up drama so commonplace to television. Beyond New York, it was said, the country was coping with its daily power problems, or, anyway, there wasn't all that publicity when it didn't.

In the case of the widely heralded TVA rescue of Consolidated Edison, it developed that the power transmitted through the PJM system to keep electric service barely alive came, not from TVA, but from private power companies which had, in fact, rescued TVA itself from serious trouble. Simultaneously—or, to resort to a better word in the language of electricity—concurrently, private utilities beyond New York were subjected to questioning they felt was undeserved when Con Ed's and New York's problems became public property.

Senator Edmund S. Muskie called a Senate subcommittee hearing on the power situation after the Con Ed generator breakdown and declared that the absence of a national power policy and especially of a national grid system was "ridiculous." Thus, the unstable New York issue once more incited a threat of legislative intervention as a means of guaranteeing reliability. Donald Cook, presiding over the nation's largest utility holding company, American Electric Power, questioned the need of any such intervention and argued that a national grid system simply would not work. The issue was academic, anyway, since no national grid would be established in the first place, let alone function, unless required by law.

Mr. Cook's seven-state utility system had been in a position daily during the New York emergency to transmit power into Con Ed's lines and had notified the AEC, biggest customer of TVA, to that effect. Mr. Cook's companies were supplying TVA in amounts up to 350,000 kilowatts at precisely the time TVA was releasing 200,000 to Con Ed. And the 200,000 kilowatts went through the Cook network to *get* to New York.

Therefore, it was a private utility holding company that "saved" New York in its hours and days of need, since TVA was dispensing to the city 200,000 of the 350,000 kilowatts it was picking up from the IOUs. James E. Watson, manager of power for TVA, confirmed the fact. Normally, TVA "exchanged" power with other systems on a balance-of-payments basis that brought the federal system a "modest" net income However, things had gone so badly, what with the delay in the completion of the big nuclear plant at Browns Ferry, Alabama, and the crippling coal shortage, that the exchange system resulted in power purchases that had cost, not netted, TVA a good deal of money. Purchasing power outside the TVA system had cost TVA $15 million "more than we anticipated," Mr. Watson said.

"It is a matter of great interest to us," Mr. Cook said, speaking of the power that saved New York and Con Ed from immeasurable discontent, "that all of this power was transmitted over lines of the private utilities. Without this transmission network, delivery to New York would not have been possible."

Consolidated Edison would have to face the music later when the year's balance sheet was computed. The purchased power, plant breakdowns, and tax increases of $30 million all in one year had cost it so much money that it was granted a rate increase of $102 million at the end of the summer. While setting the record straight, however, Mr. Cook and other private utility executives throughout the country sympathetic to the terrible problems of Charles Luce and Con Ed, hoped that the New York utility could begin to manage things better and stop causing bad public relations.

Attempts after 1965 to head off the crisis by federal law were efficiently and quietly aborted each time they were made in the United States Congress. The utilities united to fight all legislation, whether proposals for improved consumer protection in electrical rate increases or bills to legislate reliability, with a vigor that amounted to organized fury. They would do voluntarily, and do better, they said, what any law might direct them to do.

Neither Lyndon Johnson, who had ordered a study of the 1965 blackout, nor Richard Nixon, with his political and civilian law careers tied firmly to dominant industrial and financial interests, was very much concerned with electric power issues that only federal policy could ultimately handle. Irrespective of energy-policy reforms and the legislative hurdles they would have to leap to become effective, the question of electric power in America can never be intelligently and thoroughly examined as an issue separate from the whole industrial, investment, and marketing complex. Regulation in the national interest would follow a reexamination and perhaps a redefinition of what the national interest is. The deepest secret in America would be revealed when it is possible to determine who, through interlocking directorates in corporate power, owns and controls what. In the absence of such knowledge, regulatory palliatives will confront symptoms as they become evident and facts after they become irreversible; and disasters—like the wreckage of the railroad transport system and the cancerous decay of the cities— will be subject to postmortem study rather than to prevention.

The fate of a regulatory agency, by and large, is common-law marriage with its regulated industry through mutuality of interest. The association becomes legitimized in time by the appointment to the administrative and policy-making levels of people rewarded for political activity, fund raising, or an expertise achieved in the industry itself. Designed to respond to adversary procedures, the agencies, even when they respond with decisions reflecting the weight of valid arguments, more often than not find that industry experts outmatch in number, familiarity with research, and financial resources those opposing spokesmen, if any appear at all, representing nonindustry interests.

Numbed by bureaucracy, often subdued by powerful legislative committee chairmen or because of curtailed authority and sometimes ineptitude, regulatory agencies at times have been able to help stamp out brush fires or persuade industrialists to use restraint, but are disabled in initiating policy reform. Two primary forces chip away eternally at regulatory power: congressional funding and the laws, often riddled with exemptions, under which they function. By cumulative practice and precedent, and by the presence of presidential administrators with alliances, not to the enforcement machinery, but to the suspects, regulatory agencies routinely (with infrequent exceptions) exercise over a regulated industry only that authority and power it permits. Theoretically, and it sometimes happens, a regulatory agency at the federal level (if seldom at state level) can take decisive and significant action in the public interest or in the interest of principle. But in general practice, an agency reflects the concerns of the industry under observation, even to the extent that injustices and frustrations suffered by the public go unattended.

Much depends on the president. A regulatory agency, even swamped in bureaucracy, can best accomplish its functions and exert force on its related industry if the chief executive wants it that way. Lyndon Johnson was curiously indifferent about the agencies regulating the railroads, airlines, communications, stock markets, power, atomic energy, drugs, and so on. President Nixon's appointments showed early that partisanship and team play won his approval over originality, imagination, and regulatory concepts at variance with bureaucratic tradition.

Beyond the range of routine administration and trying to umpire contradictory objectives between contending forces, government regulatory agencies must be concerned with perpetuating their bureaucracy, holding their position in the federal hierarchy. Even with their often dedicated and individually competent professional staffs, they are frequently unable either to right trivial wrongs or to prevent catastrophe in their arena of jurisdiction.

It is a notorious fact that the Interstate Commerce Commission could not get Western Union offices and railroad passenger terminals to answer their telephones. Nor, for that matter, could the Federal Communications Commission induce Western Union, in the advanced age of electronics and computers, to deliver telegrams with anything resembling the accuracy and alacrity of the service it provided back in the era when uniformed young men pedaled them to their destinations on bicycles.

Also considered too trivial to invoke the regulatory process, or too difficult, was the matter of compelling railroads to keep fresh water in the drinking fountains, clean their passenger cars, repair their toilets, wash the train windows, and keep the heat on in winter or turn it off on unseasonably hot days.

But there were times when one public utility exercised regulatory power over another. The electric companies took no chances when the hard-up Penn Central owed them money, nor did they waste time making complaints to the Interstate Commerce Commission. They served notice through the courts and bankruptcy trustees that Penn Central had not paid $2.2 million in electric bills. Payment was demanded with some of the fervor exercised against a delinquent household. The utilities concluded that a railway empire with $6.5 billion in assets ought to be able to sell something, if necessary, to pay the power company. Thereafter, Penn Central was warned, Consolidated Edison of New York, the Philadelphia Electric Company, and Pennsylvania Power and Light wanted the bill paid every week. Otherwise, they told a caretaker judge watching over the shattered empire, Penn Central just might find its limping trains drifting to a halt between stations, there to stand cold and still until the account was settled and the juice turned on again for another week.

The fact that thousands of people might be stranded or subjected to treatment against which they had no redress, was not a concern of the law. The Interstate Commerce Commission has declared that its powers have never permitted it to interfere with or enforce quality of passenger service, which happens to be quite true. Interference with quality of service would be a transgression against that sector of the free-enterprise system over which policy dictates complete neutrality.

The Federal Power Commission, although the oldest and therefore, with age, inheritor of the right to be more moribund than newer agencies, by and large has sought valiantly to discharge its obligations over the years with reasonable sensitivity. Its shortcomings were many and at times serious, but they were rooted either in the appointment of commissioners who should have been employed by electric utility corporations, as many of them were before or after their tenure, or in the contradictory philosophy imposed by Congress that forbade adjustment to new times and new public requirements.

With the emergence of nuclear power in the utilities industry (nuclear power being to a utility nothing more or less than a way to fuel a boiler), the FPC was deprived by Congress and the Atomic Energy Commission of any real opportunity to formulate a national power policy. The AEC was primarily an armaments cult, so shielded from anything but the world of research and war and so intent upon promoting its secret product that the philosophy of public interest was alien to it. It was a hindsight judgment, to be sure, to suppose that the Federal Power Commission rather than the AEC might have translated the cosmic energy of the atom into kilowatts with more responsive concern for public sensibilities, but the results could hardly have been worse.

After World War II, the Atomic Energy Commission was, in theory at least, taken out of the clutches of the military and presumably subjected to civilian management. It remains, however, a superagency operating under a CIA concept of secrecy and the powerful Joint Committee on Atomic Energy. The AEC is a closed society, evaluating and reporting on itself, disclosing such information as might comfort the public and withholding, for the most part, whatever is not convertible to favorable publicity. Its empire involves manufacturing, research, scientific experimentation, armament systems, atomic explosions, grants to universities and industry, and a massive output of published material devoted to "peaceful" uses of nuclear power. Because of its absolute dominance over nuclear energy and its cultlike insularity that is a natural legacy of a classified armaments complex, it looms large and mighty in both the world of weaponry and the generation of electric power.

For it was the electric power industry that was destined to become the prime consumer and converter of nonmilitary nuclear power. Thus, the power industry was opened up to nuclear engineers and specialists who constitute a new breed of experts with ties to the military-industrial complex. The AEC is the supplier of atomic energy expertise, a promoter of its services, a regulatory agency, and the guardian over radioactive and safety standards. The overwhelming political and bureaucratic strength of the AEC could, and no doubt will, prevent any fragmentation or dilution of its authority and thus forestall development of a national energy policy. The electric utilities industry, which made no concentrated move to prevent control of the fuels under conglomerate ownership, can scarcely be expected to initiate or support a policy opposed by an agency like the AEC to which it must look for construction and operating permits.

Far more than the Federal Power Commission, the AEC resists public participation in its affairs. In the face of public insistence that the AEC concern itself with esthetic, scenic, and environmental issues when issuing construction permits for nuclear power plants, the agency has declared that such matters were none of its business. As the AEC sees it, its fundamental obligation to the public at large is to safeguard it from radioactive contamination, a task carried out virtually to perfection, as the AEC itself appraised the matter. As fears of nuclear power proliferation grew and pressures mounted against what a good many people damned as AEC arrogance, the agency capitulated and announced that it would thereafter consider, in addition to radioactive safeguards, the impact of nuclear reactors on the environment in general. Passage of the Environmental Protection Act reinforced public concern over the issue.

Even on the matter of radiation, the AEC in June, 1971, ordered nuclear plants to conform to tightened emission requirements. The order meant that eight nuclear plants in seven states would either have to make substantial installations of new equipment or upgrade their existing facilities with new design features, or else face loss of permission to operate. Although the AEC had contended that the previous standards were perfectly safe and that critics seeking tighter safeguards were unreasoning, if not paranoid, new emission standards allowed only one one-hundredth of the previously acceptable radioactivity in cooling water. Although it was an astonishing change, the AEC was careful to point out that the new standards were not the result of public criticism. They came about, said agency spokesmen, because new technology made them possible.

In any case, irrational fears about the extension of radiation, thermal pollution, and nuclear plant siting across America will not be reconciled by the Atomic Energy Commission as it is presently constituted, nor will those more moderate, rational objections held by both scientists and laymen professing some expertise with AEC operations.

Thus, the AEC, as a regulatory agency, is probably beyond public acceptance, regardless of the objectivity of the judgment, and is simply marking time until it is reorganized. The future of its nonmilitary operations will be decided in part by an energy policy applicable to all forms of power production. Or it had better be.

The fifty-year-old Federal Power Commission itself has been reduced to presiding over a mountainous mass of detail, administering rate schedules, and issuing permits for utilities to increase borrowing and issue bonds.

As an administrative and regulatory agency, it served with fair competence, if not distinction, over the expanding power industry in the period from the end of World War I to the 1940s. With the termination of old hydroelectric franchises, the FPC encouraged and persuaded electric utilities that renewal of expiring franchises might be more readily allowed under conditions that had been generally ignored in the past. The utilities in many instances obliged the FPC by dressing up their hydro sites, making boating and fishing more accessible, installing campsites, and expanding recreational facilities. More attention was paid to ecology and esthetics along waterways occupied by utilities.

But by and large, the FPC was not empowered to initiate useful action except in circumscribed areas. In spite of the fact that hundreds of thousands of citizens opposed Consolidated Edison's proposal in New York to build a hydroelectric pumped storage plant in the scenic Hudson River gorge at Cornwall, New York, the FPC granted the permit. It took private organizations and aroused citizens six years and a half-million dollars to get a federal court decision that ordered the case back to the FPC to consider such issues as scenic destruction and the value of natural resources.

A second FPC examiner's decision was nearly the same as the original one, in that it rejected the public protests and gave the nod of approval again to Consolidated Edison. To be sure, the Federal Power Commission staff was piqued by the court's criticism of the way it went about granting such permits. The court reminded the agency that its function was a loftier one than deciding balls and strikes as they might be tossed by the utility and dissidents. There were other values in a scenic fjord, other possible alternative sites for the utility to consider, the court declared, before an irreplaceable resource could be defiled.

In the Cornwall siting case, Consolidated Edison had the backing of the vast Rockefeller interests, including the support of Governor Nelson Rockefeller, and various state and institutional officials who flourish on family and gubernatorial largesse. This support diminished as the breadth of public opposition grew and as litigation was prolonged. New York's Mayor John Lindsay, who at first favored the project, subsequently decided against it on the grounds that it would probably endanger the city's water supply conduits.

After Charles Ross, a Vermont lawyer who served on the FPC, left the commission, he said privately that he knew from experience that a federal court decision which remanded the case to the agency would have no bearing on the outcome. "Reasons can be found to support the original decision, and they will be," he said. Sure enough, on August 18, 1970, the commission again authorized the Con Ed project by unanimous vote. In the earlier vote, there had been a single dissenter: Charles Ross himself.

John N. Nassikas, the newest Nixon appointee to the FPC and its chairman, wrote the 116-page decision which held invalid the contention of opponents that the Storm King plant and a huge storage reservoir in the forests at the top of it would damage a historic scenic resource or endanger a public water supply aqueduct. Mr. Nassikas said, too, that the $235-million project would not cause appreciable harm and would even do some good by producing "less air pollution than the Con Ed system would otherwise generate through any other feasible alternatives." Besides, it was argued, no other alternatives were suitable.

Consolidated Edison and its board chairman, Charles Luce, were pleased with the decision, although acknowledging that opponents would probably continue court fights against it. Joseph C. Swidler, former Con Ed consultant, formerly of the FPC and chairman of New York State's Public Service Commission, was pleased. The Storm King pumped storage plant, which would be the world's largest when its six or seven years of construction were completed, could not be expected to alleviate the metropolis's power shortage in that long interim. Litigation, in any case, would almost certainly delay construction beyond seven years. But if built, it would indeed provide reserve, or peak-load, power in the long run.

Regardless of the merits of the opponents' costly and protracted case, the fact of the matter was that the FPC, as Charles Ross knew, was simply not conditioned or prepared to serve as a regulatory response to the new thrust of ecological and natural resource considerations. The kinds of people capable of such response rarely make their way onto governing commissions. In the Cornwall case, it could be argued with strength that the power was necessary, an argument inevitably valid and one that will become increasingly so.

The FPC was not obliged to respond to a federal court's conclusion that values other than the need for power were its concern. True, the commission, in its final findings, said it did "consider" the issue but dismissed it as insufficiently bearing on other, more immediate issues such as the emergency need for more power in the New York metropolitan area.

There were other issues in the Con Ed case, one of the most famed and prolonged in the history of power in America. Over the years, op-

ponents cited excessive costs that had increased every time a new projection was computed and had doubled between 1963, when deliberations
started, and 1970, when the FPC issued its second authorization. Opponents also argued that the pumped storage plant would be obsolete
by the time it began operations and that, therefore, a nuclear plant was
to be preferred. This argument caught conservationists with their contradictions showing, since every subsequent nuclear plant Con Ed
wanted to build was opposed, too.

In the spring of 1972 the United States Supreme Court, which by
then contained four justices appointed by Richard Nixon, all but doomed
Storm King Mountain. The court upheld the FPC ruling. Unless some
new form of litigation or intervention within the state developed—
unlikely in any case, but especially so in view of Nelson Rockefeller's
power over state agencies and conservation policy—Consolidated Edison
could be expected to get on with the most gigantic engineering and
construction project ever to invade the Hudson Valley.

The Storm King case showed clearly that the FPC was incapable of
assimilating new conditions and values. Yet heaping blame on the FPC
was perhaps more futile than it was unfair. As Charles Ross had suggested, the idea of the new chairman, Mr. Nassikas, an old private utility
man, interpreting regulatory procedures *against* a power company bor-
dered on the preposterous. People are not dispatched to regulatory
agencies to institute change or initiate new concepts of regulation. And,
anyway, Con Ed was in a dreadful state; it needed enormous quantities of
new power and new money. Regulatory agencies functioned to expedite
both.

With every good reason, the public has come to recognize that regulatory agencies, conceived in the past to provide consumer protection, enforce ethical management, and balance corporate development against
human well-being, are nothing (or very little) of the kind. The government itself is a power failure in this respect.

Under a soundly developed federal policy recognizing that the
expansionist concepts of the past reflect less reality than ruin, the utility
monopolies could form a union of electric power. They could plan
production on some basis other than maximum market absorption and
maximum generating capacity, increasing without end. Production
would balance power generation and consumption against a value
system acknowledging that less use of power or a stabilized kilowatt usage across a part of the market spectrum is better than more, better than
commanding all the power anyone wanted anytime a use could be devised for it. The policy would assert that the wasteful and needless consumption of power is an assault against life and resources.

No regulatory agency can be designed to accomplish such a monumental change of values, but sooner or later, a government responding to real problems already in existence and increasing in danger will have to take up the challenge.

But before it does so, it will have to guarantee a large sector of society—the blacks, Puerto Ricans, Indians, the whole economic class existing below the fair comfort level—that any pause in the expansionist process will not strike at them. Any policy that may regulate the production of energy to a controlled and possibly predictable rate will have to retain, with increased emphasis, the concept of dispersing a disproportionate share of year-by-year resources to people who have in the past received the least.

The great fear among the leadership of minority groups in response to the ecology wave that became so popular at the end of the 1960s was that a national unity in support of wildlife and scenery would once again militate against society's victims. Since no government devoting so much of its resources to war in Asia could hope to convince the whole electorate of its reverence for life and human dignity at every economic and ethnic level of society, it could not successfully advocate curtailment of the rate of energy production while such conditions of waste and war prevailed.

The cause of conservation and a balanced ecology, of preserving scenic seashores and mountains, purifying lakes, and creating wilderness parks will never soothe the rage of people fighting vermin and rats in a ghetto or living two days a week on pet food while working as seasonal serfs on a marginal farm. Any reverence for life expressed in national policy, which control of energy production might reflect, would have to be convincing. And the sacrifices, if a reduction in the accumulation of material possessions could be called such, must come first from those who have the most and last from those possessing so little in resources and promise.

For many years and especially since World War II, there existed through successive administrations what the economist, scholar, and writer Robert Lekachman has called the "sunny confidence in growth as the universal solvent of social ills."

In a searing assault on the absurdity of the gross national product* Professor Lekachman wrote:

> It is true that political choices are easier when they concentrate upon redistribution of increments to national income rather than upon a static national income itself. It is easier to divide something new than to take something away from one group and give it to another. . . . It would make excellent sense to raise higher-bracket

* *Harper's*, August 1970.

tax rates, impose punitive inheritance levies, and really plug tax loopholes. An awful lot of money would be collected, enough both to repress inflation and to do something for the cities, the poor, and the unemployed.

Admittedly, he concluded, such a scenario was "implausible."

Socialism has long existed in the American economy but ironically a corporation or a family must accumulate a good deal of wealth and power to share in the security of its benefits. The large power companies, the wealthy dynastic families, vast oil and mining interests with their tax-depletion allowances, inhabit a world of socialism although, of course, they define it by euphemisms that mask a generalized truth. What remains of the free-enterprise system, which is substantial, encompasses all small businesses for the most part, service enterprises, overcrowded and undercapitalized operations dominated by giants and conglomerates in the same fields. But mostly it embraces some 50 million poor, low-income, and depressed middle-income people who scrounge and scramble for homes, jobs, space, recreation, mobility, and marginal security. Here competition is real and unending. It includes those living on pensions that shrink with each penny of inflation and rising prices and welfare and medicare clients receiving "benefits" of a socialism that is pretty threadbare at this level. These are the people who strive or resign themseves in an often-hostile environment incapable of providing quantitatively or qualitatively those modest, sometimes-unworthy consumer rewards they are persuaded by marketing ingenuity to seek. Theirs is the true world of competition, of indenture to debt, of remoteness from the exaltation of esteem and success.

The implications of the developing energy crisis were so far-reaching and economically important that the whole question merited the personal acknowledgment of the president, if only because political acuity dictated recognition of an issue of such magnitude. President Nixon dutifully recognized it without being able to do much about it, or perhaps without being willing to provoke an awesome battle for bureaucratic power among Washington agencies and their corporate domains as a prelude to reforms.

Mr. Nixon announced on June 10, 1970, that his administration had come to grips with the national energy problem. Little audible or visible response greeted his disclosure. In fact, so little was known across the country of the need for a reorganization and reappraisal of the production of power that administration proposals seemed bland and disinteresting, except to insiders of the power community and government people directly involved. The significance of, and the need for, a comprehensive policy encompassing all sources of energy was then lost on the general public. The issue had no glamour.

Mr. Nixon said the administration was "seriously considering" a plan to break up the Atomic Energy Commission and turn it into an agency dealing with all forms of energy. Nuclear military programs would be shifted to the Department of Defense, a development which had been prevented by the law that created the AEC under civilian administration. It was not, to be sure, an open form of civilian control, any more than the CIA was; but that was presumed, inaccurately, to have been the intent.

With military programs delivered to the Defense Department, research activities of the AEC would be moved to the National Science Foundation. Then the AEC would be expanded into a civilian energy agency, presumably to help the electric utilities get nuclear power plants built with more dispatch than had previously been possible. The fate of regulation over other fuels (oil, gas, coal) awaited other fragments of whatever inclusive energy plan the administration was developing. Where the Federal Power Commission might fit into the scheme was not made clear—then or since. Nor did the proposal suggest whether the National Science Foundation, in charge of energy research, would be funded to study how to make electricity without pollution—or to determine how to consume it in astronomically increased volume without chaos. That, for the moment, was the end of the energy-policy plan.

Mr. Nixon had indicated earlier that the Atomic Energy Commission might be whittled down a bit when he urged the sale of the government's nuclear-fuel-producing plants at Oak Ridge, Tennessee; Portsmouth, Ohio; and Paducah, Kentucky. Built at a cost of $2.5 billion, the gaseous-diffusion systems separate fissionable uranium 235 from uranium 238. (It should be noted that although fuel thus produced for use in power plant reactors is not sufficiently "enriched," as the process is described, for use in bombs and weapons, it is far from benign.) The plants were to be sold to private industry, taking the government out of the biggest industry over which it ever had exclusive ownership. It was felt that the AEC, with jurisdiction over a single but vast technology, had no claim on immortal bureaucratic life. But the AEC itself, with extraordinary support power dispersed through the government, cannot easily be stamped out.

As long as Chet Holifield is in Congress, subduing or subtracting authority from the AEC will be difficult, indeed. A California congressman, Mr. Holifield was chairman of the Joint Committee on Atomic Energy, a rich and rewarding repository of power itself. He rose to eminence through his proprietary interest in the single technology of nuclear energy. And he was not overjoyed at Mr. Nixon's proposals. Mr. Holifield was satisfied with the AEC's regulatory and promotional programs, despite the unique contradiction of such a mandate. He was also generous with his compliments to the electric utilities, the promising industrial consumer of what the AEC had to sell or, if it came to that, give away.

Once, addressing an assembly of power company people, Mr. Holifield had said that when God had bestowed blessings on America, He had a special smile for the electric utilities. The power companies were encountering difficulties with protesting mortal ratepayers and purchasers of securities, and it was nice to be told that a heavenly authority, remote from regulatory agencies, found them in favor.

Congressman Holifield, it was reported, was unhappy at the prospects of President Nixon fooling around with the AEC. If some new commission was established, it would be Mr. Nixon who would be appointing its members. In the improbable event that the joint committee was dissolved (improbable because Congress does not lightly break up a powerful institutional monument), Mr. Holifield's own power would be terminated. Under the law that established the AEC, Mr. Holifield in 1971 yielded the rotating chairmanship of the joint committee to Senator John Pastore of Rhode Island. He remained, of course, a member of the committee itself.

It appeared that neither the AEC nor Mr. Holifield had much to worry about. Mr. Nixon had simply dusted off the proposal for review. It had been advanced once before, by President John F. Kennedy, who found soon enough that the sacrosanct AEC was considered too well armed with heavy political fire power. He scuttled the whole idea.

The likelihood of a coherent energy policy emerging from the Nixon administration was highly improbable, although with the departure of Dr. Glenn T. Seaborg as chairman of the AEC in the summer of 1971, some measure of change became possible. Dr. Seaborg, Nobel laureate chemist, was succeeded, after ten years in one of the nation's most powerful jobs, by Dr. James Rodney Schlesinger, a government economist previously concerned with national security affairs, who promised to be more candid with the public and more responsive to environmental considerations than the old armaments-oriented crowd in the AEC bureaucracy.

It depended more on President Nixon and his successor than on Dr. Schlesinger whether the latter can and will be able to keep his promises. For nothing short of the full weight of the executive branch brought to bear on the AEC empire is likely to bring about sufficient change to permit an exchange of mutual trust between the public and the agency that has never escaped from the symbolic implications of atomic bomb fallout.

8

Flame, Fuel, and Crisis

It was no wonder that the development of electric power, with its miracle of incandescent light and its saturation of industry, produced a profound change in individual and national life. Neither the gift of fire and the discovery of water power, nor the energy of wind and steam had made the cumulative impact on the world equal to electricity.

Its effect on life, on its prospects, and on social and industrial advancement lifted the hopes and spirit of humanity beyond anything that had evolved before. Although the use of gunpowder and explosives had brought energy to commerce, especially mining, primarily it brought power and technology to warfare. Gunpowder, an invention of the Chinese, was not converted to use in armaments in the land of its origin; it remained in the Orient for use in firecrackers and festivals, for pleasure and spectacles, until Europeans discovered it and converted it to the deadly tasks of conquest. Electricity, too, energized war production, but initially and essentially it was applied to peaceful development. It was a true product of enterprise for nonlethal purposes, civilization's most productive and rewarding accomplishment, a liberating gift from nature, the most miraculous since the first flame.

Philosophically, men who devoted themselves to its generation and distribution understandably might have felt like instruments of a bountiful and creative God. They were, on the contrary, all business—and they still are. The electric utilities absorbed their expanding and operational concepts from an old, combative style of business that adapted *its* standards from lethal games and war: go forward or die, win or lose, conquer or be conquered.

In an era of rampant technology, of overpopulation and an overlooted planet, this antiquated concept of business has become dangerous, a worn-out philosophy from a feral time. Its archaic ideology is not applicable, in spite of its prevalence in the character and style of a good deal of industrial leadership, to the present or the future. The old style seemed to find expression in the counsel, for example, conveyed to the Manufacturing Chemists Association in New York in 1970 by Mr. H. D. Doan, president of Dow Chemical Company.

Mr. Doan thought industry should "quit bellyaching about new government pollution restrictions" and devote itself to thinking about ways of making money out of them. Government tax incentives would be helpful in motivating industry to comply with antipollution standards, he said, but he did not "think we can afford to dream about this as a method of bailing us out when avenues within our controls are available to us and haven't been given a real workout. . . . If we believe in competitive processes, we have to remember some people have to lose if others are going to win."

Other expressions of the old war-games style of industrial conduct led to more combat with previously unarmed adversaries than corporate commanders could tolerate. Conservationists goaded local and state governments into taking action against large corporations that in the past had avoided responsibility for environmental and ecological damage. Having gouged the land and polluted the air and water, most corporations were slow to learn that new rules might be applied against them.

In one such instance, the Oregon Environmental Council chided the entrenched lumber industry, long sacrosanct and long vitally important to the state's economy, for its transgressions. Larry Williams, executive director of the council, said in December, 1971, that "the industry has not been responsive to the damage it has caused—erosion, water quality, degradation, fish habitat destruction, gradual elimination of all natural areas of recreation."

This kind of talk from an agency of a state dependent on the lumber industry for much of its commercial life aroused the indignation of William H. Hunt, president of the Georgia-Pacific Corporation, with headquarters in Portland, and employer of 5,400 Oregon workers. Mr. Hunt denounced such criticism as the work of "woodsy witch doctors of a revived nature cult that insults the intelligence of those they would sway." Robert Pamplin, chairman of the board of Georgia-Pacific, in a letter to a newspaper complained of "the current environmental hysteria, the state's tax structure, inflation, labor unrest, fiscal irresponsibility, monetary mismanagement, and escalating welfare schemes."

The electric utilities, with a few exceptions, had changed their ways and their public manners and, although hardly emerging as an industry responsive to liberalism and enlightenment, treated the public with the appearance of respect, conceding that the production of power and installation of transmission lines caused pollution and havoc while deploring the necessity for it and giving the impression that they would like to improve their old ogre image.

Electric utility spokesmen were generally a good deal more sensitive than the timber, oil, mining, chemical, auto, steel, and textile industries to public outcries against pollution and ruin. It was altogether likely that the utilities, which developed some of the systems and schemes for deluding the public, refined their public relations without undergoing anything more than a cosmetic change in policy, but they had learned for the most part not to attribute ulterior motives or foolish objectives to reform-oriented citizens.

It was in their private conversations, in their sometimes genuine respect for the feelings of sophisticated conservationists and for people hit by power dislocations, that an occasional utility executive betrayed the hidden facets of his soul. But no chief of a utility holding company, looking to three or four years of gloomy prospects of raising $400 or $500 million annually for new plants, condemning sites, running transmission lines across forty miles of countryside, and fending off pickets on a death march around a nuclear reactor, could be expected to indulge in prolonged sentimentality. Although utility executives were as interested in exploiting the environmental issue for possible profits as Mr. Doan at Dow Chemical, and as loath to confront public indignation as the officers of Georgia-Pacific, they did not address themselves to the public in the old bellicose and heavy-handed style that had once characterized electrical monopolies. For power company management at least, the environmental issue had softened their voices and increased their sensitivity to the words and the sincerity, if not the reasoning, of their antagonists.

They had dwelt upon the land-use concepts of Ian McHarg, author of *Design with Nature,* and told one another about some extraordinary advice Professor McHarg had once given to a Philadelphia matron.*

---

* Ian McHarg is head of the Department of Landscape Architecture and Regional Planning at the University of Pennsylvania and a noted ecological planner. At a public forum on pollution in Philadelphia, a socially pretentious woman criticized with some vehemence the air-pollution conditions of the Delaware Valley.

"Do you know the president of the Pennsylvania Electric Company?" Mr. McHarg asked her.

"Yes," she responded.

"Well, the next time you see him don't shake hands. Leap upon him and bite his jugular vein."

They had observed their own power companies polluting the air and water, offending the esthetics of a considerable area, and neglecting to plan ahead for those devastating emergency conditions that inevitably occurred. Some utility executives were known to wince at lugubrious trade association statements attributing sacrificial patriotism to utility management and imputing Bolshevik alliances to proponents of public power. True, they maintained a low profile at power conventions and among large assemblies of their fellows where any consorting with hairy heretics who happened to wander in was undertaken with caution. Although they seldom outraged the official dogma of their monopolies, some were quick enough to agree that not all virtue was possessed by one of the two or more antagonists in siting and nuclear plant controversies.

As corporate officials, they were at times capable of immunizing themselves against painful history that, as private individuals, they were loath to see repeated. For their corporations or in the fulfillment of workaday jobs, men and women often suppress conscience, bypass principle, pretend acquiescence to conduct that in their private selves they disdain. Preferences and private ethics are all too rarely transferred to commercial life, where objectives that contradict individual taste are rationalized as the price to be paid for benefits received. Unless this rationalization was possible, only a charlatan or a psychopath would tolerate the sale and marketing of products they do not need to people scarcely able to afford them and which, in use, pollute the environment and when obsolete, require public subsidy for proper disposal.

The public pretensions of power, as in government, are often formalized communications perpetuating policy that is no longer supportable. Electric utilities, as components of the industrial process, are not what they claim or seem to be.

The first thing the electric utility is not is an industry of free-enterprise capitalism. Although he knows this to be the case, nothing pains an old-fashioned electric power executive quite so much as this fact: that he is, by and large, not within the meaning of competitive enterprise, but in socialism. His is a risk-free exercise shielded from the vicissitudes of winning and losing. He may be guilty of, or the victim of, inept management, bureaucratic bumbling, or conditions inducing darkness instead of light in the homes of his captive customers, and he may be fired for justifiable or dubious reasons, but his power plants and transmission systems will go on, in success or failure, through the seasons, as government itself goes on. His domain is a state, not a business in the conventional sense.

Early in the era of electric power, a competitive environment prevailed, with gas companies battling to retain the lighting business and coal producers bidding against one another to supply central station power plants. For years, gas mantle lighting was more reliable and less expensive than electricity. Rival companies trying to market electric and telephone service fought to attract customers in the same community until people like Samuel Insull created local and regional monopolies and until government stabilized public utility operations by chartering one company to serve a defined area. Variations of the system applied to rail transportation and, in time, to airline systems, with regulatory rate-setting powers included.

In the matter of rates charged for public utility services, telephone monopolies acquired an extraordinary distinction. By taking in a rental fee for installed telephones, then charging on the basis of time consumed and the distance between connections, adding fees for telephones of designated design and color, and the like, the telephone company enjoyed something equivalent to an open-season license in setting rates. An hour of conversation between two people separated by several states might easily cost the price of an airplane trip between the two points. Even a local toll call as often as not exceeded the cost of a bus ride to the destination called. Nothing remotely resembling such service or energy charges was imposed by even the most voracious electric utility.

For years critics of utility monopolies have grumbled that telephone companies seem able to escape the sort of scrutiny, casual as it often was, that regulatory bodies hold over power companies. This special favoritism to telephone systems was more or less officially acknowledged when, early in 1972, the Federal Communications Commission disclosed that it was simply incapable of investigating long-distance rate schedules, the Bell system, and the American Telephone and Telegraph corporation. The company and its services were too big and too complex for the staff, funds, and facilities of the federal agency charged with regulating phone service. The FCC said it would be dependent solely on data furnished by A.T. & T. to provide the criteria for determination of rates. Two FCC members dissented, and one of them, Nicholas Johnson, expressed his disgust in public at this total escape of a monopoly from regulation. Other members of the commission did not seem to mind. Nor did any comment at this highly exposed breakdown in government emerge from the White House.

Investor-owned utilities no less than municipally owned, both being chartered monopolies, are free of the threat and the inspiration of competition in generating and selling electricity to their retail customers. Where competition exists at all, it is limited to the wholesaling of power to systems that transmit it for a retail markup to customers. Federal power operations, such as the Tennessee Valley Authority and others in the northwestern and southwestern regions of the country, sell not to retail consumers but to other systems, privately and municipally owned, and to such enormous federal users as atomic energy installations. Thus, it is always erroneous when writers or opponents of public power suggest that the United States government is in the "business" of marketing power in competition with some harassed, against-the-wall utility patriotically financed by hopeful investors. Federal generating plants transmit electricity to all types of systems, including those not publicly owned, which meter it and sell it and collect for it.

There is some regional competition between fuels, but not much. It is necessary to remember that ownership of all fuels is heavily concentrated among a few corporations. Fifty percent of American uranium interests are owned by oil companies, which in turn have taken possession of vast coal lands and which own or control nearly all the natural-gas production. Occasional assertions that competitive forces exercise a stabilizing influence over power plant fuels are falsehoods. Oil supplies 75 percent of all the energy (electric, automotive, and so forth) in the country. The figure includes gas, too. Coal supplies 20 percent; hydroelectric power, 4 percent; and nuclear power, a shade over 1 percent and growing fast.

Of the energy produced by the electric power industry, data for 1969 showed that 59.2 percent of it was generated by coal; 11.6 percent, by fuel oil; 28 percent, by gas; and 1.2 percent, by nuclear fission. Hydroelectric power does not show here, of course, because it consumes no fuel.

Ten years earlier, in 1959, coal produced 66.2 percent of electric power; oil, only 8.2 percent; gas, 25.6 percent; and nuclear fission, 1 percent. To go back earlier, to 1951, oil then produced 10.6 percent; there was no nuclear power at all in the field; and coal was accounting for 68.5 percent of the electric power. Thus, coal fell from 68.5 in 1951 to 59.2 in 1969, and oil dropped from 10.6 in 1959 to a low of under 7 percent in the early 1960s, then moving back up to 11.6 percent in 1969. In terms of total power produced, nuclear power was insignificant; but in terms of its future outlook, it appeared destined to overtake just about everything else serving as fuel in the decades after the seventies.

Since seventy-eight of the largest electric utilities sell both electricity and gas in the same area, the factor of competition is further diluted, giving rise to well-founded suspicions of dual monopoly, first among the fuel owners and second among the utilities selling both gas and electricity in the same market. There is nothing to prevent a two-fuel utility from concentrating on marketing campaigns for one over the other, depending on where the better prospects of profits are. Some pressure has emerged in Congress to compel the utilities to divest themselves of one or the other forms of energy, but little has come of the divestiture idea.* The political and economic power of oil conglomerates in government is so overwhelming, virtually beyond examination, that no move to induce them to divest themselves of operations in more than one fuel is in prospect.

For all the criticism directed at the utilities, they were not initially responsible for developments that largely killed off competition among energy fuels. They aided the condition by faults of omission rather than the overt stealth sometimes attributed to them. By their failure to initiate effective research programs in their own interest and to fight for freedom in the fuel markets, utilities over the years became painfully subordinate to conglomerates dominating the energy field and to manufacturers of heavy, enormously costly turbines, generators, and nuclear reactors.

The most ominous of deplorable developments in the nation's largest industry was the corporate cornering of energy fuels by a handful of companies, a contradiction, if not a violation, of fundamental principles that both sophisticated economists and Fourth of July orators have traditionally defined as essential to a free market. Perhaps only in an era in which television networks buy baseball and football teams, computer companies buy food chains, and banks buy up their corporate customers, could language become so distorted that when oil companies purchased coal and uranium mines, it was called *diversification*.

While the largest electric utilities have been merging over the years, swallowing each other up, and combining into holding companies that the reform laws of the 1930s sought to forbid, heavily moneyed oil and financial interests have come into possession of just about everything convertible into energy fuel. One of the reasons authorities despair of imposing controls, sanity, and fairness on the fuel market is the nearly insurmountable, superhuman task of unraveling the industrial and economic fabric woven by the power of oil and money around the electric energy business. And while it cannot be accurately charged that the utilities initiated or even benefited extensively from the development, they remained needlessly relaxed and unstruggling while they and their electricity customers were being stretched out for ravishment.

In the twenty years after World War II, when the country lost its greatest opportunity to align its most sustained period of economic growth with the amelioration of its environmental and social ills, the

---

* With respect to systems operating entirely within the borders of a single state, divestiture is probably as far off as state utility commissions permit, but in interstate utilities, freedom to market both gas and electricity might be limited. Both the courts and the Securities and Exchange Commission have examined the problem and indicated favorable response to divestiture. Legislation in the Senate to compel divestiture is under study in a subcommittee.

total number of electric utilities in the United States decreased from 4,051 to 3,614, which means that 437 of them were eaten up by purchase and merger. During the same period, the number of separate investor-owned companies was cut to 472 from 1,060, for a loss of 588. The number of local public power systems remained generally stable at around 2,100, some of them being gobbled up by private utilities while others were being formed.

Rural electric cooperatives, which developed by individual initiative in partnership with government, grew from 800 to nearly 1,000. The cooperatives came into existence when large power companies neglected, usually on the grounds that it did not pay, to extend service to outlying farms and hamlets. Once a cooperative was established and grew a bit, with power consumption assured, nearby utilities sometimes opened a woo-and-promise technique to take it over. The co-ops have been generally successful in preventing this fate, however, although many municipal systems have succumbed to it. Having become successful, some co-ops have been charged with the same uncaring outlook they once attributed to private companies. They have declined, for example, to tie in the huts of impoverished Indians on western reservations to their service on the grounds that there isn't any money in it. There isn't—but, lo, the poor Indian!

The sweep toward concentration, which concurrently reduced the concept of pluralism and decentralized responsibility for such public services and necessities as electric power, has continued beyond the period to which the foregoing figures are related. Between 1965 and 1970, forty-three mergers and acquisitions were reported to the Federal Power Commission, six of them representing mergers of private power companies. Sixteen were acquisitions by purchase of one utility by another, and significantly, twenty-one publicly owned power systems were lost to the private sector, three of them being cooperatives. In fact, for the first time, it appears that antitrust law will be invoked to restrict private utilities to some extent from invading and possessing power systems that are the property of, not holding companies and absentee stockholders, but of the taxpayers and customers who finance and own them.

All utilities face two choices on the question of acquiring bulk power. Either they generate it, or they buy it. They can also generate some and buy some, purchase being made at a wholesale rate. When a private utility has an acquisitive eye on a small power company or a municipally owned one, it sometimes declines to sell it power. When purchase is thus withheld, the deprived company has only one choice, which is to install its own generating facilities, even though the resultant cost may exceed the cost of power supplied by an existing system. It can then correctly be alleged by the withholding company that the higher-cost utility ought to sell out to the adjacent private utility on the grounds of economics. Thus, it is possible for a utility to create higher costs within a small public system, then cite the condition as a reason for absorbing it.

The Department of Justice filed suit against the pleasantly named Otter Tail Power Company in Minnesota, which was charged with a number of offenses, including refusal to sell power to the community of Elbow Lake. Thus, "Otter Tail has been able to preserve a monopoly of retail distribution in towns in its service area," the Justice Department said in its citations. "Competition for local electric power distribution franchises has been eliminated . . . [and] competition in the wholesale sale of electric power has been restrained."

The borough of Pitcairn, Pennsylvania, brought suit against Duquesne Light Company under the Sherman Act, charging: "Duquesne has consistently taken the position that it would like to buy out Pitcairn's system, but it would not sell or exchange power with Pitcairn at any price." Thus, conditions that could prevent efficient operation of the Pitcairn system were created, and the possibility of Duquesne taking it over became a serious threat. By successfully isolating municipal systems, an investor-owned utility extends its retail monopoly, limited by law, to the wholesale level, where antitrust action may be invoked. The "natural monopoly" position conferred on a utility in retailing power is disallowed in wholesaling. A company is not supposed to pick and choose its wholesale customers, isolating them at will, although the practice is old and commonplace. Sometimes the offended power system simply gives up, and at other times, as in the cases of Elbow Lake, Pitcairn, and Danville, Virginia, they go into battle.

Danville's municipal system is surrounded by Appalachian Power Company, one of the holding company family of American Electric Power administered by Donald C. Cook. When Danville sought in 1969 to float bonds to expand its facilities, a citizens' committee fought the bond referendum with the help of an expensive advertising campaign. The city's attempt was defeated, and complaints to the Federal Power Commission charged that Appalachian had misled the public on the issues involved. When evidence developed that the private utility had channeled funds to the so-called citizens' committee, in contradiction to earlier denials of such assistance, a period of review followed, and the Danville power system, seeking alternative ways of raising funds, remained for the time being in possession of the public. The case was considered a classic example of a private utility's attempt to promote isolation and take-over, with the final result remaining inconclusive. Antitrust action in the Pitcairn and Elbow Lake cases was quite naturally welcomed by the harassed Danville power administrators.

One of Danville's city councilmen, incensed at American Electric

Power's successful effort to defeat a city bond issue for local plant expansion, went to Washington to testify in favor of a Senate bill (S. 607) establishing a Utility Consumers' Council. The proposed legislation would offer university grants for study and research in utilities and regulation and allow consumers to intervene in rate proceedings in all monopoly public services. The Danville councilman was John W. Carter, who was wholly familiar with power company financing of a "citizens'" committee to set the stage for taking over the publicly owned system. He said:

> I think there is something morally reprehensible when such a juggernaut of a cartel goes into a municipality and undertakes to confuse and disseminate information that is not true or which is half true for the purpose of gaining from the people who own an asset in common . . . for their stockholders.

In an unusual but unsuccessful move to equalize the combat between the small city of Danville and American Electric Power Company, the city made a direct appeal to the United States Congress to investigate the holding company. As the parent of Appalachian, American Electric Power had assets "approximately 15 times greater than the total assessed valuation of all the real estate in the city," the Congress was told in a resolution pleading for a public inquiry. American Electric Power and its subsidiaries were, the resolution asserted, "exerting the same tactics used in Danville in many other communities throughout the nation to gain control of the municipally owned electric systems."

Mayor W. C. McCubbins said Danville "and other communities similarly situated are defenseless against these intrusions, and have no recourse but to ask the Congress of the United States for protection."

The defeated city government charged that the city's attempt to raise capital was opposed by Appalachian and its holding company solely to precipitate shortages and conditions that the private utility could promise to solve by buying out the system. Even so, some of the people said, the democratic system is the way of life; the referendum was beaten by a majority, and the city ought to abide by the majority decision. However, local public power authorities were convinced that the private utilities exploited them. "On several occasions," the resolution to Congress said, American Electric Power and Appalachian "used economic might to inject its views into the political affairs of the city . . . and to engulf the electorate with propaganda for defeating [bond issues]."

A year and a half after the Danville plea, nothing was forthcoming from Congress in the way of action or inquiry. Nor would the Federal Power Commission intervene, beyond looking into the case and turning up evidence that local anti–public power forces had an unsavory connection with the private utilities. An earlier vote on a $9,000,000 bond issue had been defeated by 375 votes in 1967. After the second defeat in November, 1969, the city, which had generated and distributed much of its own power since 1886, had to plan new tactics. Unable to expand with borrowed money, it sought to install gas generators out of current funds, which would enable it to reduce considerably the power it had to purchase from Appalachian to meet its needs. In any case, the city avoided thus far being absorbed after seventy-four years of public ownership.

Whereas Danville obtained an extended lease on life and proceeded to search for other ways to increase its capacity, the case of Huron, Ohio, was terminated with more dispatch.

When Mr. E. E. Fournace, vice-president of Ohio Power Company, testified before the Senate subcommittee on antitrust and monopoly in its 1970 hearings, he said Ohio utilities were pledged to sell power wholesale to any electric system in a service area, whether municipally or privately owned. He went on to describe conditions under which Ohio would sell to any "interconnected electric system" outside its service area if "such arrangements are beneficial to both parties."

A document submitted with Mr. Fournace's statement described the wholesale contract with the town of Huron:

"Customers using electric motors above a certain size were served by Ohio Edison directly, according to terms of the utility company's contract with the village. Ohio Edison also supplied industry in Huron."

Alex Radin, general manager of American Public Power Association, later testifying before the committee, said of the Huron case:

> It is obvious that when a wholesale supplier can enter into a contract which allows it to serve the larger customers in the area of the purchasing, competing utility, the purchaser is deprived of necessary revenues and, in the case of industrial loads, of customers whose demands economically complement residential service. In the face of such restrictive provisions, it is not surprising that Ohio Edison Company eventually was able to purchase the town of Huron's electric system, and eliminate some municipal competition in its service area.

Wide dispersion of control characterizes consumer-owned systems. Ownership among the IOUs is becoming less dispersed as concentration of power spreads through all but a few of the largest industries.

A study undertaken in 1969 by Arthur D. Little, Inc., disclosed that:

> The 35 largest private utility decision makers, measured by total assets at the end of 1966, included 20 independent operating companies, and 15 holding companies with control over 58 subsidiary operating companies. Thus, these 35 decision makers, with con-

trol over 78 operating companies, represented all of the *big* * 70 electric utilities ... and accounted for almost 70 percent of all assets held by the private utility sector. The ten largest private utilities accounted for over 35 percent of private sector assets.

The report, which sent tremors through power company managements, indicated by inference at least that mergers and concentration had not guaranteed reliability or even reduced electricity rates, both of which are usually offered as the underlying reasons for such developments. Critics of concentration were increasingly skeptical that the amalgamation of power companies held out promises of anything but more trouble.

The Arthur D. Little study dwelt, too, on the concentration of ownership of energy fuels, adding to the general nervousness and extending it to some of the oil corporations, whose leaders entertained visions of growth and wealth from dividing the income from the doubling and redoubling of power generation, whether the sprouting new plants and the polluting old ones burned gas, coal, oil, uranium, or plutonium. They were arranging things to suit themselves while regulatory agencies and the federal government stood idly by. "A number of major oil companies, by entering other energy producing industries, are becoming full-line energy companies," the Little report warned. "Eleven of the top twenty oil companies are now in uranium exploration or mining, and five are in coal mining."

Actually, a subsequent economic analysis by National Economic Research Associates in Washington, D.C., showed the ownership concentration situation to be even worse than the earlier Little report indicated. Seven of the nation's ten largest coal companies are now owned by oil interests, and an eighth was taken over by a conglomerate. Of the twenty "diversified" energy companies, as the petroleum giants call themselves, five are in the top ten on *Fortune*'s list of the 500 largest American industries.

The most lasting effects of the concentration of ownership are in the coal and uranium industries. With the four largest of fifteen major coal-mining operations already owned by oil companies, the move toward acquisition of untapped coal reserves was under way. Humble and Kerr-McGee bought into this unmined reserve. A substantial portion of remaining reserves in Illinois also fell into Humble hands, making the oil company "one of the two largest owners of coal reserves in the nation,"

---

* The word *big* refers to those utilities producing upper kilowatt levels and so categorized by the Federal Power Commission. Most local power systems are classified as *small*, meaning they have a system-wide peak load of about 25,000 kilowatts or less. Of the nation's 2,168 publicly owned utilities, just under 2,000 are in the small category.

according to economist Bruce C. Netschert in testimony before the Senate antitrust subcommittee. Humble has called on some of those reserves to establish a mining venture supplying coal to the Chicago private utilities market, a development that gave the smaller municipal systems the shudders for fear their own coal supply would be cut off by the oil giant. Kerr-McGee has begun production of metallurgical coal from mines in the late Senator Kerr's home state of Oklahoma.

Quite aside from the very largest petroleum companies, the euphemistic diversification was contagious, if not epidemic, in lesser oil empires. A survey of forty-two oil companies, undertaken by Continental Oil Company early in 1969, disclosed the following results among twenty-six corporations responding: *

ENERGY SOURCE	NUMBER OF COMPANIES WITH ACTIVE OR PLANNED PRODUCTION	OIL COMPANIES WITH INVESTMENTS IN ENERGY SOURCE	TOTAL
Oil shale	3	14	17
Tar sands	3	13	16
Coal	7	9	16
Uranium	6	18	24

Thus far, oil shale and tar sands remain insignificant sources of energy fuel, but future demands and production technology promise to make them important. In uranium, petroleum interests command mining and milling operations and are expanding into other stages of the uranium fuel cycle. Kerr-McGee is the largest producer, with 23 percent of total uranium-milling capacity owned directly and another 4 percent held in half ownership. Humble has plans for milling about 8 percent of total United States capacity by 1973.

The full extent of oil company dominance of the nuclear industry was probably understated in view of the fact that all individual corporate plans were not disclosed. The move toward capture of the processing market remained apparent but not fully revealed. Kerr-McGee is one of two companies in the business of converting uranium oxide to uranium hexafluoride (UF_6) and will have approximately one-half of total national capacity now planned.

The eleven companies "entering other energy-producing industries" have bought up or into coal-producing corporations. Twenty percent of total coal production is accounted for by petroleum company subsidiaries. Only two coal companies have sufficient reserves to guarantee

* The tabulation appeared in the February 24, 1969, issue (p. 37) of *Oil and Gas Journal,* as part of an article published under the name of L. C. Rogers. It was incorporated into the testimony before the Senate subcommittee by Bruce C. Netschert of National Economic Research Associates, Inc.

supplies for electric utilities in the heavily industrialized eastern part of the country. They are Humble Oil, the Jersey Standard subsidiary, which has tracts in southern Ohio and which supplies the utility market in Chicago; and Consolidation Coal Corporation, a subsidiary of Continental Oil, the largest coal producer in the country.

Vast quantities of coal rest beneath public lands in the Mountain States, most of it under lease to oil companies (Sun Oil, Atlantic Richfield, Mobil, Gulf, and Kerr-McGee Corporation). Kerr-McGee is the legacy of the late Senator Robert Kerr, an oil millionaire who effectively expanded the family fortune while he was in public office. Mr. Kerr scorned occasional suggestions of conflict of interest, moving about the Senate as though it was a branch office of his extensive mining operations, organizing governmental support, and neutralizing objections by exercise of senatorial power. He is, understandably, remembered with awe among colleagues who marveled at his audacity and confidence. His sureness and confidence never lagged, and considering his straightforward manner of resolving conflicts of interest in his own favor, no reason for loss of confidence ever developed, nor did any effective Senate protest.

In its leasing policies, the federal government handed over large western coal reserves to corporations that, possessing a primary interest in the more profitable oil, were in a position to keep coal lands out of production as long as it suited them. Meanwhile, the power wielded by petroleum giants and the collective hopes of the corporate community for a windfall from their acquisition of the atomic energy industry (which the government was committed to deliver to private industry) helped produce a coal shortage that amounted to a scandal. It also reflected badly on the electric utilities that, enticed into exaggerated dependence on nuclear energy, had allowed themselves to be badly served by the corporate cult determined to develop it as it comes into their hands.

The nuclear energy industry has had some bad years, but if the public and the government can be persuaded that atomically fueled reactors are "clean," safe, and not impossibly expensive, a relatively small fraternity of entrepreneurs, corporations, and opportunists remain convinced that with electric power expanding like the galaxies, an endless intake of billions of dollars is their prize.

The serious implications of a coal shortage deeply concerned electric utilities, as well as the railway systems that haul it from pits to power plants; but the cause of it was not totally attributable to conglomerate oil company strategy. The coal industry was plagued by labor problems, technological and investment costs, and a new body of laws that set production and safety standards previously, and dangerously, nonexistent.

Coal producers protested that safety reforms in mining had become "too stringent." Substantial investment was required by producers to comply with the new laws, and miners were quick to strike when safety conditions were not met. The National Coal Association said labor resistance, combined with other restricting factors, could cripple the entire industry. Some companies prepared to shut down.

Until recent years, all a coal company needed to open a mine was a sufficient quantity of rudimentary equipment, access to a railroad siding, and manpower. But such days are past, and the prime deterrent to new coal production is investment money at high credit costs. Even this factor might have been overcome had it not been for the depressing and sustained impact of nuclear power on coal production.

What the National Coal Association called the wild "over-sell" of nuclear plants, starting in 1963 and 1964, induced large utility systems to contract for the installation of nuclear reactors before they were fully tested and at a time when heavy equipment manufacturers like General Electric and Westinghouse seemed willing to commit loss-leader investments to get the industry started and to file a proprietary claim on it. The nuclear program drove investment money out of the coal market. Except in instances where an occasional utility was willing to enter into a long-term contract assuring recovery of investment capital, new money all but disappeared from the coal development business. Of course, ownership of vast coal properties by oil interests inhibited investment in new coal production, too. "Now we are feeling the effects of the utilities jumping on the atomic energy bandwagon before it was ready to roll," the Coal Association reported as the 1969 coal outlook became clearly depressing.

In a report entitled *The Brownout—and Why?*, privately published in the summer of 1970 by a Washington consulting firm, domestic consumption of coal for that year was computed at an estimated 583 million tons, of which 55 percent or thereabouts (about 330 million tons) was eaten up by the utilities. A shortage of 12 million tons was predicted, which produced an intense scramble for all the coal available. Some systems stepped up the use of gas-fired generators, and others squeaked by with lower reserve supplies of power than prudence would have otherwise allowed. The outlook for the next couple of years was desolate, prompting some utilities to hoard natural gas when possible (thereby aggravating *that* shortage) as a hedge against loss of coal. Gas producers responded by threatening to curtail the gas flow to utilities and, in fact, disallowed increases in natural gas as utility fuel to new electric power business. Some state regulatory commissions, notably the Public Service Commission in New York, warned power companies not to depend on expanded use of gas fuel and not to contract for it with producers.

The report, too, blamed atomic energy speculators for the fuel crisis.

But it chastised the government for failing to take into consideration pollution and radiation factors "or the outcry from the people who didn't want an atomic reactor next door to them."

As it developed, coal production predictions for 1970 were just enough off and the caution exercised by utilities sufficiently protective to eke out the year. Production reached, not the expected 583 million, but 602.9 million tons, enough to cover the 12-million-ton shortage and to leave a few million tons in the distribution pipelines. But it was a frighteningly close call that continued into 1971 and 1972 and will go beyond that. What might ease the coal crisis is the dreadful spectacle of suddenly increased strip mining in Kentucky, West Virginia, and the western states. But the price of resolving the coal shortage by mining methods so utterly brutalizing to the land from which it is stripped—if, in fact, the added production relieves the crisis rather than trails behind increased demands—is a sorry legacy to be endured. In 1970 alone, nearly half of the 129.3 million tons of strip-mined coal in the country was gouged out of the Kentucky hills, which led to the destruction of 17,300 acres of land. Since the prospects for an annual increase in strip mining in Appalachia as well as in western states seems certain, unless long-overdue law controls it, the systematic ruin of more of the earth is inevitable.

The coal shortage and the escalating prices it produced are a marketing and economic scandal that is evidence of the failure of regulatory controls to function when most critically needed. No governmental force intervened to prevent a needless concentration of ownership of the energy fuels, which in turn produced a contrived or manipulated shortage that is nonetheless real. The production of simultaneous shortages of fuels that ought to be competing in the marketplace and simultaneously creating conditions compelling rising prices for those fuels was an extraordinary accomplishment for a small collective of very large corporations. The resultant conditions are unnecessary and inevitable, predictable and deplorable, as all fuels begin to fall into the same hands.

Historically, oil producers have controlled production of natural gas, which is subject to no federal regulation at the retail level. Gas is discovered in tandem with oil. A lively and increasing demand exists for gas because it is relatively innocent as a pollutant factor, especially since it does not spill all over bays and harbors or, save when a leaky pipeline explodes, kill people and wildlife. Both the Federal Power Commission, which regulates gas production at the source level, and the petroleum companies have insisted that gas supplies are diminished and must be conserved. Sales to utilities have been restricted in some cases and are likely to be curbed to an increasing extent if petroleum companies have their way, as they generally do. The petroleum companies blamed the alleged shortage on the FPC for being ungenerous about price increases, and talk of a gas shortage, like talk of an impending shortage of anything, drove prices upward.

Shortages in both coal and gas exist largely in reality contrived by the unity of interests radiating with the glow of nuclear energy and lubricated with the ooze of money from oil. With measured coal reserves on hand, or at least underground, for 600 years or more at this century's rate of energy use, according to Resources for the Future, Inc., a Washington research group, and other authoritative projections, how could a coal shortage develop at this time? And how could a gas shortage develop, too, with vast untapped fields available?

There is no real shortage of the existence of these fuels. The shortage applies, not to their presence, but to their production, which can, unfortunately but quite legally, be curtailed by owners and leaseholders if they are so disposed and if the same collective owners elect to go to the market with other fuels. As the largest consumers of energy fuels, exclusive of the automobile, the electric utilities might be expected to exercise a decisive role in influencing fuel policy. They prefer to be led, rather than do the leading. When Con Ed in New York and Humble Oil got together to introduce low-sulphur oil in that polluted metropolitan area, it was an exception that should have been an earlier rule.

To learn why the utilities remained passive to what appears to be abusive treatment on the part of energy conglomerates, it is necessary for the nation to learn who owns what and whether ownership of such vital resources extends also to money and credit power over the utilities themselves. There is no sinister inference that some secret combine of mad scientists has dulled the wits of power company management. Nor is there an alternative implication that utility management has been supine or stupid, which is beyond credibility except in random instances. Dependence on the conspiratorial school of economics would be necessary to conclude that the power companies hoped to get something out of a concentration of fuel ownership. All they got out of it was higher costs and infinite troubles. Any combination of electric utilities could have invoked Department of Justice antitrust action against the great international oil companies, or could have tried to, if only to point out that the fuels market ought to be kept open and free. But it was not in the nature of electric utility leadership, chary about inviting Justice Department attention in the first place, to call in the law to frisk the oil companies.

Nevertheless, the conspiratorial concept of fuel-resources control was as hard to obliterate as Lady Macbeth's damned spot. In Congress, Lee Metcalf, with a small corps of allies, tried repeatedly to raise the question and to get enacted proposed consumer legislation that would enable private organizations and utility customers to initiate lawsuits, even financing them with public or earmarked funds elicited from the power companies. Even with former federal power commissioners like Charles Ross and Lee White and experts within the FPC itself supporting such legislation, nobody with real power in the Congress or the executive branch cared much for it. The proposal remained just that.

On the issue of the real but possibly unnecessary shortages of fuels, it was possible that the energy conglomerates did not feel the time was economically appropriate to develop adequate gas supplies. The chances of higher prices improved with the imminence of crisis. An economist for the National Economic Research Associates, testifying before a Senate Interior subcommittee, was unawed and unmoved by official corporate allegations of the gas shortage. Bruce Netschert told the senators in 1970 that petroleum leaseholders had discovered gas in 500 different wells on the outer continental shelf in the Gulf of Mexico off Louisiana. Mr. Netschert testified that the sealed wells could provide enough gas to heat 4 million households, extending service from the 29 million customers to 33 million. Instead of connecting the wells to pipelines, he said, the companies shut them off, the inference being that they would keep nicely until such time as FPC generosity on price-increase requests might be more in line with corporate expectations. That generosity was soon to be elicited.

The chairman of the Federal Power Commission, John Nassikas, a sympathetic friend of both the aggressive oil producers and the uncomplaining utilities, ordered higher Louisiana gas prices to stimulate petroleum companies to find more wells and, possibly, plug them into their pipelines. Mr. Nassikas, a New Hampshire partisan of the Nixon political mold, also deplored the possibility of reorganizing energy regulatory procedures under one agency roof, as opposed to the fragmentary system that developed layer on layer in the interdepartmental bureaucracy that now prevails. His feeling was that things would work out as they were, with the power of the rigged market correcting shortages as incentives were applied. Since it was official that price increases would, under Mr. Nassikas, be allowed, he was no doubt right.

Yet, raising prices can scarcely help the situation if there is, in fact, no new gas. Since the companies that drill for gas are generally oil companies anyway, it can be expected the price increase is more likely to be used to help whichever division of the conglomerate needs its benefits than it is to be used to finance more gas exploration.

A preferred method of finding new gas might be, as James Ridgeway, an investigator and writer of considerable resourcefulness, suggested in a published summary of the situation, authorization of an improved leasing policy under which smaller operators, not just large oil combines, would be encouraged to get to work on the problem. Since evidence is abundant that vast supplies of gas exist beneath the continental shelf, the leasing policy ought to allow companies other than huge conglomerates to take a crack at discovering it, especially if the shortage is real and if the government truly wants it alleviated.

Mr. Nassikas would find the suggestion distasteful, and so, perhaps, might Mr. Nixon; but if a gas-fuel shortage is a determinant of the electric power crisis, the thing to do is find an answer to the shortage. Smaller companies can find gas, if it is there, just as they found oil before conglomerates did. They do not, ordinarily, have access to the millions of dollars in cash-bonus payments that are required of bidders under the federal leasing program that seems to be predicated on money, rather than the solution to the problem. The cash-bonus principle, in an era when the cost of money is the predominant issue in resources development, favors the powerful conglomerates, which, as has been observed, have other fish on the hook: oil, which has a record of profits longer than its record of pollution, and nuclear power development which promises gigantic income and a whole new heavy industry if it can be harnessed for nonmilitary uses.

The conspiratorial school of analysis in power development concludes that the petroleum interests—which now call themselves "energy companies" for the good reason that they have come to wallow in many other things besides oil—have set in motion marketing strategies that are predicated on an artificial inhibition of gas and coal usage.

Although hardly a member in good standing of the conspiratorial club, one of the most highly respected theoreticians and administrators in the electric power industry has acknowledged the presence of evidence to support it. In acknowledging it, however, he insisted that the strategy was a failure. He is Philip Sporn, perhaps the major contributor to the technical and planning literature of electric power. He was formerly chairman of the board of the nation's largest utility holding company, American Electric Power Company, a job in which he was succeeded by Donald C. Cook, a noted and even notorious leader among power system empire builders, who would like to see all the electric utility companies in the United States reduced to about a dozen kingdom-sized monopolies. Thus, what pluralists and decentralizers looked upon with dismay—the loss of local and regional systems—Mr. Cook viewed as industrial progress of the sort that saw four automobile manufacturers emerge from a hundred or so.

Philip Sporn was one of the few power men who did not appear to turn off the switches of reason at the prospects of nuclear power. He was, at his age and with his vast range of experience, not easily seducible, which gave him time to reflect, especially since he was under no compulsion to perform on command, save by choice, from fuels and investment councils.

Moreover, he had been for years a proponent of exotic, low-toxic forms of producing power in which he thought the utilities and the government ought to be investing substantial research funds, an idea evoking something less than room-temperature response, in general, and a good deal of passive resistance, in particular, from power people. Sporn liked to take hold of the future, where possible, rather than be engulfed by it. It was one of the advantages of being old and out of the struggle, if not out of the running.

Mr. Sporn argued in testimony before Washington hearings and in published reports that nuclear power had lost for the time being its battle to supplant coal. While the cost of coal, under market curtailment, had risen as the supply diminished, the cost of delivering nuclear reactors had gone through the stratosphere. Economies of scale to the contrary, nuclear plants scheduled to go into production at 3.5 mills per kilowatt-hour would, in his estimate, cost 100 percent above that. Such "dismal economics," as one observer called them, caused cancellations of reactor orders and prolonged delays in the confirmation of others. Where intuition, research, and appropriate planning failed to cool management's premature infatuation with nuclear power, the cost of keeping the love affair in bloom induced sober reflections. It was not the first time that outbreaks of affection for new technology produced, when all the costs were analyzed, a renewed appreciation for more stabilized, if less romantic, conditions in the industrial household.

Mr. Sporn cited statistics to show that previously attentive suitors of atomic power had drifted away with revived fervor for disdained possibilities back in the fossil-fuel pits. In 1967, he reminded the defectors, orders for atomic plants added up to 25,780 megawatts. Each year from 1966 to 1968, the average capacity placed on order was 19,150 megawatts. In 1968 itself, orders declined to 16,044 megawatts. The following year was a debacle, with 7,190 megawatts. None of this was absolute evidence that the heavily courted source of power could not, with a public relations face-lift and a reorganization of economics, aided by the promotional capabilities of the Atomic Energy Commission and the "energy" companies floating on oil, present a new body of promise later on. The blemishes might, indeed, be buffed off and costs brought more reasonably into line with coal, especially if coal continued in short supply, and more especially because it already had advanced to the spendthrift class. With the cost of all fuels going up and supplies falling behind demand, nuclear power would, in time, start looking better economically. It might be out of favor with the public for environmental reasons, but that was not explicitly the reason the utilities lost faith in it. It was simply geting too expensive, on one hand; and the equipment manufacturers could not deliver the plants and get them operating on schedule, on the other.

Bruce Mansfield, the Ohio Edison president who succeeded to the presidency of Edison Electric Institute in 1970, complained in public about the poor quality of workmanship and long-overdue delivery of generating equipment not only of nuclear installations but of conventional plants as well. He blamed faulty equipment for a significant number of power failures the preceding autumn. On March 9, 1971, Mrs. Virginia H. Knauer, special assistant to President Nixon on consumer affairs, with nominal power of persuasion and little authority, reported that during the extensive dimouts and load shedding which occurred in the eastern part of the United States six months earlier, eight generating plants with a total of 5 million kilowatts were out of operation because of malfunction. One million kilowatts were out of service with the collapse of the "Big Allis" generator in the Con Ed system, whose Indian Point nuclear plant had been dead as well.

The unreliability of generating equipment was so serious, Mrs. Knauer declared, that four utilities and nine insurance companies were suing the manufacturer for failure to meet standards. Mrs. Knauer suggested that the electric utilities would have been better advised to devote less money to promotion and advertising and more to research and development, rather than depending on General Electric, Westinghouse, and component suppliers for the creative engineering and design essential to power plant operation. It might result, she said, in solving some of the "problems of both the consumer who is not getting electricity and the corporate customer who is unable to produce it."

The whole nuclear industry had lost points and prestige, which would no doubt be recovered, since the determination to generate power by atomic fission was supported by vast interests. In a trade document published in 1963, when the utilities were persuaded by heavy-reactor manufacturers and the AEC that nuclear power held out the greater glory among fuels, the following appeared for the enlightenment of power plant managers:

> In the next five to ten years, the way atomic fuel will make its contribution to the energy economy of the United States will be in helping to stabilize and/or reduce the cost of electric power generation. . . . But for the most part atomic energy will have its effect through the impact its emergence as a competitive means of power generation *is certain to have on the price structure of fossil fuel* (emphasis added). . . . Also, it will act as a further stimulus

for improvements in existing methods of transporting fuel, notably coal.

In the years since 1963, nuclear fuel has stabilized no part of the power economy, has not reduced the cost of electricity, and if it had any bearing on the price structure of fuels, it contributed toward driving all costs upward. As for stimulating improvements in "methods of transporting fuel, notably coal," whatever that meant at the time, it failed to develop. In fact, the whole promise and projection could scarcely have been more wildly in error.

No industrial consumer in the world buys more coal than the Tennessee Valley Authority, serving 6 million people in seven states. Because it was in the heart of the coal country, TVA was never a customer of the oil companies. Its network of generating plants was powered by hydroelectric penstocks, coal, and to a minuscule but increasing degree, nuclear fuel.

Coal requirements for 1970, said TVA experts, approached 350 million tons for the utilities, making the shortage a good deal more severe than other estimates indicated. For 1972, these coal requirements would climb to 450 million tons, which could become available only by accelerating and extending the ecologically destructive stripmining operations in western and Appalachian states.

While there was, indeed, an impending crisis in energy fuels, and in coal especially, it was utilized as an opportunity by fuel producers themselves and by a number of large investment and banking institutions. It seemed, at times, that the shortages were publicized and promoted in the manner of a public relations campaign to persuade the regulatory agencies to permit—and condition the public to accept—substantial price increases across the board for every aspect of energy production and distribution.

In one regulatory agency act alone, an increase in the price of natural gas at the wellhead, presumably allowed to provide corporate motivation to discover and open up more producing fields, would cost consumers $4 billion. There is nothing like a good impending crisis, if it is properly promoted, to get the prices up, to keep the public mollified, and the regulators acquiescent. It is prudent, if possible, to keep the crisis from becoming needlessly acute—that is, to keep it as a prolonged and immediate threat, never fully realized—lest a few watchdog senators and congressmen start insisting on public ownership of energy fuels as a preferred means of protecting public well being.

Nevertheless, the coal shortage was a real and continuing threat to many electric utilities. Because of the special character of its contracts,

TVA might just possibly squeak through, even if it has to depend more than usual on the destructive strip-mining process to do so. But other utilities will not, even though they are prepared, or have to get prepared, to meet coal costs rising as much as 100 percent in little more than a year.

One plant alone in the TVA system, the Bull Run steam-generating facility five miles southeast of the atomic energy town of Oak Ridge, Tennessee, was using 7,600 tons of coal a day, 5.3 tons a minute, in normal operation.* This supply called for the arrival of a unit-car train a mile and a half long from the eastern Kentucky coal fields every day. With scarcely more than a few days' stockpile on hand in the worst of times, a week or so of bad winter weather would cripple the Bull Run operation, regardless of coal pricing economics.

In a single year, coal costs for TVA rose $60 million. Here is an example of the kind of arithmetic affecting the enormous power operation: Its Widow's Creek steam plant, in 1969, paid $4.80 a ton for coal delivered to the storage yard. Twelve months later, coal cost $8.80 a ton. Even before this startling increase, TVA filed notice that its rates to power systems would be increased by 23 percent. It was a sad and bitter reality for TVA power administrators, worse even than the southern Duke Power Company's request for an 18 percent increase, but comforting compared with the application by Georgia Power Company for a wholesale rate increase of 40 percent. It was a bad time, economically, for both public and private utilities caught in the compression of rising costs and fuel shortages.

On the basis of two factors—the runaway cost of fuel and the excessive cost of borrowed capital—the whole country faces increased electrical rates. Taxes and wage increases will add to the burden. In New York, Consolidated Edison was granted a rate increase of $102 million even as it was reducing power output on occasion by 5 to 8 percent in the late summer of 1970. By April of the following year, it asked for a 14.2 percent increase on top of that, to bring in an estimated $154 million by 1972. The utility needs $1.05 billion in 1972 for construction alone. The average city-apartment family is paying $12.61, an in-

---

* Much larger coal-burning plants than this were in prospect in the western part of the United States as enormous strip-mining operations developed in 1970–1971. One new plant in the Southwest, where New Mexico, Arizona, Colorado, and Utah meet, will consume at capacity operation 14.5 tons of strip-mined coal a minute, or 21,000 tons a day. Five other plants of similar size are scheduled for construction in a project organized by twenty-three power companies and are already (early in 1972) about half complete. Even at a near-perfect pollution-free operation of 99 per cent, the remaining particulate and toxic material ejected from the smokestacks of six power plants, all within a radius of 200 miles, will lay a perpetual dirty haze over the great clear and open skies of this sparsely populated land.

crease of up to $2.70 a month over the previous bill. Three million customers are affected, including a million or more people on welfare. And company spokesmen concede that more dimouts and loss of voltage are in prospect, even with all that new money. It should be noted that the electrical bills New Yorkers are paying are distinguished by two factors. It is the highest rate in the continental United States and there is not the slightest possibility that the cost of power will remain at this high arrested rate. Consolidated Edison has thirty-eight old and unreliable generating plants in its system, and some of the newer plants, including the famous Big Allis generator and the showcase nuclear plant at Indian Point along the Hudson River, cannot be relied upon, either. The nation's energy problems are intensified, prolonged, and expensive in New York.

Alarm over fuel costs, which exerted pressure on rates, spread to the realm of international trade policy. Coal exports to Japan, which was paying top prices that in special cases drove the cost of a ton of domestic industrial coal in 1970 to $9 and $11, irked utility management. Donald Cook of American Electric Power called for "immediate and severe restrictions" on shipments to foreign buyers.

A certain retributive justice has come home to haunt the electric utilities. For many years, coal industry spokesmen recalled, the utilities that produced half the nation's power supply in coal-burning plants had the upper hand. They would contract only for their measured needs, declining to guarantee a continued coal market, ready to abandon coal at any opportunity. "The coal operators couldn't get financing for new mines," one coal authority said. Distressed operators had to settle for $3 a ton, even when losing money, because creditors were chasing them for cash. His thesis was that because the utilities invested little in a stable coal market, they helped cause the inevitable conditions.

The Tennessee Valley Authority had two huge nuclear plants under construction, the Sequoyah near Chattanooga, with a capacity of 2.2 million kilowatts, and another at Browns Ferry in Alabama, which at 3.5 million kilowatts was for the time being the largest in the world. TVA needed bids at once on another couple of million kilowatts and decided on a coal-burning steam facility in Rhea County, Tennessee, a mile and a half down river from the famed and beautiful Watts Bar hydroelectric plant below Knoxville.

Invitations to the coal industry in 1970 to supply the fuel produced not a single bid, even though the price of coal had nearly doubled in a year. With absolutely no prospects of coal, TVA was compelled to turn to a third nuclear plant at a cost of $400 million for 2.2 million kilowatts. With 2 million customers in seven states to take care of, surrounded by the coal-producing country, TVA was driven further into nuclear power.

It seemed quite clear that something strange had occurred to the energy market. With a 600-year supply of coal on hand and a preference for using it, TVA found it wholly unobtainable. Other utilities were faced with the same unprojected and perhaps inexcusable conditions.

With the winter of 1972-73 approaching, fuel costs continued upward to levels that dictated further increases in the cost of electricity. No one referred any longer to economies of scale under which the cost per kilowatt was supposed to go down as the capacity of generating plants increased. Even after the Nixon administration, responding to years of inflationary pressures that had the country thoroughly frightened, established price-freeze machinery in the autumn of 1971, public utility monopolies expected to encounter only short-term governmental resistance to increasing rates. Electric utility spokesmen, at first horrified at the prospects of perhaps not being allowed to raise rates and possibly not being able to guarantee the expected return on investment capital, were soon comforted. Their fears that utilities might have to get authority for rate increases from some new and possibly unsympathetic agency were calmed when it became clear that the same old regulatory agencies that had always allowed rate increases all along would still be in charge. In fact, Senator Lee Metcalf charged in the Senate that if the inflation-control program turned out to be successful, the utility monopolies would enjoy profit windfalls because their own costs would be controlled and probably reduced while their income would go up. He said:

> Many of the pending rate increase requests were based upon projections of costs and prices that are being reduced. If the administration is going to let these rate increases, based on outdated financial projections, go into effect, it will be saying that either, first, its wage-price controls are ineffective, or second, it does not object to inflation created by the utility corporations.

Metcalf charged the Nixon wage-price control team with being uninformed about "the magnitude of rate hikes pending" and for failure to develop machinery for evaluating the inflationary impact of such increases on the country. As a result, he said, the main permission for exemptions and for authorizing rate increases would continue to be made by traditional regulatory bodies, or none at all. "The new utility price regulations are no more than business as usual."

Senator Metcalf thought that in the first six months of 1972 utility rate increases would approach $4 billion and that "the additional billions in annual increases which may go forward thereafter defy the imagination. . . . That will be a sledgehammer blow to our economy." All utility bills make up 5 percent of the cost-of-living index, Congress was told by the president's Price Commission. Introducing an amendment to the

Economic Stabilization Act of 1971, the law that established what it was hoped were inflationary controls, Metcalf wanted the "President or his delegate," not a federal agency predisposed to industry influence, empowered and held responsible for utility rate increases. He said:

> Because of the special impact of regulated public utilities on our economy, and because of the inability of Federal and State regulation agencies to coordinate a national anti-inflationary policy, we say put the responsibility for permitting utility rate increases where it belongs—at the Presidential level. And in order to assist the Chief Executive in managing the increases in a rational way, put back the freeze, so that he may start with a clear slate, with the reins in his hands. Only in this way can we avert a tidal wave of public utility rate increases, those already approved and waiting to be put into effect, and those to be launched by the regulatory agencies.

Prior to the federal venture into inflation management, some utility experts had recognized the need for administrative reform in establishing rate schedules. Joseph C. Swidler, former FPC chairman, concluded that government agencies were inadequate to deal with market forces driving prices and fuel demands upward. He thought some kind of a new agency regulating energy *and* rates ought to be organized.

Alex Radin, general manager of the American Public Power Association, to which some 1,400 consumer-owned systems belonged, warned President Nixon in a letter that something "drastic" had to be done about the fuel and energy problem or blackouts and breakdowns would be unpreventable. Mr. Radin enclosed in his letter a telegram from the public system in Vineland, New Jersey, stating that unless the government ordered priorities for coal, 80 percent of Vineland's power system would be shut down. Nothing short of enforced fuel allocation could begin to alleviate the problem, which was moving toward blacked-out communities and rationing of any power obtainable.

Astronomical increases in fuel costs had become commonplace. In the East, some utilities were paying $5 a barrel for oil that had cost them $1.87 a year earlier. Coal was up from $4 and $5 a ton to $11.

The quest for utility coal nearly verged on panic. Duke Power Company bought outright two coal companies in Harlan County, Kentucky, but there were few coal companies on the market for others to buy.

In nearly every part of the United States, excluding only slow-growth areas, the prospects of insufficient power became more and more ominous. In TVA country, which even after an expansion that brought 5,000 industrial operations to the seven-state watershed was a relatively slow-growth territory, failure of producers to deliver some 5 million of the 35 million tons needed in the twelve-month period ending in mid-1970 was a threat to the system. Tracing the causes of this failure, TVA people encountered some dismal facts.

One of the facts was shocking, indeed. "Poor management of the [railroad] cars and locomotives available, and the inability of regulatory bodies to do anything about it," was a primary cause of the shortage that left TVA endangered.

Cars carrying coal from the Appalachian fields to Atlantic coastal ports for export "are used for storage," it was explained by Aubrey J. Wagner, chairman of the TVA board in May, 1970.

> If a vessel designated to carry a certain cargo overseas is delayed, the coal remains in cars on the track waiting for as long as 40 to 60 days, in some cases, for the ship to come in. Thousands of cars are immobilized in this way, and others are similarly affected in other coal movements. Paradoxically, in some cases where cars have been available, there was no motive power to move them.

At about the same time, one railroad informed Mr. Wagner that it did not intend "to buy any more coal cars at all." Transportation of coal, he was told, was a low-profit item. If a large consumer of coal cared to buy cars on its own account, the railroad might consider hauling them. "And," Mr. Wagner said, "it may come to that."

Utilities dependent on coal began to get the feeling that the railroads were adopting the same attitude toward low-profit coal that they reflected all too clearly toward low-profit passengers, whom they drove from their lines. "Such an attitude," said Mr. Wagner, "demeans the public interest in rail transportation and endangers the country's electric power supply which depends so heavily upon it."

In a mild reference to the concentration of ownership in energy fuels, with oil companies wielding power over markets, Mr. Wagner allowed that "the implications of such a concentration of control over basic energy sources are far-reaching."

Perhaps the TVA system, which despite intermittent failures has had a good record of complying with power demands, would not be in such desperate straits had its Browns Ferry nuclear plant, under construction in Alabama, been completed. It was two, perhaps three, years behind schedule because of delays in delivery and faulty equipment. Browns Ferry, in northern Alabama, was, at 3.4 million kilowatts, nearly twice as large as any nuclear plant in the world projected for its delayed birthday in 1972. Contracted for years ago, it was intended to meet an orderly and predictable demand for power. But TVA, not unlike private utilities, had been smitten with the prospects of nuclear power and was vulnerable to the promotion tactics of heavy-equipment manufacturers with economic interests in the nuclear industry. It had been caught in the seduction process launched by Westinghouse, General Electric, United Nuclear, Combustion Engineering, Babcock and Wilcox, Union Carbide, and other corporate suitors associated with the Atomic Industrial Forum, the trade association of the nuclear industry, which is located in New York. The penalty for such vulnerability to promotion was as embarrassing as it was to an anxious bride stranded at the church.

No one can balance one fuel industry off against another with predictable results, to be sure; but with the electric utilities so insouciant initially, when they were not tripping over themselves trying to book dances with nuclear power, they added to their multiple woes by inattention to fuel policy in which they had a blood relationship. What the utilities live on, produce with, build with is fuel and money. What the fuel business did to them, and what the money business accomplished in interest rates to everybody, produced severe problems for them on top of critical ones existing between them and their customers. They were in a sorry fix, damned indeed for nearly everything they did and everything they failed to do.

The petroleum companies were in a commanding position over the electric utilities. Philip Sporn expressed the hope that oil under the ice and tundra of Alaska's North Slope, for which the oil companies handed over $900 million for leases in 1970, would provide abundant fuel for the power plants. This hope was not shared by certain other experts in energy matters. Lord Ritchie-Calder, the British scholar and author of numerous books dealing with scientific development, and an associate at the Center for the Study of Democratic Institutions at Santa Barbara, California, thought all the dangers of nuclear power development and the radioactive wastes thus produced offered an alternative more preferable than pumping North Slope oil into the United States through a pipeline.

The Department of the Interior, while conceding that an 800-mile pipeline through the Alaskan wilderness and probable oil spills from supertankers posed very real peril, nevertheless recommended the project as necessary to the national interest. Governor William Egan was ready, he indicated, to authorize the state of Alaska itself to undertake the oil development project if the federal government and petroleum interests backed out, which was highly unlikely.

In response to the public uproar over assaults on the environment, however, the Alaskan venture was stalled until Secretary of the Interior Rogers Morton could study the matter and prepare the position statement on which department approval would be based. There was really no question of halting the development or even delaying it for five years or so. Several hundred miles of four-foot pipeline, manufactured in Japan, has been stacked up in Alaska for more than a year. Oil rigs are standing by, along with thousands of tons of heavy equipment and a large colony of highly paid technicians and workmen.

A number of factors had combined to ease the oil supply temporarily in the United States at the end of 1971. An extraordinarily mild winter and industrial stagnation in a good many areas turned the oil shortage into a seasonal glut, without producing, of course, reductions in prices. Representatives of oil-exporting countries were, however, summoned to Geneva on January 10, 1972, to negotiate extra payments to compensate the governments for the loss of income through devaluation of the dollar. None of these developments altered the course of the North Slope pipeline and drilling project.

In order to prevent Alaskan native organizations or the state itself from acquiring any part of the land across which the line was to be built, the Interior Department designated more than 5 million acres of land out of bounds for any state or private claim that might be made on it. The 5 million acres constituted a corridor from the North Slope oil fields across the state to the Valdez shipping port. Thus, the matter was pretty well settled save for election year formalities and the settlement of certain ecological nuisances.

9

Old Power Men
and
New Attitudes

WHILE THE international petroleum corporations, the United States government, and the state of Alaska played their roles in the oil development minuet, the electric utilities and their spokesmen maintained a low profile on the North Slope issue. To the more astute among power industry observers, the invisibility of the utilities in the battle for North Slope oil, which would help fuel two-thirds of United States power production, suggested that the business had become less cluttered with executives who continued to venerate the concepts of Edwin Vennard, for many years the managing director of Edison Electric Institute and the national voice of the IOUs. Mr. Vennard was a true booster of old-fashioned Americanism and free enterprise.

After the collapse of the Insull companies, the lobbying and public relations, research, and educational programs of the industry were separated. The Edison Electric Institute took care of the intra-industry statistical and research programs, and the legislative and lobbying activities were funded and administered as a separate activity in Washington. Mr. Vennard went to New York, where his promotional and public relations doctrine was amplified for public but not for legislative consumption. He was always denied his heart's desire, which was to subject Senate and House hearings to the electrifying powers of his undoubting spirit and didactic style.

In Washington, such men as Arthur Barnett, a Republican stalwart of milder manner and adaptable ways, has for some years supervised lobbying activities with more effectiveness (considering the industry's long record of success) if perhaps less imagination, than might have been the case had Edwin Vennard been permitted to direct it all.

Mr. Vennard loved the utilities industry with undeviating devotion not only because he saw an increasing per capita use of power as the main highway to materialism and happiness but because long service as its minister of public affairs produced in him a depth of satisfaction experienced by one whose ego and sense of accomplishment came to full flower in his work. He may have been disappointed by policy that banished him from the forums of Washington lobbying and intrigue, but his loyalty and labors never flagged.

Upon retirement, Mr. Vennard opened a consulting service where utility people could go to be refreshed by his counsel and ministerial assistance. He was the embodiment of a particular kind of leadership that the awesome problems of the technological age and the multifaceted solutions they require probably will not permit again. His background and knowledge of the industry made any consultation with him memorable, whether or not it was relevant to the future.

All leadership requires perseverance, hard and often thankless work, and the recognition of, and sympathy for, common problems. It is this sincerity, this difficult work and dedication, that commands deference and mutes criticism from those who may genuinely like the leader while not necessarily sharing his convictions or shortcomings.

People in this old image are sometimes still dispatched to leadership positions in utility associations. To listen to or read the speeches of Robert H. Gerdes, president of the Edison Electric Institute in 1968 and 1969, was to be mesmerized by echoes of ultraconservative, irrelevant assessments of utilities and public affairs. Similarly, aging chief executives of some power companies—the number is diminishing, to be sure— reflect in their words, style, and administrative policy little of the depth and breadth of the realities confronting electric power expansion and its cumulative impact on all life. The power industry simply never paid much attention to equipping its management with the special sensitivity or skills that might have served them well in an era of accelerated change and overturned verities.

Nowhere in America is there a superior training ground for electric utility executives, except in the conventional fields of engineering, law, accounting, and business administration. By and large, what they learn of the art and science of politics, the dynamics of regulation, the humanism and subtleties that characterize the educated mind, they learn on the run. To be sure, other industries suffer equal shortcomings, but the world of electric power is so inexorably aligned with human and industrial life that the stakes are higher, vision is more essential, and independence and courage are more vital. Knowledge of the natural sciences, the arts and humanities, the interdependence of ecology and industry on all life is uncommon but not nonexistent among power and energy company titans. And where it is present, it is for the most part (like geologists in oil companies) subverted to industrial rather than ecosystem objectives.

Because so much of the university research financed by electric utilities is scarcely more than marketing propaganda, the power companies lost an extraordinary opportunity when they rejected the study grant proposals in particular, together with other proposals in general, in the federal Utility Consumers' Council bill (S. 607) of 1970. The grant provisions would have established funds for studies in utilities, regulations, and related research. Only the electric companies were virtually unanimous in opposition to the bill. A few other public utilities and even some Federal Power Commission people warmly favored it. One FPC commissioner testified that the study grant provisions "would be the stimulation to young people, and to others, to develop a specialization in this field, which could supplement the work that has to be done."

Douglas Gleason, executive vice-president of United Utilities, a witness for the United States Independent Telephone Association, said: "Regulators and managers of utility companies alike should welcome supported studies of regulatory matters. It would be helpful to all concerned if a broader understanding of the objectives of utility regulation could be achieved."

William Crowley, executive director and vice-president of the American Gas Association, thought that

> It would be wonderful if we could do something to stimulate public utility courses in our major universities, because we need a backlog of people both in our utility companies and in our regulatory staffs. . . . Unfortunately, there is an extreme paucity of utility economic expertise in universities. Virtually no university possesses public utility departments devoted to the education of students in public utility economics and related concepts.

Charles Ross, the former FPC Commissioner, who had also been chairman of the Vermont state regulatory body, was trying to balance his time between practicing a little law and teaching at the University of Vermont. He was clearly in favor of instituting utility studies in universities. He found the need for "objective" specialists in public utilities nearly overwhelming. For one thing, it might permit people like himself to devote his time to teaching, rather than having to take on utility clients. He said:

> For many years, both the quality and quantity of research coming out of our universities on the economics of public utilities

has been woefully lacking. . . . Research is directed where there is financial support. The private sector of the utility industry has given virtually no support to research efforts on the economic aspect of the industry. One can only wonder why. Have they been afraid to let the cold unbiased eye of the academic researcher take a good look at their operations, rates, structure, and other areas? . . . Money that the private sector has spent at the university level has largely been of a public relations type.

The tradition of purchasing, through public relations and marketing research, the viewpoint desired by private power companies had never died out, another witness said. Robert O. Marritz, executive director of the Missouri Basin Systems Group (public power), described a book financed by private utilities as "unscholarly, superficial, and often inaccurate . . . information on the history and present development of power supply in the Missouri Basin." The book was *Mid-Continent Area Power Planners,* by W. Stewart Nelson, published by the Institute of Public Utilities at Michigan State University.

Mr. Marritz, in response to questioning, conceded that all the members of the advisory committee of the Institute of Public Utilities at Michigan State Graduate School of Business were officers of investor-owned gas, electric, and telephone utilities. It was reminiscent of the old Insull days, when literature and research in the universities was bought and paid for and then promoted as authentic by the purchasers.

Even though the cost of the Utility Consumers' Council provisions would have been negligible (0.1 percent of the aggregate annual operating revenues of the electric utilities), opposition to the bill was relentless and effective.

Nevertheless, criticism of power company practice within the fraternity of managers is not uncommon. A common graveyard joke, recounted in a magazine article by John Wicklein, a television producer who put together a fine show on the utilities for an educational network, is that "we need more funerals in this industry." It is an acknowledgment that a new breed of managers, with a new outlook on the future, is desperately needed. The industry is cluttered, quite literally overstaffed, with people so deeply intent upon keeping the plants operating, expanding facilities, keeping the transmission lines in repair, and even working at the risk of their lives and well-being to keep power flowing to customers, that one is touched by their dedication and resolution. The camaraderie unites them, as does the feeling that they are harassed by hostile forces, by a public they are determined to serve, people who cannot sense the complexity and depth of their good intentions.

After a brownout in the summer of 1969, when elevators ran at half speed and subway trains barely crawled through stifling tunnels, television commentators and the press turned on New York's Consolidated Edison Company with derision. On a day when criticism reached its highest level of shrillness, a visitor to the company's dining room in the utility's headquarters in Greenwich Village could respond only with sympathy to power company engineers and management men, their faces taut from sleeplessness, not understanding how or why they had to be the target of such abuse when their dedication to the public and to the objective of restoring service was so palpable.

In emergencies that descend on a utility in a winter's blizzard, when men have been known to sit freezing on top of a high pole, keeping a live line in contact with a transformer half rooted from its perch, it cannot be said that the power company and its people are uncaring or that they put personal comfort ahead of service to those who need it.

"It was four degrees above zero, and we had to cut through two fallen elms to get the truck through, but we got the goddam juice back on in sixty-eight minutes," a Massachusetts lineman once told an interviewer. Sixty-eight minutes is a long time, perhaps, to a family in the dark and cold, but restoring power under such conditions in so little time in the night is a proud achievement to a frostbitten worker who knows in detail that without the determination, skill, highly functional equipment, and perhaps even the overtime, it could just as well have been seven or eight hours, frozen water lines, and evacuated homes that complaining customers would have had to endure.

Men on maintenance crews, once called grunts in the now-unionized trade, are rarely called upon today to strap on sharp-pointed hooks and shinny up wooden poles to cut away tree trunks and foliage after a storm. It had been a dangerous, high casualty occupation, with death by electrocution and injury from falls and burns commonplace. Training methods and safety standards have been advanced over the years, although close proximity to uninsulated wires and fallen lines remains hazardous.

Veteran workers in their late forties and beyond share memories of the kind of accidents that have diminished substantially with new maintenance technology introduced in the 1950s and thereafter. Many have helped remove burning bodies from high-tension towers and poles.

Development of the protective basket, in which workmen are raised to line level by hydraulic machinery aboard rubber-tired trucks, makes it unnecessary for them to stand on the same crosspiece with a leaking transformer. But caution and intelligence and a healthy respect for the unpredictable character of the "juice" remain the best guarantees such workmen have of dying a natural death. At the same time, the old days of climbing a pole, donning insulated gloves, and working with hot wires in hand once commanded status and attracted admiring onlookers

to a lineman's high-wire performance. Except for the nostalgia of surviving old-timers, who have mostly become supervisors anyway, electrical
workers are glad enough to work under improved conditions, and never
mind the ground-level audience of envious boys.

Cliff Newman, who advanced from grunt to supervisory status and
$12,000 a year with the Virginia Electric and Power Company, told a
magazine writer, Douglas Borah, that the worst danger was always a
poor memory: failing to remember not to *ever* come in touch with two
wires at the same time. He once climbed a pole to finish a service-attach-
ment task that a co-worker failed to do because he allowed himself to
become a conductor of the voltage. First, he made sure that his friend's
body, dangling from a safety line, was no longer in contact with the
wires, then fastened a rope around the safety belt so that workmen on
the ground could lower him out of the way.

"I don't want to mention the dead guy's name," Mr. Newman said.
"He was stupid and careless."

The young man had brushed his hand against a primary line while
the secondary line rested on his shoulder, which meant instant death.

Mr. Newman explained:

> Electricity travels in a cycle. It starts at a substation and runs
> up the primary or positive wire to the end of the power line,
> whether it's a mile long or a hundred miles long. Then it turns
> around and comes down the secondary or negative wire until it
> gets back to the transformers it started from.
>
> But there's one thing to remember: That old electricity is lazy.
> It just wants to get back to the substation the quickest way it can.
> So if you fellows maange to touch a primary *and* secondary wire
> —why, old Reddy Kilowatt is gonna take a shortcut right through
> your body, and he's gonna kill you, burn you to a crisp, while
> he's doin' it.

It was after that incident, even before he was promoted to foreman,
that Mr. Newman achieved the reputation of being a pest among the
men of his crew. He was forever talking about caution and safety. "There
are old lineman, and there are careless lineman—but there are no old,
careless lineman," he would say. After three men were maimed and disfigured in another mishap, he summoned the crew and said: "Boys, we
are going to initiate some safety rules. First of all, we're gonna start
wearing hard hats."

Working in short sleeves and hatless was part of the *machismo* of
being a lineman. The men protested.

"Skin," said Mr. Newman, "especially when it's wet, is one hell of a
conductor. So you cover up and wear hard hats."

Thus, the linemen and power plant workmen became early and identifiably part of the hard-hat labor force and, in due course, a vivid symbol of conservative middle America. Their political and social outlook, like that of utility management, did not encourage outspoken support for racial integration, civil rights, or militant demonstrations for peace. According to inquiries made by both public and private organizations in the late 1960s, only the United States telephone monopolies, over which Bell Telephone Company presided, had a more deplorable record than the electric utilities in the matter of employing and training racial minorities. By 1970, conditions began to change, especially in large urban centers, both for nonwhites and for women, who had been notoriously discriminated against as a matter of practice and policy. Backed by court decisions and a change of heart in the utility companies, men and women are changing roles and jobs in the seventies. Men are employed as telephone operators, and women are joining maintenance and linemen's gangs, further altering the old *machismo* concepts of the pre–hard-hat era.

The development and improvement of safety standards had spread simultaneously through other companies, and the record, considering the nature of their operations, showed that hazards had been substantially reduced. Yet, caution and safety is a recurrent, never-ending theme throughout the business of power plant construction and the generation of electricity. Anyone who works around or even visits a facility where power is produced or transmitted must wear a hard hat, must be well covered, and if it's a steam plant with the possibility of particulate matter in the air, must wear goggles, too.

Power company critics insist that risks and heroism would be a good deal less necessary if more transmission lines, vulnerable to the elements, were underground; if better planning, prevention, and engineering were exercised at earlier design levels; and if reserve generating capacity was kept available to back up system breakdowns. Underground transmission, pending advanced technology still on the drawing boards, is enormously costly, except for short distances. It is not likely that long-range underground transmission can become commonplace until the state of the art of cryogenics improves to the extent that electric current at high voltage can move without power loss through a low-temperature field. In many parts of the country, the practice (first made legally obligatory in Maryland) of putting electric lines underground to new businesses and individual households is growing very fast. Most midtown urban areas in metropolitan centers require all utility lines to be underground. Power companies insist they could move faster on getting rid of overhead lines to retail customers except for the fact that ratepayers balk at meeting a share of the costs.

Utility customers, of course, are people—with their contradictions and irreconcilable demands. They do, indeed, object to transmission lines cluttering the landscape and at the same time resist paying more to bury them. It is not only the quality of management of the electric utilities that has to be changed from the bumptious past; the attitudes and outlook of the customer, from the ordinary household to far-flung industry, require reevaluation, too.

Every demand for more power, every insistence that electric lines be hidden, that the air and water be unpolluted, that nuclear plant licenses be denied, involve a decision on what kind of a country, what kind of an environment, what kind of a life people want and will tolerate.

10

No Power
over
Power

It is widely conceded that one characteristic common to the inner-city ghettos and the expanding suburbs, into which millions of migrating families fled with their purchasing and political power in the 1960s, is their mutual inability to dictate or even notably influence the conditions that affect their lives and well-being.

Inertial forces set in motion long ago operate independent of necessity or good intentions. If suburbs and the cities to which they are appendages are to live rather than decay together, some mastery over the forces that bring dysfunction to the community of man has to be accomplished in an alarmingly short time.

In America, the best laboratory in which these forces might be identified, separated, redirected, and perhaps made to contribute toward the regeneration and rehabilitation of society is New York City. And the way electric power is evaluated, generated, distributed, and regulated in New York has, or could have, an important bearing on how and under what conditions the nation as a whole may arrest the course of its destruction.

In the words of Dr. Barry Commoner, a Brooklyn-born scientist transplanted to Saint Louis and an expert in the field of ecology, "New York has the worst pollution problems and the greatest collection of academies in the world; the issue is to couple what people know how to do with what has to be done."

New York, Dr. Commoner feels, is the victim of "the whole eastern

169

Metroplex—the Washington, Boston axis." Power plants and automobiles produce the whiskey-brown air, even without the influx dispatched into and outward from Delaware, New Jersey, and Pennsylvania. Although New York could not alone, perhaps, alter the course of power plant policy; since bureaucracy-bound federal agencies are involved, the city inexcusably has never forced Detroit to build a low-powered, low-compression taxi that could all but eliminate the source of a major pollutant, nitrogen dioxide. The city has control over taxi design, and exercising its control could exert leadership on the nation's most polluting industry. In total output, the electric utilities are second to the automobile in air pollution. As for "doing something" to alleviate power reduction in the city in the summer heat, let the state of New York shut down four cement plants and two upstate aluminum plants, says Dr. Commoner, and the summer crisis would be resolved.

"People seem to suffer from a paralysis of will," Dr. Commoner told *New York Times* writer Israel Shenker in September, 1971.

> If New York could make some noticeable improvement, it would have an enormous effect. People would see that it was possible to do something about their lives, that they could take their own fate into their own hands. If New York can't save itself, I don't think the rest of us can save ourselves. New York is the metaphor of the declining quality of life. It's got to be solved there, or people everywhere will give up.

Author of an important and authoritative book, *The Closing Circle,* a chilling account of environmental ruin by pollution, Dr. Commoner and a staff of eighty at the Center for the Biology of Natural Systems at Washington University in Saint Louis have added substantially to what is objectively known and have sought to persuade the country to act sanely on that knowledge. "For a number of years what we were doing was studying the natural history of environmental pollution—describing the state of affairs and grabbing people by the lapels to explain it to them," he said. "The problem was inertia.

"We now know the problem stems from the development of new production technologies which ignore ecology, and which are driven by profit. The problem is fundamentally economic, and it's not going to get cured simply by calling for recycling and cleaning up."

Whether it is possible for New York to demonstrate to other cities and the nation itself that it can apply knowledge to "what has to be done" is dependent on some unanimity between the federal, state, and city governments on what ought to be done and who pays for it. Politics aside, important changes in attitude and power policy did start to occur in New York in the late 1950s with an outbreak of public opposition to nuclear reactors in the city. Over the years, the posture and attitude of the Consolidated Edison Company, once despised as an arrogant monopolistic giant, developed into a policy of rational self-interest. The company can now be reasoned with, its opponents feel, even though it remains a formidable corporation. But both Consolidated Edison and public forces resistant to its growth have become more mature. It took a complete change in Con Ed's management, years of conflict between the utility and environmentalists, an unparallelled blackout and numerous power shortages, a federal court case, and repeated public hearings to educate the utility and the public on issues of mutual concern. What the utility and its captive customers learned was that their antipathy to one another's outlooks on more new power plants was nearly irreconcilable. What began in the 1950s as the first citizens' attack against the first proposed big commercial nuclear power plant in America spread to nearly every section of the country and expanded to include hostility to other types of power installations as well.

All over the nation—along the earthquake faults of the California coast, in Oregon, beside the waterways of Florida, in the Finger Lakes region of upstate New York, on the shore of Lake Champlain in Vermont, on the rivers of Connecticut, on Chesapeake Bay—opposition to sites for nuclear power plants that are absolutely essential, or are said to be, was and remains intractable.

Even in the midst of summer brownouts, when Consolidated Edison sought to double the capacity of a conventional fossil-fueled plant in Queens, a plant that New Yorkers could scarcely deny was needed to keep their lights and appliances operating, public objection was strident and was sustained until the city and the utility negotiated design changes and pollution limitations.

In 1955, the Atomic Energy Commission, determined to prod the power industry into using nuclear fuels, announced its Power Demonstration Reactor Program. Any utility prepared to finance the construction of a nuclear plant was offered research and development help and a waiver of fuel inventory charges for the first five years of operation. At that time, it was quite clear that the first nuclear plants could not be economical but might provide operating experience and develop the state of the art so that later plants would be commercially profitable. In most cases, the financial risks of the first reactors were shared by a number of companies. In one historic case, Consolidated Edison of New York undertook a pioneer project entirely on its own.

Con Ed wanted to put the plant in the Ravenswood section of Queens, a highly populated urban borough of New York, in contradiction to AEC policy that disallowed reactors in such areas. Con Ed and the engineers they consulted were convinced that reactors could be built to

safety standards compatible with population density. Moreover, any
utility likes to have its generating plant reasonably close to its customers
in order to avoid needless transmission costs, buying land for lines and
towers, and the like. Since New Yorkers would be consuming the power
produced, utility management reasoned that it was logical enough to
erect the generating plants on the home territory of the ratepayers.

But the customers would have none of this reasoning. What was
probably the most vociferous outpouring of indignation occurring against
an electric utility up to that time caught Con Ed off balance. The company had proposed what it called a "concept," and was ready to experiment with and finance new technology that would dump no soot, sulphur
oxides, or ash into the whiskey-brown New York air. In the meantime, a
60,000-kilowatt boiling-water reactor began generating electricity at
Shippingport, Pennsylvania; and a 140,000-kilowatt pressurized-water
unit began commercial service in Massachusetts in 1960. They were ex-
pensively out of line with electricity-generation economics, but they demonstrated nuclear technology on the utility market acceptably well. Con
Ed's plant at Indian Point on the Hudson River at Montrose in Westchester County, where it had fled with its nuclear dreams after being
run out of Queens,* went into service in 1962. Producing 270,000 kilowatts, it was the first "big" nuke designed to produce power economically
and competitively on the commercial market. The first "truly large" nuke,
as a generating plant in the 400-to-500-megawatt range was then called,
did not become operative until 1967 at San Onofre, California. It generates 428,000 kilowatts of electric power.

The Indian Point reactor, a pioneer installation in the world of
nuclear-fueled generators and focal point of ten years of embittered controversy over the new technology, is something of a continuing disaster.
It is forever killing fish in the Hudson River, at one point so many fish
that the public, especially fishermen, stormed in outrage to authorities
at state and federal levels. Charges of mass destruction of striped bass
and other edible species were for a time denied or played down as inconsequential, until a photograph showing a dump at the plant heaped
high with tons of dead fish made its way into print. The photograph had
been suppressed, the magazine *Sports Illustrated* charged, by the state's
Department of Conservation, whose administrators were fearful of
offending Con Ed's ardent friend, Governor Nelson Rockefeller.

---

* As far back as 1962, or about the time the Indian Point plant became operative,
Con Ed applied for a license, which it later withdrew, to build a million-kilowatt
plant in the heart of New York City. In the wake of its experience in Queens,
the application was an audacious move that *Scientific American*, in its issue of
February, 1968, said "was several strides ahead of its time; it served, however, as a
welcome affirmation of industry's confidence in nuclear power." Con Ed may
have been run out of Queens, but it was not intimidated.

The company, not visibly concerned that a good many authorities from the governor down to some lowly functionaries in the clerical range of the Conservation Department had sought to protect it from embarrassment, made some external design changes in its cooling-system intakes at the river's edge. It was announced that the fish kills, which Con Ed had said did not happen, would not happen again. But they did happen again, several times, probably as a result of thermal conditions, although the company has always denied that, too.

The old nuke has had other problems too. Notably, it had to be shut down in advance of the high peak load in the summer of 1970, a precarious time for Con Ed and nearly every other utility serving urban areas. It was out of action for more than a year, and for part of that time, both the Indian Point nuke and Con Ed's Big Allis generator,* with a capacity of 1 million kilowatts, were inoperative at the same time. Reserves then were in dangerously short supply, but with power imported from outside the system and with voltage reduced now and then, Con Ed and its customers got through the summer. With Governor Rockefeller running for a fourth four-year term at a time when fish kills and pollution were not convertible into his familiar, hard-sell television commercials, other state authorities relinquished their caution momentarily and threatened to shut the Indian Point plant down permanently if damaging discharges were not better controlled. Although nobody in New York needed to take *that* threat seriously, not when the loss of any power might tip the reserve balance and black out the metropolis, it did add to Con Ed's endless woes, not the least of which was trying to keep thirty-eight antiquated and erratic fossil-fuel plants in operation.

The woes continued into the summer of 1971, during which the days of voltage losses, both in New York and throughout the nation, mercifully declined from 1970. The reasons for this bit of good fortune, in terms of wavering power reliability, were the absence of prolonged heat waves that invariably exhaust power capacity in areas where reserves are slim and depressed economic conditions that in a good many industrial regions amounted to a recession. Since near-maximum demands on power were not made, near-maximum crisis conditions simply were avoided.

Oddly, the only other reactor similar in design to the historic Indian Point plant, the equally aged and smaller 170,000-kilowatt unit in a beautiful riverside setting at Rowe, Massachusetts, enjoys an impeccable record. Licensed about the same time as Indian Point, the Rowe reactor

---

* "Big Allis" is the name given the largest generator of its type in the country, built by Allis-Chalmers Corporation. It is both famous and infamous in the power industry: famous for its great size and generating capacity, and infamous because it is an example of concentrating too large a proportion of any utility's generating capacity in one piece of equipment.

has never had a breakdown worthy of note and has never, as far as can be learned, slaughtered tons of fish. To be sure, on the question of fish kills one has to be skeptical, for it is not common for a utility to make public disclosures of such disasters and bear the brunt of consequent poor public relations unless obliged to do so. Nevertheless, the Rowe reactor seems to run on and on, never making a bad name for itself and never causing its collective of New England utility company owners anything other than nominal trouble. Some utilities have only one kind of luck, it is said, bad; and Con Ed seems to be one of those. Not only did its big million-kilowatt generator break down, taking 13 percent of the company's capacity off the line through part of 1970–1971, but the power resources of a good part of the eastern United States had to be organized to rescue New York City from even the average warm summer of 1970.

When the dog days came, New York was in another of its innumerable crises. An import of power from the Tennessee Valley Authority and the holding company kingdom of American Electric Power, even from Canada, plus persuasive campaigns to customers to voluntarily reduce usage, allowed Con Ed and the urban area to stagger disconsolately through one more summer.

Charles Luce, the $150,000-a-year chief executive of Con Ed, took occasion to say that if the company had not been thwarted for seven years or so in its attempt to build a quick-starting hydroelectric plant to supply peak-load power, the people would be better served and the metropolitan area would not be repeatedly threatened with a paralytic loss of power. He was referring to the 2-million-kilowatt pumped storage plant, twice as big as any in the world, authorized by the Federal Power Commission on Storm King Mountain at Cornwall in the scenic Hudson River highlands. The project had long ago become a cause célèbre in the widening conflict between conservationists and the power industry. Con Ed had already spent more than $15 million in preliminary work and planning on what, when authorized in 1963, was to have cost $140 million. By the end of 1965, when a federal court rebuked the Federal Power Commission for willfully neglecting to consider the conservation issue and ordered it to reopen the license hearings, the cost of the project had increased to $165 million. Accused of acting like an umpire or referee between adversaries, rather than evaluating a huge pumped storage plant on the scenic river in terms of the larger public interest, the FPC was stung by the surprising court decision. With no choice open to it except to comply, the agency took the by then world-renowned Storm King case under review; and the Scenic Hudson Preservation Conference and a group of other conservation organizations momentarily celebrated the court's landmark decision.

The city of New York added its objection to the big power plant in-

stallation on the grounds of possible damage, in the course of construction, to the great nearby aqueduct carrying water from the mountains
to the city. Five years later, the Federal Power Commission again authorized Con Ed to go ahead in a decision that to opponents seemed to take
little cognizance of all the ecological and conservationist reasoning that
had become part of the national consciousness. Further litigation brought
a United States Court of Appeals judgment upholding the FPC decision.
In October, 1971, the Scenic Hudson Preservation Conference and other
litigants, who had spent $600,000 in donated money to fight the case,
declared its intention to take the case to the United States Supreme
Court.

Meanwhile, an appeal had been made to a newly titled state agency
called the Department of Environmental Conservation, which was asked
to try to stop the invasion of Storm King on a number of grounds: 8
billion gallons of water would be pumped from the Hudson River every
night and stored in a 240-acre reservoir atop the mountain. During peak
power periods in New York City, the water would be dropped 1,000 feet
through penstocks to operate generators and then back into the Hudson.
Litigants against the project contended that aside from defacing the
stone mountain and the river's edge with power installations, the New
York State Department of Environmental Conservation ought to object
to the thermal pollution and damage to the river and violation of water
standards by the enormous daily pumpout and discharge of water.

The commissioner and chief executive of the New York State Department of Environmental Conservation was Henry L. Diamond, who
moved into the post after some years in the employ of one or another of
the Rockefeller family's various foundations and philanthropic enterprises. Both Nelson Rockefeller and his brother Laurance, who together
wield considerable power in political, financial, and conservation circles,
had supported the Con Ed project; and Mr. Diamond was not disposed
to come to any decisions that might run contrary to previous Rockefeller
positions. Just the same, Mr. Diamond's decision, when it came in August,
1971, was a masterpiece among lame explanations of its kind.

Water standards would not be violated by the installation, Mr. Diamond concluded, not by thermal conditions nor by the turbulent daily
removal and reentry of 8 billion gallons of water. Everything was going
to be all right, Mr. Diamond said; but if he should be wrong in his conclusion, he would shut the plant down immediately, and it simply would
not be allowed to operate again as long as any danger to water standards persisted.

By this time, Con Ed's estimated cost of the project was up to $400
million, with the final cost over six years of construction impossible to
compute. Although Con Ed was pleased indeed with what it felt was

Mr. Diamond's reasoned and thoughtful decision, opponents all across the country were staggered that the state could sanction so costly an undertaking in the face of complete dependence on data originating elsewhere for its findings. Did not the state agency, particularly one devised and staffed to deal with conservation and environmental questions of such magnitude, have any responsibility to investigate the project and develop a record of its own?

Shutting down a 2-million-kilowatt plant "after the environmental damage would already have been done," said Albert Butzel, a member of the law firm that was fighting Con Ed in the courts, was a gross departure from reality. After handing down his decision, Mr. Diamond said that he had been "tempted" to start an investigation into the Storm King plant but demurred because the FPC had held hearings on the matter and because the issue was in the courts. He did not feel, he said, that he ought to start any procedures that might be construed as arbitrary delaying tactics. Mr. Diamond's concept of the exercise of power over environmental matters appeared, in one of the most significant and prolonged conservation battles in modern American history, to reflect such a mild and generous attitude toward one of the litigants that it was small wonder Consolidated Edison was "pleased."

Just before Christmas, 1971, six years after the first federal court ruling against the FPC, Scenic Hudson and its allies moved in the state supreme court at Albany to challenge Henry Diamond's unquestioning ruling.

Scenic Hudson declared that it was a terrible mistake to allow Con Edison to monitor its own pollution, as Mr. Diamond was willing to permit, in order to determine whether conditions justified shutting down the plant.

New York City joined in the suit, again expressing a fear that its aqueduct, 140 feet from the construction site, might be damaged and voicing its concern that the daily pumping of water from the Hudson might allow saline to extend farther up the estuary and ruin fresh-water supplies New York requires in emergencies.

Charles Luce himself had not been responsible for the Storm King Mountain controversy, which was well under way before he left a government job in Washington to go to New York. He persisted with its development, however, and in time anger over the mountain project in particular and pollution and power failures in general was directed at Mr. Luce personally. On one occasion when Mr. Luce was bicycling along Manhattan streets to demonstrate his willingness, along with other cooperating notables, to support nontoxic transportation as opposed to the automobile, a pedaling picket followed on another bicycle displaying a sign that criticized Mr. Luce and Con Ed as contaminators of the air.

Mr. Luce always contended, simply, that Con Ed needed the Storm King plant desperately and that no alternative plan for peak-load power was open to the utility. Opponents argued time and time again that Con Ed ought to stay out of the Hudson highlands and, if necessary, put a nuke somewhere else. Luce said two more nukes were being built at Indian Point, one with 870,000 kilowatts to go into service in the summer of 1972,* and a 965,000-kilowatt plant scheduled for operation in 1974. But neither of these nor any other plant construction in prospect was a substitute for a hydroelectric pumped storage installation, since the latter is swung on the line at high-load periods on two or three minutes' notice. It was explicitly designed to back up power needs on those dangerous hot New York summer afternoons that provoke brownouts and shortages. A nuclear plant cannot do this. Unlike the Cornwall reservoir and water-powered turbines, a nuke cannot be turned on and off intermittently. A nuke provides base-load, not exclusively peak-load, power. Luce thought that if people would understand and appreciate this distinction, the controversy could be resolved.

Conservationists who argued for a nuclear plant instead of the Storm King project were for the most part equally hostile when their advice was followed. When Con Ed tried to build more nukes at Indian Point, in Long Island Sound at New Rochelle, New York, and elsewhere, people by the thousands protested *their* construction, too. Since erecting a plant of any kind, with the possible exception of small gas-fired units, brought forth intense opposition in nearly every part of the country, how, then, was the demand for expanded power production to be met?

Lelan F. Sillin, chairman of the board of Northeast Utilities, a holding company of four power companies in Connecticut and Massachusetts, is one of the newer breed of executives torn between what he sees as demands for more power and a personal inclination to neutralize antagonism among people with whom he sometimes identifies.

Sillin once ordered a power line redirected to avoid disturbing a nesting osprey atop one of his company's utility poles, which the bird had simply taken possession of in an exercise of squatter's rights. He authorized the allocation of a grant to try to save ospreys from extermination as a result of DDT infestation, and did not add the donation to the rate base. Personally and with financing he could arrange through con-

* A costly fire in an auxiliary building near the 135-foot dome containing the atomic reactor for this second Indian Point plant interrupted construction work in early November, 1971. The fire, which the Westchester County sheriff said was the work of an arsonist, did about $5,000,000 worth of damage to cables, wiring panels, pumps, and electric equipment. It would require four months to make repairs and replacement, but assuming the plant met AEC operating and safety requirements, it is scheduled to begin operation in advance of the peak-load period in the summer of 1972.

nections outside the company, he sought to alleviate gruesome social and ghetto conditions in a deprived New England community. As an individual with a social conscience, as a man concerned for endangered species, whether human or fowl, he invited approval and admiration; but as a utility executive raising capital and building power plants, he was reviled, his company denounced in public forums, his colleagues criticized as members of an evil cabal.

Mr. Sillin went to New England after serving first as legal counsel, then as chief executive of Mid-Hudson Power Company across the river from Storm King Mountain. The land configuration on his side of the river was perfect for another hydroelectric pumped storage plant, and he was eager to build one there. But in the face of environmentalist objection and possible litigation, Sillin let the project go, glad enough to be rid of the controversy, and shortly thereafter departed for a bigger management job with Northeast in Hartford, Connecticut. The abandoned hydro site has since been acquired for a public park.

At Northeast, Sillin inherited a management, in April, 1968, that had marshaled the resources and lobbying strength to defeat in Congress the famous Dickey-Lincoln hydroelectric project in Maine, a historic and inevitably futile effort to get a "little TVA" going in industrial New England.

Dickey-Lincoln called for the construction of dams on the Saint Johns River and was a remnant, although a very large remnant, of the Passamaquoddy tidal power program that had captivated developers since early in the century and that Franklin D. Roosevelt looked upon as a needed national resource. A pair of huge dams, at the hamlet of Dickey and at a downriver valley where the rural Lincoln School stood, would have brought to the Northeast its first federal power complex. The private utilities, which collected the highest electric rates in the nation outside of New York, wanted no federally financed power in the region, with the certainty of lower, or "yardstick," rates that would go with it.

Dickey-Lincoln probably had a less than pure cause to present, especially with mounting concern for ecology, because of extensive flooding of wilderness country by proposed dams and because of questionable economics deriving from high and unpredictable construction costs.

During the Kennedy years and the Lyndon Johnson administration, when Stewart Udall was Secretary of the Interior, a movement grew for funding and proceeding with the Dickey-Lincoln system. Every private utility in a dozen states joined in opposition, and lobbyists were sent to Washington, where, it was rumored, the power of payoff and trade-off coldly and corruptly strangled Dickey-Lincoln and public power in New England indefinitely, perhaps for good. Northeast Utilities, under a management that preceded Lee Sillin, was the organizing force that tightened the garrote.

Lee Sillin apparently declined to join in opposition to Dickey-Lincoln, which was pretty well finished by the time he arrived in New England anyway. He concentrated on organizing six New England states into an interconnected power pool that, whatever its unfulfilled needs, encompassed both privately and municipally owned systems. When the Dickey-Lincoln debate broke out in Congress once more, as it did periodically, and when funds for design and engineering studies were voted down, the voices of Sillin and his subordinates, if present in the chorus of opposition at all, were inaudible. He was concentrating on trying to get more generating capacity into his sector of New England.

Company consultants surveyed twenty-four sites in the chartered area and selected two, one in Connecticut and another in Massachusetts, as the possible location for a hydroelectric installation to provide quick power at dangerous peak-load periods. Without purchasing either site or exercising the awesome right of eminent domain, the company announced its need to build a plant on one site or the other and invited the public to participate in the decision. It was a bold, original step and an unlikely one for a private utility. It was also risky, for it meant that the cost of acquisition would be considerably higher once it was known that one of the sites might have to be purchased.

Sillin's candid exposure of company plans and needs included a public invitation to suggest a third site from the inventory of twenty-four, if the first two were objectionable.

Lelan Sillin's venture in public participation did not endear him to the narrowly conservative element of management that is clearly dominant in the power business, nor did it win the favor of conservationists and ecology buffs.

A conservationist spokesman grumbled that the company was making a grandstand play in seeking to involve the public and denounced the proposal to acquire either of the two sites. Both, it was charged, threatened irreparable damage to marine life and the environment.

Charles R. Bragg, a Northeast Utilities executive, responded: "That's an opinion, or a judgment. It has to be resolved. If neither site merits conversion to hydroelectric power, the company will not build there."

But, obviously, it had to build somewhere or face the certainty of being unable to deliver power on demand. If there was to be no possibility of public acquiescence to any plant site at all, the utility was left with a hard and necessary decision to make alone. It was obliged by law to acquire a site and develop it. The efforts at public involvement failed.

A number of other utilities made efforts to open the decision making on plant siting to public participation and scrutiny. A year or so after Sillin's effort came to grief, Northern States Power Company in Minneapolis created the Citizens Advisory Task Force to help determine which of four fossil-fuel-plant sites would be most acceptable to environmentalists. Representatives of thirty conservation organizations, some harsh critics of the utility, participated. Weekly meetings were held with utility management, and it was made clear to the participants that new generating capacity had to be in operation by 1976.

In a study of the Northern States venture, published in December, 1971, by California Institute of Technology, it was reported that the first weekly meetings of the utility and conservationists were marked by suspicion and openly expressed hostility. After six or seven weekly encounters, however, "something significant happened." Uncompromising critics were silenced, and the actual work of deciding a plant site progressed. The group accepted a site that was the most expensive of the four to the utility, but the power company yielded and went ahead with construction.

The California Institute of Technology study recommended "new forums" of the old town-meeting style so that plant-siting questions could be resolved openly, with the public participating. It concluded that locating power plants involved far more than solving engineering problems and more than financial considerations. Open planning was offered not as a prescription for harmony but as a reasonable possibility for a workable approach.

Consolidated Edison regularly kept informed, and invited full expression from, 300 environmental lawyers, conservationist organizations, planning groups, community leaders, and power plant critics every time a new installation was planned. Thus, a few companies sought to avoid some of the antagonism common to the industry. But the effort was ad hoc and sporadic, and it seldom satisfied people holding diametrically opposing views.

In September, 1969, the power industry as a whole met to debate recommendations that experts from outside the fraternity be invited to participate in environmental policy making. The recommendations were summarily rejected in an action that was a lingering vestige of old animosities against conservationists, whom one resolute defender of insularity called "people who only muddy the water." Presumably, his own utility kept the water pure.

The utilities had met to consider establishing an Electric Power Council on Environment, whose purpose was the study of means for reconciling generating-capacity expansion with the scientists' and the public's protests against damage to the ecosystem. The council was to be an agency for serving mutual needs of the public and the power companies. Its purpose was to lay to rest what utility spokesmen felt was an excess of emotionalism and hysteria that broke out over several new nuclear plant projects, especially a $300-million nuke to be built on the shore of Chesapeake Bay in Maryland.

The Baltimore Gas and Electric Company, which was not notable for encouraging open site planning, had received a construction permit from the AEC to build a huge reactor at Calvert Cliffs on the bay south of Baltimore. Scheduled for completion in 1973, the plant was situated near a site said by scientists to contain the largest deposit of fossils in the world. Maryland watermen were horrified and admittedly a little emotional at prospects of thermal pollution and emissions further degrading the waters of the bay and depriving them of the harvests of marine life. A lot of oyster bars had been wrecked over the years by dredgers, a lot of clam beds ruined both by pollution and greedy harvesting methods; and the prospects for the future of watermen were grim before the threat of nuclear plants around the Chesapeake added to the gloom. The virulence of public reaction to the Baltimore utility's plans and the AEC license induced the power industry to establish, for the first time, a long-overdue environmental council.

When the names of the council's twelve members were finally announced, no representative of the public, no conservationist, not even a member of a single regulatory agency was among them. They had been explicitly excluded in the council's formation. The new chairman, William C. Tallman, president of the Public Service Company of New Hampshire, said the utilities had "concluded we should keep this an electricity group." It had been recommended that at least one federal power commissioner be named, "but it was not agreed to, so it was dropped," said Mr. Tallman. The National Rural Electric Cooperative Association and the American Public Power Association, made up of federally and municipally owned systems, deplored the exclusionary policy. FPC Vice-Chairman Carl E. Bagge termed the council "inadequate" and said that reconciliation of differences between the utilities and their adversaries was impossible if the latter were not to be permitted even to associate with power company management.

Up in Vermont, former Federal Power Commissioner Charles Ross walked the shore of Lake Champlain at the village of Charlotte, where yet another big nuclear plant, momentarily stalled, was proposed. Reflecting on his own frustrations in seeking regulatory reforms, throwing a stick into the lake to be retrieved by a gamboling dog, he said: "What could you expect? The companies don't want to change."

Companies were made up of people who, like the Bay people of Maryland, expressed their fears and frets by resisting change.

Lee White, thoughtful and retiring chairman of the FPC, replaced to make way for a more partisan Nixon appointee, John Nassikas, said: "It was a stupid thing to do."

Perhaps it was stupid, and surely it was regrettable; yet the utilities had done nothing particularly original in creating a council exclusive to the power industry. Their action was no worse than the government's.

When the White House created the National Industrial Pollution Control Council, its purpose was to

> allow businessmen to communicate regularly with the President, the Council on Environmental Quality and other government officials and private organizations which are working to improve the quality of the environment.

The new presidential council was composed of fifty-five members, board chairmen or presidents of major oil, automobile, electric utility, mining, timber, coal, airline, and manufacturing companies, and was further adorned with the presidents of the United States Chamber of Commerce, the National Association of Manufacturers, and the National Industrial Conference Board. "They are the leaders of the industries which contribute most to environmental pollution," said the eternally complaining Senator Lee Metcalf. He observed:

> There is not, even for window-dressing, a council composed of those ecologists, students, earth-lovers, and plain old-fashioned conservationists who have forced the administration and the big industries to take some action. . . .
> It is now six years since the Department of Health, Education and Welfare, prodded by the House Natural Resources and Power Subcommittee, first attempted to inventory industrial waste discharges. That inventory was stopped year after year by a business advisory committee similar to the one which the President has now appointed.

After six years without the necessary inventory, the Water Pollution Control Administration tried to assemble the vital information by collecting it from the fifty states, which was hopeless.

Mr. Nixon's appointees were, indeed, a register of highly placed corporate luminaries, some of them notorious to ecologists and conservationists for many years. Among them were:

> Birny Mason, Jr., chairman of Union Carbide Corporation, which for eighteen years had engulfed the Ohio Valley near Marietta, and much of West Virginia, with airborne garbage, successfully keeping legitimate government investigators off its property
> Bert S. Cross, of Saint Paul, Minnesota, chairman of the council

and chief executive of Minnesota Mining and Manufacturing Company

Willard F. Rockwell, Jr., vice-chairman of both the new council and North American Rockwell Corporation, which enjoyed lucrative government contracts and liked to sponsor adventurous television shows with their familiar commercial proclaiming that the corporation and "the future are made for each other"—which could be true

Charles H. Sommer, of Saint Louis, Missouri, chief executive of the vast Monsanto chemical operation

Clifford D. Sivert, of Wayne, New Jersey, president and chairman of American Cyanamid Company

Howard J. Morgens, of Cincinnati, Ohio, president of Procter and Gamble Company, which had some trouble with its public image for building up phosphate discharges into waterways

Milton Mumford, of New York, chairman of the board of Lever Brothers, another detergent and phosphate producer

Lelan Sillin, of Northeast Utilities, of which Senator Metcalf said that company "has been complaining about the environmentalists and the company's research and development burden. Yet the company's four affiliates spent 50 times as much on advertising as it did on research and development in 1968. And this year [1970] its officials have been advocating more expenditures on public relations."

Senator Metcalf's facts were wrong, in this instance, possibly because he failed to detect a change that had come over a very few of the utilities. Like Con Ed in New York and a few others, Northeast had second thoughts about increasing its public relations and advertising budget, as it turned out, and actually cut it back, even eliminating from its schedules a good deal of advertising.

Sillin accepted a seat among the fifty-five members of the one-sided council at the urging of Charles Luce, a former public power advocate and administrator of the Bonneville federal power district. Lacking illusions about an agency like the council, Sillin nevertheless said he was willing to make the effort in the hope that it would accomplish something.

Expenditures for advertising, as compared with investments in research and development, were indeed far out of balance, as Mr. Metcalf said. Of the 212 major private companies that took in nearly $20 billion in 1968, 51 spent *nothing at all* for research. All the investor-owned power companies, which constitute one-eighth of all the investments in the country, allotted to research and development less than one-tenth of their outlay for promotion, sales, and advertising at all levels. Although these expenditures are included in operating costs and are paid by the customers, emphasis on pollution abatement and other forms of related research was inconsequential.

Expenditures in 1970 by the IOUs for advertising, according to FPC documents, totaled $88,724,225. Sales expenses were $306,386,371. Research and development allocations within the companies for power plant technology, systems planning, engineering, nuclear systems, and so forth amounted to $25,536,246. This was an increase of $7 million over 1969. The IOUs supported research conducted outside the companies by the Electric Research Council, the Edison Electric Institute, nuclear power groups, and others, with allocations totaling $20,500,733. This was $3 million more than in 1969.

The quality and purpose of some of the research the utilities elected to support really deserved classification as sales and promotion costs. An industry with only 8 Ph.D.s among nearly 12,000 engineers ordinarily would be expected to seek extensive outside research consultants in technology and pollution abatement. The average number of doctorates among 12,000 engineers in other industries is around 600, not 8, as Lee Metcalf liked to point out.

Yet, the utilities went to a professor of marketing, Thomas R. Wotruba, of San Diego State College, for aid and consultation. Professor Wotruba suggested more market research and, according to Metcalf, called on state utility commissions to hire marketing experts, which would seem to aggravate rather than alleviate the supply-and-demand problems of the industry.

The professor had recently completed a fellowship with the San Diego Gas and Electric Company, in conjunction with the Foundation for Economic Education at Irvington-on-Hudson, New York, which has won modest fame as a proponent of market monopolies and for advocating abolition of public education and the income tax.

Established in 1946, the Westchester County foundation, with its publication called *The Freeman,* has been the recipient of substantial contributions from investor-owned utilities. Other promotional expenditures in 1968 included "good will" distribution of tickets to professional football games and subscriptions to *Industrial News Review,* an editorial service in Oregon that writes and distributes free weekly editorials to periodicals praising private utilities. Senator Metcalf kept a running account of these expenditures for insertion into the *Congressional Record.*

As Senator Metcalf correctly suggested, the president's own council inspired no hope at all among conservationists, who were excluded from its company. Probably, it was not seriously intended to interest people with expertise, since they are not easy to delude. More likely, it was intended to appeal only to what Lee Metcalf termed "the hitherto silent majority." He said:

> Let us tell it like it is: The purpose of industry advisory committees to Government is to enhance corporate image, to create an illusion of action, and to impede Government officials who are attempting to enforce law and order and gather the data on which enforcement is based. . . . business advisory councils and public relations ploys will not preserve the environment.
> They will hasten its destruction because they impede enforcement.

The utilities empire had "more power than a hundred senators," Metcalf said, charging that they even exercised it to prevent reforms intended to assist the utilities themselves to function more adequately. The industry was organized and financed to paralyze any movement looking toward reform or even grants and inquiries to study reform. Yet, as Sillin, Consolidated Edison's Charles Luce, and Donald C. Cook would concede, reform of some kind was essential both to the industry's and to the public's well-being.

Mr. Luce had called for more responsible regulation on the part of the state's Public Service Commission. In fourteen years of four consecutive Rockefeller administrations, the commission had become a rest home for politicians put out to pasture by the voters. It is held, along with Consolidated Edison itself, in the lowest possible regard and, in spite of the occasional performance of acceptable watchdog services, has acquired a reputation for becoming the expediting agency for utility-rate-increase proposals.

Charles Luce was perceptive enough to the attitudes that prevailed in New York to know that public confidence in the power system could scarcely be restored if widespread disdain for the regulatory commission continued. Thus, in response to the power crisis, not to a need that had existed for years, the governor ordered some changes and appointed Joseph C. Swidler, a Con Ed consultant and a former chairman of the Federal Power Commission, to administer the Public Utilities Commission in New York. Mr. Swidler had earned a reputation in the industry as a no-nonsense regulator at the federal level, a reputation shared by such retired FPC luminaries as Charles Ross, of Vermont, and Lee White, a Washington lawyer. They and of course some others, such as John Carver, had found that regulation, as the laws were written, was not geared to the public interest in the sense that the environment could be effectively protected or dubious practices reformed.

Asked to offer his views on an "ideal form of regulation," Mr. Swidler wrote that there isn't any: "And if someone could dream it up, I doubt that any legislature would pass it."

Having left the Federal Power Commission, Mr. Swidler devoted himself to helping private utilities cope with their production and regulatory problems. After serving a term with Consolidated Edison, his reappearance as chairman of the New York Commission put him back in an exposed position in the service of the public interest, presumably disentangled from any conflict of interest with former employers. He began cautiously suggesting that the nation was using too much power and that, perhaps, people should be encouraged not to waste it. It was a departure from the old Vennard days when the practice was to sell the maximum for any and all uses.*

Because preventing catastrophic pollution of the air in the little time, comparatively, left to do so seems possible only if the internal combustion engine is replaced with some nonpolluting source of automotive energy and if industrial plant emissions are drastically reduced, Mr. Swidler proposed in 1970 that users of power pay part of the cost of redeeming the atmosphere. The likelihood of discarding the gasoline engine, the very foundation of the American industrial economy, was remote. Nor could old polluting power and manufacturing plants, let alone enormous new coal-burning installations, be shut down without throwing the nation into joblessness and depression.

Therefore, Mr. Swidler proposed before a Senate subcommittee, consumers of power should be taxed 1 percent of their electrical bills to underwrite the cost of research and new technology to make power production compatible with the environment and the survival of living things. A 1 percent tax for research would produce $300 million a year, a figure someone computed as representing less than three weeks of General Motors' income.

"In time, no doubt, most if not all conflicts between environmental

---

* Mr. Swidler, at least, has long been associated with electric power in some manner or another. Not all state regulators are. Some very curious personages have turned up now and then in the role of regulator over public utilities. Senator Metcalf complained before a Senate antitrust hearing in June, 1970, that the Alabama Power Company had been permitted by a state agency to add $4,000,000 in bank deposits to its rate base. He thought it illegal for Alabama citizens to be paying electricity bills on an alleged capital outlay that was safely in the bank drawing interest. The power company had no right, he suggested, to be making two incomes on the same money. Asked why he had not protested to the Alabama Public Service Commission, he said he had done so, only to learn that the commission chairman had approved the peculiar arrangement. The chairman was Eugene ("Bull") Connor, who some years earlier had disappeared as public safety director in Birmingham after achieving national notoriety for using cattle prods and other forms of brutal treatment against blacks and civil rights advocates.

and energy considerations will yield to technological solutions," said Mr. Swidler, with more confidence than any expressed by alarmed scientists in other forums. The planet, an *Audubon Magazine* article was saying concurrently, was already dying from photochemical smog. New automobiles emit "more oxides and nitrogen than ever before," wrote James A. Fay, engineering professor at M.I.T. But in any case, Mr. Swidler conceded, "we do not have the time to let nature take its course." And the fact that the electrical industry had devoted only "pitifully small" sums for research, other than marketing studies and promotion, made a consumer tax necessary.

The 1 percent levy would amount to $2 a year for a modest household paying the local utility $200 a year and would raise to $6 annually the tax bill to abate air and water pollution for a $10,000-a-year wage earner with a family of four. In 1970, that taxpayer contributed more than three times $6—$19, to be exact—for space exploration, $26 for more highways, and $1 for mass transportation. His taxes to pay the cost of war were, of course, a good deal higher than the others combined.

The "idiocy of present priorities," as the *New York Times* pointed out, "is a simple threat to survival."

"We face a crisis that could stop America in its tracks," said Senator Edmund Muskie in the hearing before which Mr. Swidler and others testified.

There are steps the private utilities could take. They could begin to take the initiative for a national power grid. They could initiate negotiations or, if necessary, antitrust litigation against practices that killed competition in fuels. One can only imagine the shock waves that would sweep through the investment-banking and industrial communities some morning when the news appeared that the electric utilities were seeking in the courts recovery of billions of dollars in fuel overcharges which they had paid because energy conglomerates destroyed the free market in fuels and drove up prices in a managed market. Even more shocking would be an announcement that funds recovered from such overcharges would be rebated to power company customers.

The utilities could pool resources for research programs aimed at developing technology with increased efficiency and minimal toxicity. They could open the doors to real public representation on their boards, representation by men and women detached from the banking and industrial fraternity. Finally, they could commit their corporations to a policy of henceforth giving priority to qualitative rather than quantitative factors in expanding their systems.

The reason they will not do any of these things, except possibly, in

time, opening up the boards of directors to new people, is that utility
experts are convinced that such actions would cause the money market
to lose interest in making capital investments in power companies. So
things that need to be done or that ought to be tried will not come
from initiative developing within the power industry. This leaves it to
the government, which, alas, in matters of this kind often seems to be
an extension of industrial, rather than people, power. And in any case,
an insufficient number of people, unless political leadership undertakes
to educate them, understands such profound and remote matters anyway.

Instead of research, the utilities were using income from their customers and from financing purchased on the credit market to buy (exactly as Penn Central did) corporations unrelated to their function and
charters.

They allowed conglomerates to play around in the fuel markets in
contradiction to their vital needs, then emulated the conglomerates,
acquiring businesses that they had neither the experience nor, considering their risk-free status, the right to be in. Even relatively small utilities,
their growth limited by the boundary lines of franchises, were taking
controlling interests in nonelectrical enterprises and reporting cheerfully
that newly found sources of income were more promising than their
own slow-growth power operations. It was suggested in the Senate by
Lee Metcalf that it was only a matter of time until utility management
would be more attracted to outside monetary possibilities than those
of the regular business, very much as Penn Central management devoted
itself to buying and developing outside revenue sources and neglected
to run its railroads.

Utility corporations argue with conviction that like banks and other
public services, they are pursuing the principle of equal justice in exercising their conglomerate opportunities. A good many of the nation's
privately owned power systems have pursued this form of economic
equality or have disclosed plans to correct their oversight.

"What is happening to transportation is happening in the energy
field as well," Senator Metcalf said in presenting a resolution (SR. 426)
calling for establishment of a special committee to investigate economic
and financial concentration. After citing the Penn Central holding company for moving, virtually before the ink was dry on the merger, "into
ventures quite apart from railroading," Mr. Metcalf chided power corporations, chartered solely for the purpose of producing electricity, for
doing the same thing:

> The quasi-governmental utility apparatus brings together fi-
> nancial, business, and political muscle throughout the territory
> served by the utility. The directors and retainers come from the

banking community, other industries, the universities,* and leading law firms. Often they include legislators as well. . . . Through
interlocking directorates this hierarchy is ideally suited for business
ventures beyond the scope of the original franchise.

The utility apparatus consisted largely of twenty operating companies
and fifteen holding companies, with control over seventy-eight subsidiaries that, combined, represented 70 percent of all private utility
investments.

In a report delivered to the Senate on December 28, 1970, Senator
Metcalf was especially critical of many universities from which, he said,
the public had a right to expect a higher level of public responsibility
than from most corporations. Instead, he charged, the universities were
content to be part of the corporate hierarchy and routinely "cast their
considerable votes in corporate elections for the policies and personnel
of corporate management." It was not necessary for a university to own
a controlling interest in a utility to influence its decisions and conduct, he
said, citing the effort by the Project on Corporate Responsibility, led by
Ralph Nader, that embarrassed and induced General Motors into at
least reviewing its wayward policies on safety and pollution.

The entrance of utilities into extraneous corporate ventures poses for
the present and the future, and for the public they serve, peculiar and
unpredictable implications. The Philadelphia Electric Company, for example, without intervention from any quarter, extended its charter to
engage in "manufacturing, processing, owning, using, and dealing in

---

* At Metcalf's request, fifty-three universities, with Harvard owning the largest
equity, listed their holdings in utilities, oil companies, and other energy enterprises. Yale does not invest in power companies. Other large stockholders included
Princeton, Northwestern, and Cornell. The treasurer of Harvard, which had 9.3
million shares in energy corporations, was a board member of Commonwealth Oil
Refining Company, New England Electric, Niagara Mohawk Power Corporation,
and Middle South Utilities.

The holdings of the fifty-three universities include:

	NUMBER OF SHARES	VALUE AS OF DECEMBER 5, 1970
Oil companies (44)	11,487,949	$526,773,290
Electric utilities (85)	10,963,272	321,590,645
Gas utilities (32)	1,805,683	57,204,063
Total (161)	24,256,904	$905,567,998

This does not include the 2,062,718 shares in energy corporations, valued at
$62,996,775 at the end of 1969, held by Harvard's State Street Investment Cor-
porations.

The universities (including the State Street funds) control more than 4 percent of the votes in Middle South Utilities, the New York holding company which
controls Arkansas Power and Light, Louisiana Power and Light, Mississippi Power
and Light, and New Orleans Public Service.

Standard Oil of New Jersey attracted the largest university investment, totaling
$129,245,370.

personal property of every class and description . . . [and] acquiring, owning, using and disposing of real property of every nature whatsoever."

Thus propelled into commercial and territorial enterprises otherwise antithetical to a power company, it was not surprising that the corporation found itself in the real estate business while its management searched the horizons for other ventures that the new set of rules seemed to legalize. It was a broad field, indeed, for a company charged with generating and disbursing electricity in the southeastern sector of Pennsylvania.

"Variety may be the spice of life, but does it have any place in the life of a power company?" This question was asked by *Wall Street Journal* writer Royce Rowe, who examined the matter of electric utilities buying into outside interests. Like everyone looking into the question, Mr. Rowe saw an analogy between Penn Central and the possible fate of power companies. If its amusement parks, hockey teams, hotels, and other diversified enterprises had not kept a railroad system solvent, could the utilities expect greater salvation? Of course, it was to prevent the utilities from yielding to such temptations that the old Holding Company Act of the Roosevelt New Deal era was passed in 1935. But that law restricted interstate companies (like Sam Insull's empire) more than it did a free-wheeling power producer within the boundaries of one state or even one that was part of a holding company.

On a small scale, some utilities had tested the waters of diversification, found them too cold, and withdrawn. The Wisconsin Fuel and Light Company had bought a radio station in Manitowoc at one point, owned it a couple of years, and sold it in 1969 for a loss of $32,741. Most utilities, however, started their diversification in real estate, if only because the National Housing Act permitted them to borrow 90 percent under the Federal Housing Administration's insured mortgages. Also, a utility in real estate can promote housing, which collects new customers.

Because a utility is obliged to serve its domain, promotion of housing developments has a logic to it not necessarily related to the logic of a railroad owning a hockey team. Niagara Mohawk Power Corporation built 134 apartments, confident that each would consume $130 a year in electric current. Its $2.4 million project was possible with only $200,000 cash, under procedures possible to risk-takers using other people's money.

Similarly, the Florida Gas Company entered the business of manufacturing prefabricated homes, with plans to build a community for 35,000 people on 4,500 acres near Orlando, Florida, within easy reach of Disney World and the television dream of the future.

Northern Natural Gas Company, of Omaha, Nebraska, bought a Massachusetts company that made plastic toys, which would seem to lack the logic of real estate, considering the geographical distance involved. Otter Tail Power Company, which faced antitrust action on complaints that it was being monopolistically ill-tempered to several hundred communities, acquired a half interest in a new Holiday Inn in Fergus Falls, Minnesota.

The acquisition by utilities of small airlines, vacation resorts, appliance manufacturing, and the like was disturbing to some power producers who thought that a utility ought to stick to the business of power. One of them was Donald C. Cook, of American Electric Power. "I think it's a mistake for a utility to get into a business in which it has no experience," he said. Mr. Cook, a former chairman of the Securities and Exchange Commission, was not so much against the idea of amalgamation as he was genuinely concerned about the capability of management to get more diverted than diversified. "It's hard enough to run a utility business without running the risk of spreading your talents too thin."

As Lee Metcalf and his executive assistant, Vic Reinemer, know so well, it is extremely difficult to interest the president and the Congress in issues relating to electric utilities and virtually impossible—save in the wake of blackouts, rate increases, and a railroad bankruptcy—to interest the public. Senator Metcalf and Mr. Reinemer wrote a book called *Overcharge*, published in 1967, which is a documented account of successful methods by which private utilities over the years collected hundreds of millions of dollars from their customers over and above allowable rate charges.

Defenders of what the authors cited as overcharges argued that acceptable accounting practices legally permitted rate computations that were not, in fact, excessive at all—another instance of opposite conclusions derived from the same evidence.

In New York, after the city's last World's Fair, it was remembered that the management which preceded the arrival of Charles Luce at Consolidated Edison had allowed itself to be persuaded by Robert Moses to help finance the fair with the purchase of bonds. Mr. Moses, famed as a public administrator and builder of bridges, tunnels, parks, and highways, had been paid $1 million as chief executive of the financial and artistic fiasco that the World's Fair became. Bondholders did not, as it developed, get their money back, and Consolidated Edison's losses in the flamboyant project somehow got lumped in with costs payable by the utility's customers.

Metcalf and Reinemer found that electric companies were a continuing source of financial support to extremist conservative groups, some of them tax-exempt. This latter escape hatch was all the more interesting because the funds contributed by utilities were deductible from their earnings and deductible again from the income of the tax-exempt organizations that had the common characteristic of loathing publicly owned power systems, regulation, and other forms of bolshevist control over Americanism.

The book reported a 1964 analysis that had shown eighty instances in which higher-echelon management of about fifty power companies actually "served as officials of about a dozen extremist groups."

The utilities, in addition to their contributions of cash, had delivered their management and personnel bodily to organizations that opposed the income tax, labor unions, civil rights, antipoverty programs, the United Nations, the Supreme Court, public power, and even public education. No instance could be found of a utility executive working with, or contributions made to, the American Civil Liberties Union, integrated housing, abortion reform, human rights, law enforcement, and similar liberal nonsense. They did, however, give help to world population control and the Planned Parenthood Association.

11

Power and the
Nuclear
Era

BACK IN 1905, a German-born physics student was working in Switzerland as a patent examiner, there being at the time little work aside from teaching in his trade. He was Albert Einstein, a man with an intellect and an intuitive grasp of the universe equal to that of few human beings of the twentieth or any other century. While his job of examining and classifying patents supported him, he wrote and published several notable scientific papers that established him forever as a force that changed the world.

One of the papers speculated on earlier experiments that sought to determine the precise speed of the earth through absolute space. Another theorized that mass, or matter, was inert and that energy was something rather opposite, a force, a capability. It became known as the Einstein *Theory of Relativity,* and there were not many people in the world capable of comprehending it. It was still the horse-and-buggy era, and electric power was only twenty-three years old. Until then, matter and energy were thought to be, as Dr. C. Jackson Craven, of the University of Tennessee, once wrote, "as different from one another as, say, a square yard is different from an hour." Or, in other imagery, as disparate as a handful of rock and the time of day—something utterly beyond relationship.

But Einstein's theory expressed an equivalency between matter and energy as separate manifestations of the same fundamental reality. Each was convertible into the other.

$$E = mc^2$$

E is a quantity of energy; m, a quantity of matter; and c^2 the speed (squared) of light in a vacuum. As incredible as the theory was—and it was all but beyond acceptability even in the advanced scientific circles of the day—it proved ultimately valid in nuclear fission.

After World War I, with the availability of spectographs and the ability to determine the weight of neutrons and protons in the laboratory, it was discovered that a nucleus of helium containing two protons and two neutrons should have weighed, on the internationally used atomic scale, 4.0341. This was the combined atomic weight of the protons and neutrons. However, separately the weight was 4.0341, but the weight of the nucleus that contained them together was 4.0039. What happened to the missing 0.0302? The weight difference was energy.

When the lost 0.0302 was multiplied by the square of the velocity of light, as Einstein postulated, it represented an enormous amount of energy. Other scientists discovered and confirmed that two light nuclei, when combined to form a heavier one, did not weigh as much as the sum of the original two. Conversely, if two nuclei heavier than iron were coalesced into a single heavy nucleus at the other end of the periodic table, where uranium begins, the new nucleus weighed *more* than the sum of its components.

It could thus be concluded that if a very heavy nucleus was divided, with the sum of the weights being less than the original, the vanishing difference would reappear as a tremendous amount of energy. The little bit of difference did not seem like much in itself, but compounded by the velocity of light squared, the difference was quantitatively beyond any measure of energy previously imagined.

In the mid-1930s, Enrico Fermi, an Italian physicist, exposed different isotopes to bombardment by neutrons that, lacking either a positive or negative charge, were unaffected by electrical influence. What usually occurred in Fermi's experiments was that the bombarded nuclei would absorb the neutrons but throw off alpha, beta, or gamma rays (alpha, a positively charged particle; beta, resembling a cathode ray and consisting of electrons; gamma, similar to X-rays, but of greater penetrating power). Sometimes an atom's nuclear positive charge would be increased by one unit, which put it in the next-higher place in the periodic table.

The last known element in the periodic table was uranium, and Fermi and others suspected that sending neutrons at high velocity into *that* might create previously unknown chemical elements. These logical suspicions existed elsewhere, too. In 1939, two German chemists, Otto Hahn and Fritz Straussmann, and the physicists Lise Meitner and Otto Frisch, announced that the absorption of neutrons by a nucleus of the isotope uranium 235 could result in a splitting, or fission, into two parts that put them near the middle of the periodic table. They were off target about the position of the elements in the periodic table, but little else. They had laid the cornerstone of atomic fission, the atomic bomb, and by extension, nuclear power plants.

On the way toward the destination of the split uranium atom, something unexpected and remarkable occurred. Perhaps it was not altogether unexpected, since physicists and chemists had speculated on the possible existence of transuranic elements or isotopes, that is, something beyond uranium in the periodic table.

When Lise Meitner and Otto Frisch interpreted in 1939 the experiment in which the Berlin scientists, Otto Hahn and Fritz Straussmann, produced fission in uranium, it was apparent that "new" elements involved in the process had fitted in somewhere near the middle of the periodic table. But later on it was clear that some of the products were new isotopes at the *end* of the scale, and extraordinary transuranic elements they were. The sequel to the work of Fermi, E. Amaldi, O. D'Agostino, Franco, Rosetti, and Emilio Segrè at the University of Rome, occurred in 1940 and 1941 at the University of California at Berkeley.

In 1940, Edwin M. McMillan and Philip Abelson discovered and identified element 93, neptunium (uranium was 92), the first of a dozen or more evolving from the work on nuclear energy. A few months later, Arthur C. Wahl, Glenn T. Seaborg, and Joseph W. Kennedy bombarded uranium oxide with neutrons in a cyclotron and found an isotope of neptunium that could be chemically separated. It emitted alpha radioactive properties. The discoverers christened it plutonium. All the work at Berkeley and later developments in Chicago, New York, and at other huge installations devoted to nuclear fission over the next five years was classified in the deepest possible secrecy.

Prior to the work at Berkeley, physicists realized that uranium fission released free neutrons when the nucleus split and that each one could, if slowed down enough, strike another nucleus, release more energy, and so on and on, in a chain reaction. There did indeed exist an equivalency between matter and energy, and there it was!

Albert Einstein, knowing that the military significance of the German experiments with nuclear fission would hardly be lost on experts of the Hitler war machine, wrote a historic but then-secret letter to President Franklin D. Roosevelt. The letter set in motion the sequence of events that led to the atomic bombing of two Japanese cities.

Dr. Fermi and a team of scientists built the CP-1 (Chicago Pile No. 1) under the grandstand of the University of Chicago athletic field. Their objective was to produce a controlled nuclear chain reaction. They had to assemble enough uranium in the pile so that the released neutrons would have a good chance of finding nuclei of fissionable uranium 235 before escaping from the action and getting lost in other material. Alternate layers of graphite, containing uranium metal or uranium oxide, were separated by solid layers of graphite blocks. The graphite slowed down the neutrons sufficiently to create fission and served as a control element. By releasing and interjecting the graphite control, they incited the neutrons, which, at reduced speed, began splitting the energy-producing uranium 235, thus achieving the first sustained nuclear chain reaction.

It was an infinite moment. Death was altogether possible and half expected. No previous experience in mankind quite equaled those seconds when the control rods, which would free the impelled neutrons, were pulled upward from the pile. Everyone in the shielded, guarded place would remember it always. Consciousness of the significance of the time was intense. Glenn Seaborg recalled the elemental safety precautions, sophisticated versions of which, he said, subsequently characterized nuclear operations:

> One man had a hatchet with which to sever the rope which held up the first control rod. Another man had a hammer with which to break a bottle of boric acid which would run down into the reactor and absorb the neutrons. A third man was ready to shut down the reactor by normal means.

It was a far more astonishing phenomenon than the one that had occurred sixty years earlier when Edison's lights went on in the old Pearl Street central station in downtown New York. The date was December 2, 1942, five days before the end of the nation's first year of official engagement in World War II. The notable event was the foundation of nuclear power, as the Berlin discovery of Meitner and Frisch had been the cornerstone, and was recognized as the first day of the nuclear age.

Propelled into world war by the Japanese aerial bombardment of Pearl Harbor in Hawaii the preceding December 7, the United States was losing its merchant fleet and crews to German submarines at a formidable rate. The fleet, of course, was vital to the support of Russia and England. The German air force had half destroyed a good many British cities, and although the morale of the populace held strong, the island nation was reeling.

General Leslie Groves was dispatched by President Roosevelt to Tennessee, in the heart of the federal TVA power country, to build plants to separate and process uranium. Einstein's letter to the president brought a national commitment called the Manhattan Project, under which the multitude of far-flung operations in support of the atomic bomb objective were coordinated. The uranium installations were hidden between mountain crests because scientists believed that if a dreadful accident should occur it might be confined within the ridges, one of them being Oak Ridge, the locale of the uranium production effort.

The project involved high-speed construction—with an absolute priority on whatever materials and personnel were required—of facilities in New York, Illinois, Tennessee, New Mexico, Idaho, Washington, and a network of secret laboratories. Each had its own scientists and technical experts, many thousands in all, laboring on different aspects of the problem of developing a nuclear fission weapon.

In Germany, where physicists and chemists had unwrapped the theoretical secret, scientists were thought by American and Allied forces to be converting nuclear energy into armaments. To scientists of England, Canada, and the United States, logic dictated that discoveries made in Germany would surely lead the Hitler command to race toward completion of a fission bomb. A start in that direction was made, but it fizzled out in Hitler's preoccupation with rocketry research. Yet, the American war command, knowing the Germans had all the theoretical knowledge necessary to do so, assumed they were in a race with the Germans.

As it happened, many scientists who had not been murdered in Hitler's gas chambers were driven from Europe by his racism and madness. These creative scientific minds, plus a highly organized government commitment, gave the United States the advantage it needed to design and build the most destructive weapon of all time. Regardless of what happened to the world in the intervening years, it is safe to assume that if Adolf Hitler's government had preceded America's in the development of the fission bomb, the problems that haunted the earth a generation later would be different, indeed.

The identification of plutonium was the factor that sped the ultimate result along. It was, of course, theoretically possible to utilize uranium 235, a fissile material; but in practice, separating the fractional percentage of it from ore made up largely of fertile but then-useless uranium 238 was not very likely. No chemistry existed for the separation of the two isotopes that were chemically identical. After a number of methods were tried at Oak Ridge, the gas-diffusion technology was developed. But the probability was that it would take too many years of effort to get the necessary quantity of ^{235}U from the processed yellow cake, a uranium derivative. Thus, a duplicate and concurrent effort to make plutonium serve the same deadly function was undertaken.

Although uranium in its unseparated form was present in abundance, plutonium was so nearly nonexistent that it defied an old assumption that anything in existence at all existed in quantity. It was present in such minute measure that a Congo pitchblende concentrate, which Glenn Seaborg examined in 1951, contained seven parts of plutonium in a trillion (1×10^{12}) parts of the crude material. An ore called fergusonite, with a uranium content of 0.25 percent, contained even less. The half-lives of most plutonium isotopes are so short compared with the age of the earth that any of them present when the earth was young scarcely exist now. Thus, it had to be produced synthetically, in multiples of the technique by which Seaborg and his colleagues identified it: by directing a neutron at a nucleus of uranium 238. When the nucleus absorbed the neutron, it produced the isotope plutonium 239 and emitted two beta particles. Actually, neutrons captured by uranium 238 cause the formation of uranium 239 (neptunium), which then *decays* immediately to form plutonium 239.

It was wholly as fissile as uranium 235 itself and, from a destructive point of view, less complicated. Plutonium could do exactly what uranium could do. But altering the nature of particles on a gigantic scale was difficult because no quantity of plutonium yet created was sufficient to be visible.

Until some other way could be found, it was necessary to use the laboratory method of making a microgram (0.000001 gram) at a time by stacking uranium near the cyclotron target and bombarding it with neutrons. Two University of Chicago scientists had developed an ultra-microscale that could measure it by weight. It was so extraordinarily sensitive that it could weigh an amount as small as 0.01 microgram. Its entire load capacity was 0.5 microgram. By August, 1942, 50 micrograms of plutonium had been produced in compound form. Fifteen months later, in November, 1943, several plutonium globules were formed. It was the first plutonium metal.

Meanwhile, the manufacture of plutonium was in the process of development on a larger scale.

In the heart of another federal power area in the Northwest, at Hanford, Washington, on the Columbia River, huge piles, or nuclear reactors, were built for the explicit purpose of exposing uranium to intense neutron bombardment. The best place to find a large supply of neutrons is in the heart of a self-sustaining, chain-reacting pile of uranium, an extension and enlargement of Enrico Fermi's experiment under the Chicago stadium. It has to be remembered, in order to understand the plutonium production process, that uranium itself is the basic commodity involved. But uranium contains about 140 times as much ^{238}U as ^{235}U, and only the latter is fissionable.* However, ^{238}U *is* fertile, and it is the bombardment of neutrons that converts it to fissionable plutonium.

In the midsummer of 1945, scientists attached to Project Y at Los Alamos, New Mexico, working feverishly under the direction of Robert Oppenheimer, completed a most careful assembly of a bomb containing plutonium produced by the Hanford reactors. On July 16, near the New Mexico town of Alamogordo, the Trinity, as it was designated, became the first man-made nuclear explosion. It completely vaporized a tall steel tower and melted several acres of sand into oddly shaped, varicolored forms. The flash of light was the brightest ever to illuminate the earth.

Three weeks later, a high-flying bomber dropped a U-bomb over Hiroshima. Within another three days, a plutonium bomb, on the order of the one tested at Alamogordo, wasted Nagasaki. The Japanese might have surrendered in the interim after Hiroshima, thus deterring the drop on Nagasaki, but for the fact that the war-making power of the nation was in Tokyo, several hundred miles away. Communications out of Hiroshima were so completely destroyed that assessment of the first bomb's damage was not possible in Tokyo.

There was not, of course, much difference to be noted by the vaporized and cremated dead or the irradiated survivors of the two demonstrations. They were scarcely concerned with the phenomenal fact that with the expenditure of the total supply of fissionable uranium and plutonium existing in the world, no more such bombs existed. Many more, of course, were coming. Nor could they have known that of the two kinds of nuclear bombs remaining on earth after Alamogordo, they had been impartially exposed to one of each.

Because research to apply its energy to electric power has been under way since 1954, the thermonuclear (hydrogen) bomb likewise requires comprehension in the context of nonmilitary possibilities. Einstein's theory equates with perfection to fusion, which is thought to occur in the sun's thermonuclear phenomena. There is no other explanation for the sun, since energy supplied by gravitation, combustion, nuclear fission, and so forth, could not have kept the sun (with a temperature of 40 million degrees) going so long and promising to continue for billions

---

* The use of chemical symbols is no doubt confusing in the text because of apparent inconsistencies. Uranium 238 or uranium 235 is sometimes used for the sake of readability. Formerly, they would have been presented as U^{238} and U^{235}, which was the familiar style. But the format changed somewhere along the line because chemical elements and their isotopes needed a distinction. Although it is appropriate to use *uranium 238* in text instead of U^{238}, later international usage dictates ^{238}U instead of the old U^{238} in referring to the isotope. "U" itself, of course, means uranium, as designated in the periodic table.

of years, whether it has mankind to shine on or not. All the fossil fuels (coal, oil, and gas) are repositories of energy originating in the sun.

Thermonuclear action is called *fusion* because the nuclei of hydrogen, of which the sun largely consists, do not split, but *fuse* at extremely high temperatures to form helium nuclei. *Thermo* means, simply, "heat." The earthly question is that if the energizing power of the sun is duplicated, as it is on a trifling scale in the H-bomb, what could possibly contain it in a closed system if the objective was solely to release the energy, not in an enormous bomb, but in some controlled manner commensurate with reasonable use?

In spite of the fact that fusion of ordinary hydrogen atoms makes the sun shine, the condition is not easily transportable to designated locations on an oxygenized earth. The action is too slow, for one thing; but other isotopes of hydrogen, called *deuterium* and *tritium,* fuse more rapidly and seem, potentially at least, to be sources of controlled thermonuclear energy. Fusion of light nuclei would be infinitely "cleaner," in terms of radioactivity, for peaceful purposes. Radiation is undesirable, as well as both an expensive and a moral problem, in the generation of electric power. Simply stated, radioactive "ashes" of fission reactions (the contaminated products nobody cares for) can be murderous or genetically damaging; whereas in fusion, which deals with helium rather than plutonium or uranium, they are, insofar as any fallout is concerned, sanitary. In a "clean" fusion bomb, however, radioactive contamination remains severe because of the need for a fission trigger mechanism to make it, as a Pentagon spokesman might say, "operational."

Fusionable material would have to be heated to a temperature of more than 100 million degrees Fahrenheit and contained long enough for an appreciable amount of fusion to occur. But at such heat, and in such an occurrence, nothing yet capable of being imagined would keep it from being a bomb. The container would simply vaporize and spoil everything.

However, at such temperatures, all atoms are stripped of electrons, the resulting mixture of nuclei and free electrons being known as a *plasma.* Particles that make up plasma, however, retain an electric charge and are thus responsive to a magnetic field. If the field is powerful enough, it conceivably could contain the action without permitting the energy to break through whatever walls imprisoned it. The problem is an extremely difficult one—technically much more complicated than putting astronauts on the moon—and will take time and a good deal of money to solve. When the time comes, however, the isotope of hydrogen necessary for an earthly reproduction of the energy of the sun will be available unless something happens to make its source scarce. Deuterium, known as *heavy hydrogen,* exists in nature as a single atom in

6,500 atoms of normal hydrogen. As D_2O, it is called *heavy water,* not because it is any heavier than other water, but because it is simply water containing significantly more than the normal proportion (1 to 6,500) of hydrogen atoms.

For producing electric energy, some fusion method would present a safer and possibly less controversial technology than the dependence on highly toxic materials thus far in use. But thermonuclear power is so far off in the future, twenty years or more, that the use of uranium and plutonium, dangerous and toxic as they are, is almost certain to fuel power plants all over the world before the era of fusion develops. Scientists of the Atomic Energy Commission, which suffered a budget reduction for fusion research in 1970, believe that "no laws of nature" stand in the way but that years of experiment and engineering must precede design of a huge plant, capable of generating 5,000 megawatts, that might make the technology economically possible.

A belief in early success of fusion research efforts prevailed in Russia, where scientists are confident of developing a prototype fusion power plant by the end of the 1980s. Research is proceeding in the United States, notably at Princeton and Cornell, and in France; but a good deal of secrecy characterizes much of the effort because no one nation is disposed to reveal anything that might lead to another acquiring a compact hydrogen bomb. With nuclear power twenty-five years old, any country that has the money and the motivation to commit resources to it, can make bombs, generate electricity, desalt ocean water, or otherwise apply it as an energy source. Some countries (China, France, England, and Israel) have devoted resources to it, but after twenty-five years, its primary function remains precisely what it was created for: to vaporize and obliterate selected areas of the globe. Its secondary function might, in time, include blasting open new canals and harbors or releasing supplies of natural gas trapped beneath the earth's surface, but its largest promise involves the application of nuclear energy in the generation of electric power.

The policy of withholding in the secret recesses of government the knowledge of the nonmilitary possibilities of nuclear energy for so many years has left much of the nation misinformed and ignorant about it. Both proponents and opponents of atomic fission have to contend with the fact that with its contradictory promises and threats, it is understood by only a very small fragment of 1 percent of the populace. Of course, not many people understand electricity either, but it was developed and it proliferated in an open society, and it has a better reputation. There might be no need for a popular understanding of nuclear power if so many significant issues did not have to be resolved, sooner or later, by an electorate or by people the electorate will have to trust.

When the time came, fifteen to twenty years after World War II, that nuclear materials not necessarily different from those utilized in weaponry could fuel power generators, a wary public was not ready to believe that much good could come of it. The official argument of nuclear proponents that a children's playground on a greensward outside a uranium-fueled power plant would be as safe for idle play as any other plot of grass was greeted with skepticism.

Yet, the argument could be true, at least in a comparative sense. When things go well, with an atomic core producing steam to spin huge generators as its design specifies, people would be indubitably safer lolling about an adjoining park than they would be living beneath the high stack of a gagging, coal-burning plant emitting 275 tons a day of particulants and a stream of sulphur oxides. They would also be less endangered swimming in the otherwise-clean water downstream from one nuclear plant cooled by the same water than they would be in a cove receiving the outfall of upland sewage. But the instinctive fear of a fission-fueled installation will not be dispelled as long as dissembling, special pleading, and occasional falsehood undermine public inclination to believe the most persuasive of pronouncements.

Two primary commodities became available for exploitation with the release of nuclear energy for nonobliterative purposes: first, the fuels to run reactors for electric power; second, the by-products and radioactive substances that have to be disposed of safely and permanently to prevent them from killing and polluting on a hideous scale.

Because production of electric power by nuclear materials, unless outlawed, is destined as a matter of policy and profit to increase geometrically, it is essential that it become better understood by a maximum number of people in general and by decision-making leadership in particular. Dangerous old assumptions that the atmosphere, the oceans, and the land are inexhaustible, that the conquest of nature is the proper pursuit of man, have proved to be fearfully false. Nuclear power, like any other force applied to excess also has limitations. It could be a good or an awful thing.

All nuclear reactors in America are fueled by enriched uranium. The enriching process remains a government monopoly. But although it was once highly classified, the process has come partially into the domain of private industry, which undertakes work farmed out by the AEC. Uranium itself is mined in the rocky territory of the western United States and in many other regions of the earth. Extensive reserves exist in Canada. The natural ore contains less than 1 percent of the metal (uranium), and only 0.71 percent of that is fissionable, or fissile. Nearly all deposits contain a concentration of two to twenty pounds per ton of the isotope uranium 238, which is called *fertile* (rather than fissile) material. The minute amount, that 0.71 percent, of the more immediately desirable isotope uranium 235 is also part of the same ore. (An isotope is any one of two or more forms of the same chemical element, having the same number of protons in the nucleus.) Only the insignificant amount of uranium 235 is fissionable.

In its natural state, uranium is mildly radioactive. When processed or enriched, it becomes truly dangerous. In its natural state, when it is located and mined, good ventilation and dust-control standards are necessary for the protection of workmen. Even then, uranium mining is hazardous. A disproportionately large number of miners have suffered respiratory tract cancer, and some have died of leukemia. Even in the wake of improved safety standards, many court and compensation cases have been filed by miners or by their surviving families against mining operators.

Extracted from the original ore, 1 cubic foot of the metallic uranium contains the energy equivalent of 1,700,000 tons of coal. This image may be further clarified by recalling the TVA coal-burning plant at Bull Run in Tennessee, which consumes more than 5 tons of coal a minute, or 7,600 tons a day. It would take the Bull Run plant, operating at full capacity (950,000 kilowatt-hours), 224 days to consume the 17,000 carloads of coal represented by 1 cubic foot of uranium.

A much larger coal-burning plant at Mohave, Nevada, turning out 1.5 million kilowatts and consuming 12 tons of coal a minute, uses the same quantity of coal in just under 100 days. Gigantic plants projected for construction in the West and Southwest—all to be fed by strip-mined coal—will be fueled by 25,000 tons of coal every twenty-four hours.

The efficient use of plutonium, the world's most highly toxic substance, produces even more energy—an inspiring or an appalling improvement over uranium, depending on one's view of things.

Uranium ore is first pulverized, then dissolved by a reagent into a "leaching liquor." When recovered by a solvent extraction process, it is calcined (roasted) to remove fluids. The remaining concentrate is called *yellow cake* and contains between 70 and 90 percent ^{238}U, not the minute percentage it started with.

Some twenty or more uranium mills, all privately owned, can produce at full capacity more than 20,000 tons of ^{238}U a year, although production between 1963 and 1970 averaged about 10,000 tons annually under a stretch-out program imposed by the AEC procurement policy. Also, AEC sales promotion plans lagged a bit.

Yellow cake is then further processed to remove excess baggage and impurities, the result being essentially pure "orange oxide." Chemical conversion by reaction with hydrogen fluoride gas produces a further refined substance called *green salt,* which is shipped to one of three enormous processing plants operated by private industry under contract to the AEC at Paducah, Kentucky; Oak Ridge, Tennessee; and Portsmouth, Ohio.

At the processing plant, the green salt compound is converted in reaction with fluorine gas (F_2) into uranium hexafluoride (UF_6). At the uranium hexafluoride stage, the fuel is in a solidified state at normal room temperature; but above that temperature, it sublimes (converts into a gas). The enrichment of uranium is accomplished at elevated temperatures in what is called the *gaseous-diffusion* process. It is rather like filtration, except that instead of depending on differences in the sizes of solid particles, it makes use of variables in the mobility of gas molecules.

A law of physics rules that with certain exemptions, molecules of gas have the same kinetic energy, which is defined mathematically in terms of the mass of the molecule times the square of its velocity. This means that lighter molecules, in constant random motion, travel faster than heavier ones. In a mix of isotopes 235 and 238, the ratio of weight, or the separation factor, is slender indeed. It is 1 to 1.0043 in these identical chemical twins.

Through hundreds of stages in what is known as a *diffusion cascade,* the $U^{235}F_6$ molecules, being faster and striking a porous barrier more frequently, separate from the slightly more sluggish $U^{238}F_6$ laggards. As the gas works its way up in the cascade, the enriched material can be withdrawn at any point. What is not enriched is thus depleted, withdrawn, and stored. Since the entire process must be operated at less than atmospheric pressure, the whole plant has to be vacuum-tight. Considering that the installation, with all its stages, would, if stretched out in a straight line, be several miles long, this is an astonishing construction accomplishment.

The three gaseous-diffusion plants consume an astronomical amount of electric power. At one time, they absorbed half the total output of the TVA system; and in 1962, by consuming 47 billion kilowatt-hours, they used one-twentieth of all the electricity generated in the United States.

A commonly used nuclear fuel in a power reactor is uranium dioxide (UO_2), a powder reduced from orange oxide. A number of chemical companies supply this conversion service to the civilian power industry on a routine commercial basis.

Nuclear power people feel it would be wonderful if tiny pellets of uranium dioxide could be tossed into a reactor now and then, thereby simplifying things, like injecting a couple of bits the size of aspirin tablets into a heating unit beneath a boiler for an uncomplicated conversion of energy. Such elementary use of nuclear energy, a little shielded box to drive an individually owned nontoxic vehicle, exists thus far only in fantasy. Nevertheless, it was reported in 1971 that some strides for a more direct conversion of atomic fission into electric power had been made at the experimental or laboratory level.

Little pencil-thin pellets in short segments are stacked one on top of the other in tubes ten or more feet long. The tubes, filled with fuel, are then arranged into a bundle of rods, each precisely separated to make up a fuel assembly. This fixed spatial distribution disburses the heat-generating capacity of fissionable material in order to maintain channels through which coolant flows.

The cylindrical pellets are encircled in a thin tubular sheath. This is called *cladding* the fuel. The protecting tubes are fabricated of stainless steel or an alloy of zirconium (Zircaloy). Cladding shields the fuel from corrosion or erosion by preventing contact with the coolant. It also locks in radioactive products, a needless commodity, formed as the atoms undergo their sustained fission reaction. Good, even thermal transfer between the pellets and the cladding is an absolute essential to prevent concentrated "hot spots" from cracking or melting holes in the thin, extremely hard metallic tubes. Such breaks and melts have occurred, and with highly radioactive material cast about, there is grave danger even when it is contained within the chamber enveloping the entire core. The core is a collection of hundreds of fuel assemblies, each a bundle of pellet-filled tubes. So, it is necessary to keep heat evenly distributed and the core evenly cooled.

It is this core, within which is accumulated immense amounts of radioactivity, that fuels both the reactor and the controversy about siting nuclear plants along public waterways or within range of habitation. When it first becomes operative, a reactor, except for discharging heated water drawn into and ejected through the cooling system, presents only nominal danger, which fission technicians contend is easily guarded against. But after operating for a time, it becomes "a unique hazard to people and property in its vicinity," in the words of Dr. Ralph E. Lapp, a serious and noted student of nuclear affairs and author of the book *Arms Beyond Doubt* and many published articles. It becomes more hazardous as the concentration of radioactivity increases within the nuclear core. In time, of course, the fuel rods are removed, radioactive waste is taken away and interred in some nuclear graveyard, presumably —as the AEC crosses its heart and pledges the nation—remote and safe from contact with the ecosystem. In a reactor, one-third of the fuel is removed and replaced each year so that there is a continuing input of fresh enriched uranium and an equal removal of spent fuel destined for the salt mines, disposal tanks, or whatever destination the AEC requires.

It was in acknowledgment of toxic hazard that the Atomic Energy Commission in the past licensed reactors only when they were to be isolated from the populace, a policy subject to change, however, as more and more reactors are authorized. Where an isolated reactor, remote from reactors and from people, might be tolerated, a string of them along one river or around the shore of a lake could not. For, as Dr. Lapp wrote, each reactor becomes "a potential threat without precedent in urban life" and in a single year of operation consumes more nuclear fuel than could be detonated in a thousand A-bombs of the type dropped over Nagasaki.

With the core in place, with fresh nuclear fuel prevented from releasing energy (just as coal or oil releases no energy until consumed by fire), with the whole structural mass enveloped in a huge beehive concrete dome, how is the nuclear reactor turned on? And what happens? The massive pile could squat there on the waterfront, a more or less inert structural mass, uncontaminated and silent, until fission occurs. The phenomenon has to be started and, most significantly, stopped.

Since all nuclear reactor power plants consume uranium and will do so even when plutonium becomes a prime energy source, their operation is started and stopped by a precise but simple process of confining and releasing atomic particles. In a high-power reactor core, according to Dr. Lapp, 9 million small pellets of nuclear fuel are fitted into tubes eleven or twelve feet in length, with clusters of tubes forming a cylinder eleven feet or thereabouts in diameter. This array is sealed in a pressure vessel, into which control rods can be inserted or withdrawn, much like the graphite rods that Dr. Fermi and his associates used in the Chicago stadium in 1942. By removing the control rods, the atoms are unconfined, and fission, or chain reaction, begins with 30 billion fissions occurring each second to release a watt of energy. The whole core—its structure, rods, and pellets—weighs about 1 million pounds in an installation of this size.

The chain reaction, with control rods withdrawn, produces heat that either boils water circulating in the system or heats it far beyond the boiling point under pressure that prevents boiling, depending on the type of reactor. Steam is, in any case, produced to drive the great turbines that spin the sleek shafts of the generators that make electricity. The center of the uranium dioxide pellets rises to a temperature of 4,100 degrees Fahrenheit, a nearly molten condition. The tubes containing the pellets are cooled by water moving at high speed under pressure of 1,000 to 2,200 pounds per square inch. The reactor, then, is a contained environment in a controlled chain reaction, designed to permit a circu-lating coolant to encompass heat. In order to stop or slow down the process, the control rods are injected into the system to reduce the atom-splitting action to the degree desired.

Any interruption of the cooling process is perilous, and one of the most critical considerations in the design of a reactor is finding ways to keep the coolant flowing perfectly or to switch to an emergency method of heat reduction in a matter of seconds.

Dr. Lapp has examined the fail-safe procedures of nuclear reactors and has postulated that the "worst" thing that could happen to cause loss of coolant would require a double break in large pipes that con-duct heated water out of the reactor core. Within five to ten seconds, the temperature in the containment vessel would jump from 600 to 1,500 degrees, and the core itself would begin to collapse in two minutes. Steam explosions and a melt-through of the vessel itself would probably occur in an hour. In a day, the molten mass would break through the containment slab on which the reactor is built, an undesirable develop-ment called the *Chinese syndrome* because the sinking mass would be bound through the earth to China.

The point to stress here, as Dr. Lapp assesses it, is that the fail-safe emergency system must have coolant sprayed or flooded into the core within five to ten seconds. After that, the core as an entity no longer exists. What would exist would be a mass of molten debris no longer affected by any cooling operation. After eleven years or thereabouts, this radioactive mass would be a cooled-off glob of material about eighty feet in diameter.

Thus, the control rods that shut off the action and the coolant that regulates heat are the primary elements of a nuclear reactor. Almost everything else around a nuke core is there to contain or suppress violence released by an operational breakdown, a containment or a sup-pression that could be relatively temporary if the postulated "worst" thing that could happen did happen.

It was no wonder that the nukes, destined to increase from perhaps 25 or so at the end of 1972 to between 500 and 900 at the end of the century, depending on their kilowatt size, have people questioning the policies of the electric utilities and the Atomic Energy Commission. Aside from the fact that neither government nor industry has developed any credibility to spare since World War II, the very nature of nuclear power makes it difficult for people to be comfortable with. It is hardly possible for isolated sites to be found for 500 (or 900) big plants along water-ways. It is only a matter of time, perhaps just a couple of years, before the doctrine of isolating nuclear plants from the populace will have to give way. Already, in 1971, the Calvert Cliffs plant on Chesapeake

Bay was thought to be too close to too many people, excluding a body count of 200 souls who lived within a mile or two of it. One New Jersey plant will, when built, be five miles south of Trenton and ten miles north of Philadelphia. Plants of increased kilowatt size (dictated by economies of scale) and the envelopment of open space by urban development have put the populace and the nukes on a collision course. Some wholly new concept of regulatory procedures and electric power management is overdue.

Apprehension about radioactivity has not so much diminished so far in the decade of the seventies as it has altered in character. The severity of other problems impending around the world—excess population, famine, depletion of resources, uncontrolled pollution, unrelieved poverty—have made genetic damage by radiation seem somewhat far away and less threatening than more immediate disasters.

In spite of the years of secrecy, and in part because the Atomic Energy Commission itself has become slightly less insular, public appraisal of radioactive dangers has become more reasonable, if not quieter. Fear of the damage of heat to marine life and the waterways in most areas provokes more opposition to nukes than radioactive emissions do.

At one point in the early development of nuclear power, some people were concerned about the possibility of electricity itself, if generated in a uranium-fueled plant, being more dangerous or different from power produced by other fuels or by water. That is not so, of course, since uranium is not at all a substitute for anything except the energy that runs the machinery. The radioactive fuel remains always within the core. And although many people, perhaps millions, insist that the amount of irradiated material that emerges into the air or cooling water is dangerous, the fact of the matter is that it is so minute that it is normally difficult to detect and measure, at least in the case of emissions from one installation. It is the prospect of many installations that justifies apprehension, and many indeed are coming.

A visitor to a nuke is given a measuring device highly sensitive to the presence of radioactivity. Sensors in doorways and at checkpoints are designed to sound an alarm if and when any radioactive emissions contaminate the atmosphere, the plant, or the person of a workman or visitor. The alarms are inevitably silent save on the rare occasions when someone arrives wearing an old-fashioned watch with a radium dial. In such instances, the detecting systems are so delicate that the watch on the wrist or in a pocket of an unsuspecting tourist will set off a warning gong, to the visitor's chagrin and, after a fashion, to the relief of impressed witnesses of the inadvertent demonstration of the alarm system. They are generally reassured that so mild and harmless a form of radiation is noted at all and that nothing emerging from the hundreds of highly contaminated uranium fuel elements can throw off rays of one sort or another to equal an old five-dollar timepiece.

These instances also serve as a kind of fire drill for people around the power plant, who are required to be ready to reduce or shut down in a matter of seconds the controlled chain reaction unless the equivalent of an all-clear signal immediately follows the tripping of an alarm. Monitoring devices are buried in many places deep within the nuclear center, as well as around it; and if anything unusual occurs, long before an external manifestation of it, flashing lights and disclosure instruments, under the gaze of attendants at a central operating console, instantly report the condition.

Nuclear plants on occasion have allowed a guide taking touring visitors around installations to show them his radium-dial watch after they gather in a reception area at the completion of the inspection. Having checked the radioactivity instruments carried on the tour and found them showing the presence of no emissions whatsoever, they are impressed to hear a clanging warning bell when the guide holds the watch (kept on the place for just such a purpose) over the threshold of the last doorway through which the visitors emerge.

Critics of the utilities, and especially of those operating nukes, find such demonstrations insufferable, charging them off to fraudulent public relations calculated to lull the public into acceptance of nuclear technology. Two of the more persistent critics of plants in the East, Larry Bogart of Allendale, New Jersey, and Leo Goodman, an implacable opponent of nuclear power, who is employed as a consultant by the United Automobile Workers in Washington, thought the radium-dial-watch demonstration ought to remind people, not of its harmlessness, but rather of its historical relationship to ignorance about radioactivity.

Mr. Bogart, chairman of an ad hoc citizens' organization that fights nuclear plants wherever and whenever they are proposed, recalls in public appearances the once-famous case of a New Jersey watch company whose women employees died mysterious and painful deaths over a period of years, ending in the early 1930s. The women were employed to paint the faces and numerals on watches with luminescent material containing radium. Using small artist's brushes, some of the women developed the habit of wetting the tips of the brushes with their tongues, intensifying an occupational hazard that, as it developed, was lethal enough to be in the same room with. One by one, the women became ill and died, death being attributed directly to cancer caused by radium.

The deaths of the women after prolonged illness and the lawsuits that followed, during which the country was given further education in the hazards of radioactivity, shocked the public into its first appreciation of carcinogenic elements. The education of the public had begun with earlier accounts of the use of short-range X rays. Discovered by a German physicist, Wilhelm Conrad Roentgen, the X ray (so named because its nature was unknown at the time) could penetrate solids and act on a photographic plate. X-ray technology, which was called *roentgenology*, became, and remains, significant in diagnostic work and anatomical therapy. But until X-ray technicians learned to shield themselves against repeated exposure and to use the technique sparingly on patients, some suffered progressively injurious wounds that necessitated amputation of fingers and hands, and some died prematurely.

With indisputable evidence that radioactivity was indeed dangerous, public health authorities and regulatory agencies established "permissible limits" of radioactivity exposure that experience year after year inevitably proved to be inadequate to the point of guesswork. The limits were reduced time and time again and are applicable in uranium mines, laboratories, weapons manufacture, or wherever any form of emissions is likely to present hazards. Although some radiation is normally present in nature, especially in rock-faced cliffs and nonfoliage areas, an articulate fraternity of both lay and scientific critics has long maintained that no such thing as a permissible dose of radioactive exposure, other than its inescapable presence in nature, should be authorized outside medical treatment and diagnostic investigation.

Plants consuming uranium fuel are probably the most carefully, exhaustively safeguarded of any commercial or industrial operation in the country, not excluding those in which volatile explosives and highly toxic chemicals are manufactured. But there is evidence that the time is approaching when the treatment and isolation of contaminated substances produced by an increasing number of reactors might produce impossible problems. The cost, the maintenance, and security administration over radioactive wastes that might not become harmless for thousands of years looms over the whole concept of nuclear power, whether utilized for war or for peace.

If nuclear fuel is the prime commodity of the split atom, the secondary commodity is radioactive garbage, the disposal and isolation of which presents difficulties remote from anything the human race has ever encountered. Yet the Atomic Energy Commission is confident of its ability to bury safely all the waste that could accumulate for a hundred thousand years. Considering the results of the careless disposal of radioactive sands, for which the AEC was responsible, around the area of Grand Junction, Colorado, in the period of a few years, AEC confidence encompassing a hundred thousand years will have to be discounted. For twenty-five years, the AEC has put radioactive wastes in sealed containers and stored it, as the agency explains it, "near the surface of the earth." It is disturbing to reflect upon, but the AEC in some instances has taken no better care of its deadly trash than littering louts who throw beer cans from automobiles.

The AEC has to handle its irradiated wastes in liquid form for some time, and it has to be looked after pretty carefully, monitored at all times, with tanks replaced when corrosion and other nuisances make it necessary. Constituents of such wastes take centuries, in some cases, to decay to safety. Improvements in handling wastes include technology to convert them into solids resembling a claylike substance, so that they can be buried without fear at least that they will leach into the ecosystem.

It is a cumbersome process. Power plants have to budget 3 percent or more of the gross cost of nuclear power generation just to handle the stuff, and those costs are certain to increase. In fact, some students of the radioactive-waste problem have suggested that handling, monitoring, and maintaining security over this increasing toxic tonnage could develop into a very large and costly service business. With a couple of hundred nukes in operation, costs of waste treatment and disposal might equal the original cost of the nuclear fuel itself. Even finding something to do with these materials would not solve anything in the long run, since they would just turn up again in some other way, in view of their resistance to decay.

Plutonium is particularly troublesome. A dozen or so pounds of it can be made to form a critical mass under the correct conditions, with both immediate and genetically mutative results extending into whatever generations remain. In an aqueous state, twenty ounces could "go critical" with similar unpredictable results. Elaborate precautions have to be taken: tanks, vats, reaction vessels, and the like are kept to dimensions unlikely to permit a critical volume of it to collect under "normal conditions." The batch process (a batch being less than the few ounces or pounds capable of getting out of hand) characterizes the production method. One batch goes through the line before another batch is admitted to the operation.

Even amounts so small that they elude visibility are inadmissible. Although the rays do not penetrate the skin, the stuff could be inhaled or enter through cuts, to destroy blood-forming organs of the body, where 80 percent of anything ingested would remain for fifty or more years. Ten percent of it would head straight for the interior of a human being's bones, or the bones of any other living thing, for that matter.

Because of the "undiscernible nature of the health hazard" presented by plutonium, as the AEC puts it, a limit necessarily has to be placed on the quantity any one person ought to be exposed to. Of course, any limit is pretty arbitrary because nobody has much experience with it. A determination was made that one body might take in 0.6 microgram or less "without eventually producing undue risk to health." The maximum atmospheric concentration was set at 0.00003 microgram per cubic meter of air, the assumption always being in such cases that each submicroscopic fragment would somehow get evenly distributed through the various meters of air to which a wandering victim was exposed.

Experience will, as in the case of the permissible limits relating to earlier radioactive substances, determine whether everyone has figured appropriately the quantity of a previously nonexisting and genetically destructive poison that one might take on without becoming unhealthy —or dead. Plutonium 239, with its half-life of 24,360 years, may require considerable experience indeed to meet a purist's complete satisfaction.

Plutonium, known on the list of chemical elements somewhat understandably as Pu, remains the most threatening of radioactive elements as far as electric power production, not to mention bombs, is concerned. In due course, utility reactors are going to be producing it in many places for a long time in increasing volume. The source of this production approaches in reality the development of a romantic old dream that has haunted inventors since Leonardo da Vinci: an energized perpetual motion machine. It is called a *breeder reactor,* and it produces, in addition to electric power, more nuclear fuel than it consumes. This is not a probability; it is an established certainty, tested and operative. The reactor's sustained chain reaction uses uranium 235 in its initial stages, creating plutonium out of its fertile 238 as it fissions along. Plutonium will thus become, in addition to electricity, a salable product of the breeder reactor, a fuel that the electric utilities may own themselves if the oil companies do not manage, in some manner, to get possession of it. It would be the first time in many years that the utilities controlled their own fuel supply. Petroleum interests, merging and purchasing their way into control of the energy market, might then have to buy up the electric companies in order to own the plutonium-producing reactors. Nor is it illogical to assume they would do so as an extended exercise in diversification.

The breeder reactor doubles the energy fuels it consumes in a fifteen-year operating cycle. *Doubling time* means that new fissionable material produced in fifteen or so years equals the total amount consumed in the same period, including the amount contained in its fuel core plus any tied up in fabrication.

The only commercial breeder reactor plant ever built in the United States was a dangerous and financial fiasco that cost the customers of the Detroit Edison Company a good deal of money, provided them with very little power, and scared the wits out of people for miles around the area of Lagoona Beach, Michigan. It was the Enrico Fermi plant, intended to be a monument to the Italian physicist. It became less a monument than a tombstone for a premature dream of Walker Cisler, chairman of the board at Detroit Edison, who won a certain distinction from its construction and erratic operation that he might have preferred to do without. Even so, the Detroit utility is likely to win a footnote in history as the owner of the sole commercial breeder reactor, dead or alive, in the world for twenty-five years. The period will be up in 1980, by which time the age of the breeder reactors is expected, exclusive of Mr. Cisler's persistent if dubious effort, to be under way.

The history of the Fermi plant is noteworthy, especially to nuclear power opponents who have cited it over the years as a horrible example of forcing into existence technology for which only Mr. Cisler, Admiral Lewis L. Strauss, chairman of the AEC, and a collective of corporate empire builders were ready. Admiral Strauss, a former partner in Kuhn, Loeb, the investment-banking house and an important institution in the money business, was an advocate of delivering nuclear energy, which he administered presumably as a public servant, into the hands of private industry. He remains, historically, a prototype of the kind of man presidents ought not to select for positions that carry with them decision-making authority.

Nevertheless, he was in the government when Walker Lee Cisler served as a power consultant in World War II. Cisler also met General K. D. Nichols, an engineer attached to the atom bomb project. In 1947, one of those industrial advisory groups of which Lee Metcalf complains frequently was set up to expedite the use of nuclear power in the electric utilities. Cisler became its executive secretary. It was a traditional situation in which people seeking the rewards of government policy were commissioned to make it.

A year or so later, the advisory group proposed that utilities be given the right to produce electricity with the technology developed to win the war. In 1950, five combinations of industry-utility companies decided to build conventional uranium water reactors. One of the five, made up of Dow Chemical Company and Detroit Edison, elected to study the breeder reactor on the grounds that the sale of the plutonium it would produce would bring in profits over and above the sale of electric power. In effect, a breeder held out the possibility not only of "costless" power but also of extending a utility into the nuclear fuel business as well. This was before the petroleum business bought so deeply into the nuclear field.

The AEC approved the Dow-Edison plan in 1952. Strauss, at that point, was chairman of the AEC in the Eisenhower administration. The Fermi breeder proposed by Dow-Edison "could be turned from civilian to military requirements on very short notice," said Mr. Cisler, in praise of the flexibility of free enterprise.

Representative Chet Holifield of California and Senator Clinton Anderson of New Mexico, cochairmen of the Joint Congressional Committee on Atomic Energy, were outraged at Strauss and the AEC for readily accommodating themselves to private industry. In later years, they be-

came pretty accommodating themselves, but then they were incensed
at Dow-Edison's breeder project, which they thought premature. Cisler's
compelling drive to get the reactor constructed exceeded only Lewis
Strauss's determination to take over the civilian nuclear energy complex.
The project, with money and industries lined up by Cisler to form a
"nonprofit" corporation, went forward. Cisler won a ruling from the Internal Revenue Service that made contributions to the new corporation
deductible, an extension of the risk-free benefits in private enterprise.
He also had approval from the Michigan Public Service Commission to
charge to Detroit Edison customers unlimited costs, part of operating
expenses, on the ground that Fermi was a research and development
operation.

Meanwhile, General Nichols left the Atomic Energy Commission to
work for the Atomic Industrial Forum, the nuclear business trade association. Cisler brought him into Detroit Edison as a director in 1955 and
nine years later named him to the board of Freuhauf Corporation, of
which Cisler himself was chairman.

With a "Q" clearance giving him access to the deepest secrets of
nuclear technology, he had a pretty clear idea of the value of plutonium,
the price of which was secret on the grounds that if the Communists did
not know what the government was paying for it, they might not assess
its importance. Cisler figured that his Fermi reactor could ask $90 a
gram, according to Saul Friedman, a Detroit newspaperman who made
an exhaustive study of the Fermi case. The price was later computed in
less heady circumstances at $46 a gram.

In the preliminary planning, Cisler tried to get the Public Utilities
Holding Company Act of 1935 changed, since Detroit Edison and other
utilities, along with their equipment suppliers, were acting in concert,
contradictory to the Holding Act. Failing in that move, he nevertheless
got Justice Department assurance that an antitrust prosecution would not
be undertaken against the new nonprofit, tax-exempt corporation.

Late in 1955, the corporation (Power Reactor Development Company) had its application before the AEC for a construction permit.
Since the economy of the plant had been based on $90 a gram for its
plutonium, the projected figures had to be revised downward, in view
of the fixed price of $46. Cisler had to take out a $15-million loan for
plant construction. He had a $3-million subsidy from the AEC for
uranium 235 fuel. Operation of the plant was to begin in 1961. By 1970,
the plant was to have earned $43.4 million from the sale of steam to
Detroit Edison's own turbines and $48.6 million from plutonium sales to
the government. It figured out to a little over $9 million a year in earn-
ings for ten years.

Then, in late 1955, a frightening accident occurred. Near Idaho Falls,
the AEC had an experimental breeder reactor in operation. A "meltdown"

occurred when the reactor's fail-safe system appeared to malfunction. The fuel core was destroyed, but the fissionable material mercifully did not collect into a critical mass to produce a bomb-like explosion. A couple of men were killed in the rare accident, which involved a buildup of more heat than the internal mechanism could bear. The reactor in Idaho was isolated from any population. Fermi was to be in the heart of the metropolitan area. The Idaho meltdown was so hard to explain that one official of the Atomic Industrial Forum in New York speculated that one of the reactor attendants must have wanted it to self-destruct as a method of committing suicide. It was an option that critics felt fail-safe procedures should have denied him.

Before the AEC granted the construction permit, Lewis Strauss blunderingly revealed in Washington that he was going to give a speech at the ceremonial groundbreaking for the Fermi plant on August 8, 1956. The permit was not, it appeared, just under consideration, as the AEC implied. The Strauss remark was evidence of a sure fix, highly offensive to others who had been asking questions about the Idaho accident. One reason why Strauss was a poor choice for AEC chairman immediately emerged. He had overruled and classified as secret a report from the commission's own Advisory Committee on Reactor Safeguards, which said that "the Committee believes there is insufficient information available at this time to give assurance that the [Fermi] reactor can be operated at this site without public hazard." Further study was proposed, and the construction permit was opposed. There was simply too much "risk to the health and safety of the public."

Thomas E. Murray, a member of the AEC, went before a House subcommittee to reveal that Strauss had suppressed the report from his own advisers and to oppose the permit. Four days before the groundbreaking and the scheduled Strauss speech, with Mr. Murray dissenting, the permit was granted.

Representative Holifield called the decision "reckless and arrogant." He said the tax-exempt reactor corporation could not get insurance. In due course, the government itself provided, in the 1957 passage of the Price-Anderson Act, nuclear reactor insurance in the amount of $486 million. It was another of those public subsidies that so often eliminate the risks in private enterprise by assessing the costs to the taxpayers.

Back in 1957, the Brookhaven National Laboratory prepared a study for the AEC (a document known as Wash. 740) that attempted to assess the possible damage resulting from a maximum predictable accident in a large nuclear installation. It was determined that a blowup of a reactor in the 100-to-200-megaton range could kill 3,400 people, injure 43,000, and cause property damage of $7 billion, possibly necessitating agricultural quarantines over an area of 150,000 square miles.

One reactor at the Windscale Works in England spewed radioactive

fission material over the countryside on October 10, 1957, after which
authorities seized milk and foodstuffs in a 400-mile area. It seemed that
nearly all the reactor's containment safeguards had failed in an unpredictable situation.

No underwriter and no pool of them would provide coverage on the
scale projected in the Brookhaven report. The insurance industry in the
United States devised a plan to cover $74 million, or a little more than
1 percent, to indemnify a utility and equipment manufacturers against
damage suits. Under the Price-Anderson Act, the government put up $486
million, for a total of $560 million, leaving $6.4 billion to be picked up
by the victims themselves in a mishap of the size projected in the AEC's
own Brookhaven study.

Senator Clinton Anderson, whose name was memorialized in the insurance bill, reflected on the successful effort by Admiral Strauss to bull-
doze the Fermi permit through all obstacles and called the AEC a "star
chamber." It was closer to a denunciation of the arrogance of Mr. Strauss
than of the Atomic Energy Commission as a whole. The affair was galling
to both Anderson and Chet Holifield, who, as cochairman of the joint
committee, might have been expected to wield at least some neutralizing
influence. But Mr. Strauss was favored by President Eisenhower, who
frowned on public power as "creeping socialism" anyway, and by the
Establishment of his time. At the groundbreaking, he made it clear that
critics of the Fermi plant lacked an appreciation of patriotism and suggested that their deeper motive was to undermine the nation. Said Mr.
Strauss, without reference to the suppressed report, Fermi critics were
"aiding the attack which is being directed against the free enterprise development of nuclear power in this country. . . . The attack would, if
successful, have the effect of weakening, if not eliminating, such free
competition and of returning atomic energy to its former condition of
government monopoly and operation." It was clear that Mr. Strauss felt
obliged, as administrator of that federal monopoly, to put it into private
hands.

The Fermi plant never produced more than a trickle of electricity or
a gram of plutonium. Licensed to generate 200,000 kilowatts, its maximum at any point was 67,000. A nearby conventional system made ten
times that amount at a fraction of the cost, which, in any case, Detroit
customers paid.

The United Automobile Workers, with AEC critic Leo Goodman
gathering and presenting a good deal of testimony, took the AEC to
court on the grounds that the plant endangered 3 million people and
would never be safe. The circuit court of appeals agreed and ruled
against the plant, but the United States Supreme Court reversed the
decision. In a dissenting opinion, Justice Hugo Black and Justice William

Douglas wrote: "The time when the issue of safety must be resolved is before the Commission issues a construction permit." They said, further, that the AEC's construction of the law which established it was "a light-hearted approach to the most awesome, the most deadly, the most dangerous process that man has ever conceived."

On October 5, 1966, Fermi was lumbering along at 37,000 kilowatts when the radiation alarms sounded throughout the plant. Six control rods were inserted their full distance, absorbing the neutrons and stopping the chain reaction. The power was shut off. A half ton of uranium 235 was in the core, cooled by liquid sodium. It was a meltdown, with its danger that the fuel might collect into a critical, explosive mass. Misshapen zirconium metal, looking like a flattened beer can, blocked one or two of the openings admitting the cooling sodium. Heat intensified, the assemblies buckled, and two subassemblies melted.

It took a year to diagnose the cause. The interior was highly radioactive. A forty-foot periscope was dropped into the interior to take photographs, which revealed the beer-can outline of molten metal. It was worse than the "maximum credible accident" allowed for in the design, but fortunately radiation leakage occurred to set off the alarms and disengage the chain reaction.

Fermi lay on the beach of Lake Michigan for nearly four years. Digging out the lethal material was complicated and expensive. Preliminary test operations were begun again, and in the late summer of 1970, Fermi "went critical" once more. In one ironic way. Walker Cisler was correct. It *was* a research project that proved what its critics had said: that the technology was not ready for it. On the other hand, it did not blow up 3 million people. It was back in token operation in 1971, faltering and subsidized, unlikely to produce any plutonium or to generate very much electricity, but demonstrating some kind of a point that by then eluded everybody.

Walker Cisler showed up at the White House early in 1971, still pursuing his dream of successfully operating the world's first breeder reactor to produce electric power. At seventy-three, he had won high favor and many friends as a fund raiser for President Nixon and the Republican party. He moved about trying to raise $50 million to keep Fermi going. The plant had sold in its stormy life, not the electricity to produce earnings of $43.4 million by 1970 that Mr. Cisler had foreseen but an estimated $300,000 worth. Nor had it produced the projected $48.6 million worth of plutonium. It had produced none. Yet, because the federal government had spent $1 billion or so on breeder reactor development, Mr. Cisler thought another $50 million was justified.

Perhaps Mr. Cisler had been getting reports about the big plutonium breeder reactor nearing completion in the Soviet Union. It would be a splendid vindication of his own vision and determination if the Fermi plant, which in seven years had not operated at full power for more than five days, could become fully operative and produce some plutonium before the Russians unveiled their big new facility.

Thomas O'Toole, a writer and investigator for the *Washington Post,* reported that Mr. Cisler's request to the White House to divert to Fermi some available AEC funds had made some Washington luminaries nervous. Why this was so seemed curious, in view of the fact that before many months had passed the government was handing out $250 million to keep the Lockheed Corporation afloat.

Senator Henry M. Jackson, who was then busy trying to persuade the government to keep pouring money into the supersonic transport aircraft project, queried AEC Chairman Glenn Seaborg on that agency's dealings with Cisler and was assured that the AEC did not "contemplate" bailing out the Fermi plant. Cisler could see that hope was fading and changed his tactics. He sought a waiver on $11 million worth of nuclear fuel needed at the Fermi reactor. With the fuel supplied by the AEC, Cisler would export it to Japan or Belgium for fabrication into a core for $3 million, which was $7 million less than it would cost in the United States. If this could be accomplished, it was reported, original backers among the utilities and equipment manufacturers would put up another $39 million and the Fermi plant, which had cost $128 million to begin with, might not have to be junked.

Even Chet Holifield, who as a California congressman was under assault by constituents angry about nuclear plants being planned over earthquake faults, did not care much for the proposal to send uranium abroad for processing. "I would not look favorably on this plan," he said.

The plutonium breeder reactor, it seemed, was doomed. By the end of the year, the Soviet Union announced that its 350,000-kilowatt fast breeder electric plant was about to become operative along the coast of the Caspian Sea. In Scotland, another fast breeder power plant was nearing completion. In the United States, in mid-January, 1972, the AEC announced that the era of the fast breeder would begin on schedule—if eight years or so behind the Russians. The agency and the Tennessee Valley Authority would build a 350,000-kilowatt plutonium producer in eastern Tennessee for about $500 million. It would begin generating electric power in 1980. Fermi had not been successful and not, as it turned out, very commercial. All it had been was the first. Then Mr. Cisler's dream had melted down.

12

The Protestants

of

Power

By 1976, when the nation is 200 years old and electric power itself is rounding out its first hundred years, 300 nuclear-powered plants will be producing 147,000,000 megawatts of electricity in twenty-eight countries. Not long after, plutonium breeders will begin making their appearance.

The old Idaho plant was abandoned, but the Atomic Energy Commission continued to operate two experimental plutonium reactors, one at another Idaho site and the second at Fayetteville, Arkansas. By 1971, $1 billion of government money had gone into breeder reactor research, a good deal of it directed to safety measures and radioactivity controls.

It is the plutonium-producing plants, far more than the hot-water uranium reactors, that are the despair of nuclear power opponents. In anticipation of mounting opposition, designers hope to make plutonium plants "even more beautiful," as one advocate expressed it, than the generally despised water-cooled installations. The plutonium-producing monsters call for use of liquid metal and other more highly sophisticated coolant systems that will, nevertheless, still discharge heat into the air and water. Thermal pollution is becoming so pervasive that by 1972, most authorities on the subject were predicting that within twenty years half of all the runoff water in America would be drawn into and expelled from power plants. Electric companies and the industrial complex that depended on them were determined to proceed with all forms of nuclear energy development but conceded that the issue of water heating plagued them more and more.

The whole question of heat discharge is complicated by the fact that although one nuclear reactor on a fast-flowing river or along the shore of a lake or tidal waterway might create imperceptible damage, multiples of reactors were ecologically threatening indeed. Like the automobile, perhaps, many millions could be tolerated if sufficiently dispersed, but too many in one place were measurably destructive to air and space resources.

For all their apparent cleanliness and promise, nuclear and plutonium plants suggest violence against nature. Beyond that, the nukes and fossil-fuel plants are simply not much fun to see.

A hydroelectric power plant, on the other hand, is sometimes beautiful to see, a majestic work of colossal simplicity in which one feels and observes the phenomenon of power being created. The action of a continually replenished volume of water responding to the law of gravity and itself providing the energy to turn generators that, in turning, create electric energy, can be an inspiring experience. In this creation of power, nothing is lost or dirtied; the water is not polluted; no smoke or oxides emerge from stacks; no radioactive emissions spill into the water or the air—nothing evil or damaging happens. Rushing water presses in its passage against steel blades that turn a shaft to which the blades are attached, and the shaft spins to act upon an invisible magnetic field, creating a movement of electrons that is power.

The most gigantic hydroelectric operation in the world is in Siberia, a 6-million-kilowatt complex on the Yenisei River that is three times larger than the Grand Coulee Dam output that feeds the American West. Twelve 500,000-kilowatt generating units of the eastern Soviet project, known as the Krasnoyarsk power station, were built and started up over a period of fifteen years and completed in 1971. The Krasnoyarsk station overpowers another Russian hydroelectric complex, the Bratsk, on the Angara River, which, at 4.1 million kilowatts, was for years the world's largest hydro producer. Two more power stations are under construction along the Siberian rivers in 1972.

In North America, the billion-dollar hydro complex under development in northeastern Canada at Churchill Falls will probably remain the largest waterpower producer of electricity indefinitely, once it is completed, because sites in remote locations have about run out.

In the United States, it was the Federal Power Act of 1920 that set off the development of hydroelectric power, the only source of electricity over which the Federal Power Commission has anything approaching complete jurisdiction. Hydroelectric power, however, adds up to only 4 percent of the electric energy generated in the United States, and it will become less and less, in percentage terms, in the future. The greatest sites are in the Grand Canyon, the northwestern mountain ranges, on the

Snake River, in the TVA system. But great natural sites that had not yet been condemned for hydroelectric or pumped storage power production by the 1970s are a lot less likely to fall to the power companies than they would have been in the past. The Storm King Mountain case gave national impetus to the movement to salvage what is left of scenic lands and waterways.

Perhaps the most effective individual agent against hydro development in America is the implacable David Brower, for some years president of the formidable Sierra Club, and an advocate of the idea that rivers were intended by nature, not to be dammed up, but to flow. Quite a few dams proposed by the Federal Bureau of Land Reclamation remain unbuilt because of Brower's articulate opposition to them.

But it is not only in the United States that there is opposition; in the Soviet Union, an otherwise harmonious assembly in 1971 of the twenty-fourth Communist Party Congress was riven by dissension between power plant developers and the Ministry of Agriculture over condemnation of fertile farm valleys for hydroelectric reservoirs. The same conflicting questions about environmental desecration that are familiar to militant conservationists in the United States were answered by Soviet power system promoters in much the same language that electric utilities spokesmen have used for many years in the United States.

"It is the sacred duty of every Soviet citizen to preserve the land," said Minister of Agriculture Vladimir Matskevich, to a roar of applause. "We power workers are taking steps to conserve land. We love our dear land, comrade farm workers," retorted Minister of Power Pyotr S. Neporozhny, who nevertheless insisted that vast reservoirs had to be constructed both for the generation of power and as a source of water for populated industrial areas.*

Generate power in coal, oil, gas, and nuclear plants and save the land, said the farm people. The Soviet Union's nuclear power program calls for a nuclear output of 30 million kilowatts in the next ten to twelve years. It is uncommon for such conflict to break out in public forums in Russia, and the intensity of the argument over the management of natural resources suggests that government-run electric utilities in the land of communism have to face opposition common to the IOUs of the United States. Perhaps the difficulties in America are more varied. Although the Soviet Ministry of Power might have to placate the farm bloc, it is spared embarrassing confrontations with stockholders.

Grave concern existed over a monumental project covering a kingdom-sized area in the United Arab Republic, where the Aswan Dam

---

* The conflict over Soviet power policy was reported from the Communist Party Congress by Theodore Shabad, correspondent for the *New York Times,* in a dispatch published in that newspaper on April 9, 1971.

caused dislocations and heartbreak while promising long-range industrial and economic benefits. For thousands of years, the annually flooding Nile River carried silt and topsoil from the uplands into the Nile valley to replenish farmlands and feed the marshes and shallow water of the Mediterranean coastal plane. A thriving shrimp industry depended on the life chain nourished by the Nile. With the Aswan Dam holding back the vast Lake Nasser reservoir, 310 miles long, fishing and farming at the mouth of the Nile were severely disrupted and the shrimp industry threatened with ruin. Lake Nasser flooded 122,000 Nubian villagers out of their homes into forty-three relocated towns. The Aswan Dam will produce 10 billion kilowatt-hours of hydroelectric energy a year and has added 2 million acres of irrigated, arable lands to the nation to make up for ending an ancient way of life along the lower Nile.

Although no utility would be interested in constructing new hydro plants generating as little as 4,000 to 7,000 kilowatts, a number of them remain in operation around the country. They were built forty to sixty years ago, in the early days of power development, when people were content to consume 400 to 500 kilowatt-hours a year, as opposed to an average of 8,000 by 1971.

In New England, the dammed rivers created cherished lakes with valuable and much-sought-after land around their shorelines. Because of their insignificance in terms of output, utilities care little about them beyond the fact that they are licensed by the FPC and must be maintained as part of a regional system. Feeding their small, reliable output into the network, the hydro plants are fully automated, requiring little more than an occasional inspection and nominal maintenance. As a condition of license renewals after long years of operation, power companies added landscaping and recreational facilities that made them highly valuable resources far beyond their importance in power generation.

In some cases, strenuous objections were made when they were built because they flooded lands, eliminated isolated fishing streams, intruded on the wilderness, and deprived some people of their back-country freedom. If, however, one were to suggest that they be removed (as has been done on occasion) because they were no longer essential, which they are not, Yankee residents along their waterfronts would fight tenaciously against the proposal.

The half-million acres of lakes, dams, and coves created by the TVA system were accompanied by reforestation that produced a brand-new hardwood timber industry, carefully harvested and carefully preserved. They restored pasture land, provided extensive recreational and sports facilities like those developed in the Northwest by both private and public utilities developments, and added incalculable ecological and monetary value. For $20 a month, one may anchor a houseboat at a mooring site in a cove along any number of TVA dams, get electricity and pollution-free sewage disposal while docked, and cruise at will waterways probing into wilderness or extending from northeastern Tennessee, south into Alabama, and north to the Ohio and Mississippi rivers through locks safely bypassing once-impassable shoals.

Once it was thought that extensive construction of dams—nine major installations and forty or more smaller ones scattered throughout seven states—in the TVA system would destroy much of the fishing and otherwise cause irreparable harm to marine life. Large investments were made in rearing fish in pens along the waterway. They were fed and nourished until, reaching appropriate size and age, the pens were opened and the fish emerged to replenish life in the dams and rivers. Locks and bypasses around high dam breastworks gave marine life access to a broad world of fresh, although, alas, often polluted water. For some years, water pollution was not a problem throughout the great system; but as industries grew in size and number (paper and pulp mills, chemical companies, food and lumber processing, and coal-burning power plants), the vast network of dams and waterways suffered the fate common to water everywhere.

The need to raise fish for restocking the dams and rivers has long since been eliminated. Field after field of wide, shallow gutters in which fish were reared have been planted in pastures, where passing observers wonder at the strange, evenly corrugated shape of the green land on which fine cattle graze, making their way across the peculiarly undulating, man-shaped landscape.

Fish life proliferated so remarkably in the chain of dams and waterways that catch limits were raised and the fishing season extended. An ecological balance was restored and, if one can make a judgment from statistical studies and observation, improved. In the rising wave of criticism against utilities and against the expansion of electric power, it has to be remembered that some beautiful and remarkable developments went hand in hand with the excesses that brought the nation to its time of peril.

The immediate and future threats of atomic waste disposal and heat discharge into the waterways remain the most frightening aspects of continued power development. Part of the AEC's problem in dealing with the public in these matters is a simple one of bureaucracy and the stultifying tradition of secrecy, needless and otherwise, that tempts politically oriented leadership to hide what is not easily arguable. Another part of the problem is that there are many dangerous and troublesome aspects of nuclear power which the AEC, in its contradictory roles as press agent and arbiter, studies and worries about no less than its detractors.

In all the years of Atomic Energy Commission functions, it did not authorize its administrators and experts to participate in free public dialogue until September, 1969. And when it did so, it resorted to a kind of show-biz promotion and public relations, complete with chicks in miniskirts and sales convention hoopla, that might have been appropriate for a new model 350-horsepower, eight-cylinder Snarling Brute engine from Detroit; but it did not evoke a welcome response from the Vermont audience it was calculated to impress. Nevertheless, Glenn Seaborg himself showed up and made a learned, persuasive speech glorifying nuclear-fueled power plants, several of which had been proposed in the state. But the prospects of a uranium fission plant on Lake Champlain, south of Burlington, and others strung along Vermont's cool rivers aroused in New England a response equivalent to that which might greet an interracial free sex festival in a Mississippi high school.

In two days of open public seminars at the University of Vermont, the AEC contingent had crossed over into hostile territory. Faced with unsentimental questioners skilled in the detection of dissembling in the town-meeting school of democracy, the AEC contingent was subjected to a cold grilling and a good deal of acid response to their warmly worded generalizations. They emerged from the conflict nursing their wounds but enriched by the experience and better prepared to confront subsequent bodies of restless natives elsewhere in the country.

Senator George Aiken, the state's perennial export to Washington and as durable as a block of Vermont granite, its other leading export, had almost single-handedly won some concessions from the private utilities industry that they would have liked to withhold. Since small publicly owned municipal power systems, such as one in Burlington and others in Vermont, could never raise the capital to build large economy-of-scale nuclear plants nor consume the production that one of them could generate, the big IOUs, which already had two such plants on the Connecticut River, were prepared to envelop the municipals in a sea of power. Largely because of the municipals and a comparatively frugally minded Public Service Commission, Vermont had the lowest electrical rates in New England. But without access to huge new generating capacity, the situation could easily change in favor of the IOUs, with probable loss of sovereignty to locally owned power.

Senator Aiken was, with the announced retirement of Senator Bourke B. Hickenlooper, destined to become the ranking Republican on the Joint Atomic Energy Commission. A no-nonsense conservative, Aiken had an independent bent and a certain disdain for any excessive display of avarice, which he detected on the part of private utilities in developing nuclear technology while leaving the municipals at a grave disadvantage. It was his feeling that high electrical rates had been a factor in the departure of a good many New England textile and other manufacturing operations to the southern states. The fact was that the exodus was stimulated by low southern labor costs as much as by power rates. In any event, Aiken's status on the joint committee gave him a little power of his own to apply now and then.

He forced the private utilities to allow municipals and cooperatives to buy their way into the nuclear combines on a pro rata basis that allowed them to file a claim on nuclear power generation commensurate with their contribution to the equity. In some measure, this was, from the point of view of the big IOUs, not altogether fair, although the presumption that justice itself is not uniformly fair supported the municipals' case. Or so Aiken and the public power systems' managers thought.

The complaint of the private utilities was that in a large system composed of many old, inefficient plants in need of retirement, and in view of their own need for heavily increased generation, they ended up with a mix of all kinds of facilities, cost variables, and operating problems. A small municipal, on the other hand, with limited growth capacity, could buy into a big new nuke for 5 or 10 percent of the action and get a guaranteed supply of low-cost power that would cover its expansion needs for a long time without sharing any of the higher costs charged to old facilities they had no claim on. Thus, the big private utilities felt they had been shaken down to some extent by having to open up a part of their best economy-of-scale power. Yet what was a valid point was yielded under the pressure of larger realities, for as Aiken said, it would have been grossly unjust for municipals to lose everything while the big IOUs stood to suffer only little losses that they would no doubt reconcile somewhere in their accounting procedures anyway.

The nuclear age, then, brought the small public systems into its fold, and Senator Aiken, with assistance from Lee Metcalf and traditional private-power foes in Congress, was largely responsible for it. His Senate seat from Vermont was so secure, anyway, that any opposition developing against him out beyond the sugar maple groves was insignificant. It was said that his expenses in his last reelection campaign were less than a dollar.

In addition to the change of practice that compelled the IOUs to share a percentage of nuclear output with the municipals, the proposed nuclear plant on the shore of Lake Champlain in Charlotte was withdrawn. Both the Vermont and the New York legislatures passed bills making nukes highly unwelcome on the lake that joins and separates the two states. Moreover, both states filed a brief supporting the Minnesota court case seeking to set radiation and thermal emission standards at more restrictive levels than the federal government decided was permissible.

When Glenn Seaborg and James T. Ramey had been reappointed in

1968 to the Atomic Energy Commission, Senator Aiken, who never voted against a presidential appointment no matter how mediocre or offensive others may have thought the nominee to be, stood up in the Senate and rebuked them. He did not reject the appointments, just some aspects of their philosophy and conduct in office. On the day of the vote for confirmation in July, 1968, the Vermont senator delivered the strongest reprimand against presidential nominees he had ever uttered in his long tenure in Washington.

> I simply want to express the hope that from now on they will give greater consideration to the public welfare and somewhat less solicitude to the private power companies of the United States. I believe they are doing a great disservice to the people of this country by, day after day, licensing $100 million atomic power plants under the medical therapy and research clause of the law instead of under that part of the law which would automatically put these people under the anti-trust laws. . . . I believe they have done wrong; they are continuing to do wrong.

Senator Aiken was referring to the procedural anomaly, which had been traditional AEC practice, of licensing nuclear installations not as commercial enterprises but as medical and research reactors. The AEC was permitted to do this under the law—as the AEC interpreted it.

Just that very morning, Aiken said, he had received notice that the Atomic Energy Commission had licensed three more plants under the medical therapy section of the law. He went on:

> I do not believe they are medical therapists in any sense of the word, particularly when they construct plants costing $100 million and $150 million each.
>
> After licensing by the AEC, the power companies go down the street to the Securities and Exchange Commission, which finds they are profit-making enterprises and authorizes them to sell stock and borrow money running into billions of dollars.

But by being licensed under the medical and research section of the law, the nukes were absolved from antitrust action that the Department of Justice could initiate if they had been more correctly licensed as the commercial power producers they were.

A month or two earlier, Senator Aiken had made a suggestion that, for a conservative senator, was extraordinarily uncharacteristic. He hinted directly that socialism in the private utility industry might be in the public interest. It was the sort of thing that could easily have drawn a "Heavens to Betsy!" gasp from any number of his Republican constituents.

In a hearing on Senator Aiken's bill requiring the private power utilities to coexist with public systems and to let the municipals have a share of nuclear-produced power, an assistant secretary of the Department of the Interior came forward to testify that he was highly in favor of the Aiken proposals. He was Kenneth Holum, who has since become a former assistant secretary, and who had earlier tried to get the government interested in creating an interconnected power grid over half the nation. Such a grid, linking together all sources of electric power, would reduce the likelihood of failures and brownouts and the necessity for unilateral decisions to build more power plants in each franchised monopoly area.

In addition to preventing the exclusion of municipal systems from the benefits of nuclear energy, Aiken wanted a single federal agency with power to regulate environmental effects: thermal pollution, radiological hazards, stack emissions, water and land damage, and the like. He did not accomplish that, nor did Mr. Holum make appreciable inroads in trying to establish a federal grid system, although the objectives of both Aiken and Holum were essential and long overdue.

Aiken was one of very few officials anywhere in the federal government, one of perhaps half a dozen, who acknowledged the generally ignored capture of the energy fuels market by the oil interests. When the prices of coal, oil, and gas began to soar, Senator Aiken began to suspect that forces of collusion and conspiracy were at work in the marketplace. The well-being of the nation was under threat, "a very serious threat to political democracy," he said, "because when you control energy—and oil interests now control coal and are on their way to controlling nuclear fuel—then you control the nation." This group, as Aiken saw the evidence, "is determined to get control of electric energy" in the United States. To less conservative critics than Mr. Aiken, the evidence was convincing that energy control was already a pretty well established fact, with the private power companies serving as passive participants in the arrangement, rather than as objectors.

Most protestants of power policy addressed themselves less to the issue of fuels and energy control than to environmental destruction for which the utilities, their industrial customers, and retail ratepayers were responsible. Although Norman Clapp of the Rural Electric Cooperative, which produces power as a publicly owned entity, repeatedly deplored Donald Cook's program for organizing the country into twelve to fifteen regional utility monopolies, and although Aiken denounced the energy trust, the main public outcry has dealt with environmental hazards. And although most protestors are citizens of no special cachet, many recognized authorities have given validity to their complaints. Around the AEC empire, a lot of them have to be accorded a certain measure of respect: Barry Commoner, of Washington University in Saint Louis; French anthropologist Claude Lévi-Strauss; René J. Dubos, of Rockefeller University; Eugene P. Odum, of the University of Georgia; Paul R. Erlich, of Stanford University; Kenneth E. F. Watt, of the University of California; Daniel Merriman, of Yale University; Ian MacHarg, of the University of Pennsylvania; and a host of others.

Lamont C. Cole, of Cornell University, was thought by AEC people to be a bit shrill, always seeing the doomsday side of things, as, indeed, Paul Erlich was with his occasionally alarmist talk about a dying universe. John Gofman and Arthur Tamplin, two AEC scientists harshly critical of nuclear power, were brushed off as special pleaders and malcontents; and Ernest J. Sternglass, who accused the AEC of contempt for human life, was openly despised. George Wald, the Nobel biologist at Harvard, was thought to be misguided or perhaps just seeking applause from the young who idolized him.

The AEC and its fraternity of experts presents something close to a unified chorus of optimism in contrast with the views of individuals outside the nuclear energy fold. Scientists who, in some cases, have been associated with the AEC are now and then disdainful of their former professional colleagues; but by and large, the AEC presents an institutional viewpoint asserting that all is well in the field of nuclear reactor technology and that it will continue to be.

Dr. Glenn Seaborg, who served the AEC as chairman under three presidents until Nixon replaced him in 1971, was the nation's most prestigious spokesman for, and an unrelenting proponent of, nuclear power. He was supremely confident as AEC chairman and as a scientist and panelist at worldwide meetings in the United States and abroad, that nuclear technology would solve most of the major problems confronting the century.

Twenty-five years after Trinity, Dr. Seaborg presented an elaborately reasoned view of fission and fusion in the June, 1970, issue of *Bulletin of the Atomic Scientists*, which commemorated the twenty-fifth anniversary of the nuclear age. The essay allayed all fears and projected a world of enormous "nuplexes" set in serene parks, providing illimitable power for food production, desalting water, purifying air and water, reclaiming and recycling wastes, serving mankind as "an extension of nature."

Reviewing history from 1995, Dr. Seaborg noted that ten years earlier, nuclear plants "accounted for a reduction in the atmosphere of almost one billion tons of carbon dioxide and about ten billion tons of sulphur dioxide." One of the big installations in the Seaborg vision was named for Dr. Edward Teller, creator of the hydrogen bomb. It was to be the first giant breeder reactor and was to win distinction for bringing down the cost of electricity to a fraction of what it is in the decade of the seventies, when rate increases were running $4 billion in a six-month period. Under such attractive economic conditions, Dr. Seaborg saw many new industrial processes becoming "economically feasible."

There were details in the Seaborg projection that escaped the understanding of candid utility executives. The prospect of power costs dropping to a fraction of the 1970 level is, indeed, likely only in a vision. The best chance a ratepayer has of getting power for less money would be under marketing conditions that might charge him less per watt but compel the use of four or five times *more* watts than he could previously consume. As for a lot of new industrial processes becoming "economically feasible" with a superabundance of nuclear power, people long before 1995 are going to be asked some hard and pertinent questions about whether any new industrial process is necessary, or serves a useful and life-preserving purpose.

Dr. Seaborg, the National Academy of Sciences, and the whole vast array of educated professionals populating what former Secretary of the Interior Stewart Udall called the science Establishment, were severely censured in an outbreak that disrupted the 1970 meetings of the American Association for the Advancement of Science.

Mr. Udall, addressing the association in Chicago on December 29, 1970, called for "a dispassionate and intensive study of the National Academy of Sciences and the whole scientific enterprise in this country." The science Establishment, he charged, did nothing to alert the nation to its environmental crisis. "Science, lacking any foresighted ethical or social vision, can be a menace to man as well as a beneficence." The National Academy, a government-chartered society of leading scientists, functioned "all too often as a virtual puppet of the government."

Dr. Seaborg was quite bitterly criticized preceding and during the assembly of scientists. He was slated to move up, in an election that was little more than a formality, to the presidency of the association. The fact that the chairman of the AEC, regardless of his stature as a scientist, would almost certainly become the association's president, disturbed many of the 130,000 members and at least several members of a 13-man governing board.

When the news editor of the association's publication, *Science* magazine, directed a writer to prepare an article about the possible conflict of interest a man like Dr. Seaborg might face and about the related issues of the nuclear power controversy, the article was ordered suppressed by the editor, Dr. Philip H. Abelson. The news editor, Daniel S. Greenberg, resigned; and the dialogue that followed was heated enough to provoke demands for a review of the election procedures of the association.

A lot of scientists were upset, and rather a few were indignant, at the prospects of having as their president a man who had headed the AEC for ten years. A substantial body of younger scientists was particularly incensed about the matter, and some of them wondered how the association, with Dr. Seaborg as its president, could sit in judgment on the issue of nuclear power plant pollution when the AEC chairman was in the business of promoting the nuclear technology involved. Dr. Seaborg said he would not have been involved in any such conflict of interest at all.

"I would absent myself," he said.

When Dr. Seaborg, as president-elect, appeared in Chicago to address an AAAS session, a group of perhaps forty people, whom the press described as radical scientists, appeared with the apparent intent of interrupting or confronting the AEC chairman. Dr. Seaborg left without making his speech, which had been released earlier to newsmen. The militants said they were members of a loosely organized group called Scientists and Engineers for Social and Political Action. In the prepared speech that Dr. Seaborg did not make, he said:

> I think we must realize that science is suffering today from a kind of dislocation and disunity brought on by its own success. That is, it has fostered changes in our society faster and with far more impact than our social and political institutions can absorb and manage them.

He thought scientists would have to be "more aggressive in bringing the issues, deliberations, and thinking of science to the public." He did not dwell at all on the allegations and censure against the science Establishment that Stewart Udall had cataloged rather explicitly.

As the leading American proponent of nuclear power reactors, Dr. Seaborg could be convincing. He was absolutely confident that reactors and their contribution to electric power offered salvation and redemption to the industrial world and felt that "emotional outcries" on the thermal pollution theme were nonsense. He liked to mention a joke that illustrated to those overly exercised about nuclear power plants that before the internal combustion engine, the horse had caused a little pollution, too.

There was nothing whatsoever to fear from radiation in a nuclear power plant, Dr. Seaborg declared without equivocation. Danger from accident was not significant, with so many safeguards and independent, sequential protective devices that apprehension was virtually without justification. Besides, people were needlessly apprehensive about radiation anyway, since it "is in the air we breathe, the food we eat, the water we drink, and the ground we walk upon. Indeed, the tissue of our bodies contains radioisotopes which decay with the production of radiation."

Natural radiation comes from cosmic rays, nuclear particles of high energy that strike the earth from outer space. The atmosphere acts as a barrier against them. "The natural radiation you would receive at sea level is about half of what you would receive in the mile-high city of Denver."

On the issue of disposal of radioactive wastes, Dr. Seaborg's confidence was unwavering. Each hundred gallons of high-radioactivity contaminated wastes could be reduced to a cubic foot of solids, thence transferred to a "federal repository" (abandoned salt mines in Kansas, probably) for isolation from man's environment for thousands of years. Nothing to worry about in a salt mine; it was deep, dry, out of the way, and would never "mix" with anything leaching into the life chain. "It is estimated," said Dr. Seaborg, "that the volume of solidified radioactive waste requiring disposal through the year 2000 would occupy less than a fraction of one percent of the salt mine reserves."

Finally, "thermal effects," which was the phrase he preferred to "thermal pollution," are equally insignificant; or, anyway, they can be "good, bad, *or* insignificant, depending on the specific site and the measures taken in the design of the plant. The addition of the heated water from the plant does raise the temperature somewhat."

In any case:

> With respect to the regulation of the thermal effects of cooling water discharges, we do not at present have legal authority in this area. We have cooperated with the Department of the Interior and *sent copies of applications* [emphasis added] to build nuclear plants to the Department for comment. We transmit these comments to the applicant and urge him to cooperate.

The Atomic Energy Commission not only lacked authority in the area of thermal standards but irritated conservationists and some state authorities by its disinclination to seek jurisdiction on the question. As much as any other issue, if precise standards had been spelled out early, the thermal effects of nuclear plants might have militated against the promotion of reactors in the utilities industry. The result was that until the stormy outbreak of interest in environmental matters caught the fancy of editors, publicists, and television producers at the end of the 1960s, nothing definitive about heating public waterways got into the law at all. The Atomic Energy Commission made no notable efforts to bring the problem within the range of its own authority, as it had every obligation, if not much interest, to do.

Dr. Seaborg, scientist, over the years became, his critics said, a federal bureaucrat in an insular world, defensive over his domain, a committed adversary in the development of multipurpose atomic power.

As a codiscoverer of plutonium, which he once called "an ornery element," it was suggested that he had a conflict of interest, if not a vested interest, in its extended usage. As the dominant personage administering nuclear energy, he was one of the insiders, impatient with questioning and protective about nuclear programs. He was deeply and significantly involved in the beginning, when bombs and armaments were devised; and for ten years, he was one of the leading figures in the Western world trying to make plutonium commonplace as a fuel in the electric utility business and in other levels of industry and experimental research where he and fellow experts thought it might be applicable. He departed from Washington at the end of the summer of 1971 to go back to research and teaching at the University of California at Berkeley.

In the months prior to his departure, Dr. Seaborg presided over the most highly controversial and internationally protested AEC explosion ever to take place: the $200-million, five-megaton Cannikin project at Amchitka Island in the Aleutians. Concurrently with preparations to set off the explosion 6,000 feet beneath the island's surface, the AEC, quite astonishing some of its more audible critics, announced new safety standards for all power reactors and radiation limitations that would reduce emissions to 1 percent of what was previously allowable.

Two weeks later, on June 19, eight nuclear plants in seven states were ordered by the AEC to make safety improvements to reduce risk of accidents to cooling systems. Five plants were directed to modernize their cooling systems, and three were told to lower their peak operating temperatures. Those ordered to get their temperatures down could probably comply while remaining in operation, the AEC reported; but the five compelled to upgrade their cooling systems would have to shut down. One of the eight that would have to close down again was the luckless old fish killer on the Hudson River, Consolidated Edison's Indian Point Number 1, which was cited for both the high temperatures and the coolant design problems. The other four that would have to suspend operations were Commonwealth Edison's Dresden Number 1 plant at Morris, Illinois; the Yankee Atomic Electric Company's reactor at Rowe, Massachusetts, which had run up such a favorable record for uninterrupted power production; Consumers Power Company's Big Rock Point plant at Charlevoix, Michigan; and the California Edison plant next door to President Nixon's "western White House" at San Clemente, California.

In addition to the beleaguered Indian Point plant, the temperature-reduction order went out to Carolina Power and Light's nuke at Hartsville, South Carolina, and to the Turkey Point Plant of the Florida Power and Light Company near Miami.

The AEC had asserted time and time again that its standards for radioactive emissions were so exacting and so abundantly safe that fears to the contrary were irrational. In all the years of Dr. Seaborg's tenure, the commission took the position that thermal effects of power reactors were none of its concern and that its jurisdiction over radioactive safeguards was absolute. Several states (Minnesota and Maryland, for example) did not feel that the AEC limitations on radioactive output were sufficiently strict and passed laws more restrictive than AEC regulations. The commission objected to these state "intrusions" into the AEC domain, but the state legislatures in effect said they could intrude anyway and the commission be damned. Any broadening of AEC powers over thermal pollution or even a more responsive attitude by the agency to the issue surely would have served the public interest. But the AEC seemed to feel that it would probably inhibit the promotion of reactors.

Conservationist organizations started court suits to compel the AEC to concern itself with thermal pollution safeguards, especially in the hundred or so nukes under construction or in the design and planning stage by 1971.

The AEC argued that although no law compelled it to bother with thermal matters, it had in fact become concerned about them. Commissioner James T. Ramey complained in a letter to the *New York Times,* following a knuckle-rapping editorial citing AEC lethargy over the hotwater question, that the agency was being unfairly criticized. "For many years," he wrote, the AEC "followed the practice of requesting comments from appropriate federal agencies on the environmental and safety aspects of proposed nuclear power plants." Furthermore, the "requested" comments were passed along to applicants for nuclear power plants who were then "urged" to comply with any good ideas they contained. After all those years of collecting comments and sending them to the electric utilities, how could anyone believe that the AEC had not taken a concerned, lively interest in protecting water resources? What, one wondered, was the commission expected to do? Stop licensing nuclear plants just because some zealots were forever hollering about thermal pollution?

In a paragraph-long sentence conceived in a mating between bureaucracy and injured innocence, Mr. Ramey said AEC watchdogging procedures in the future would become even better than they had been in all those years of comment collecting:

The AEC now does have authority and responsibility under the Water Quality Improvement Act [the Muskie act] with respect to non-radiological matters affecting water quality, such as thermal effects, to require the licensee of a nuclear power plant to provide a certification by the appropriate state or Federal agency that there is reasonable assurance he will comply with applicable water standards.

In addition to the "reasonable assurance" thus expected from electric utilities, the AEC had budgeted $3.2 million in 1971 for research projects dealing with the whole question of "thermal effects." The research program would "provide the basis for sound technological decisions on what additional steps may be required to protect the quality of our waters."

A little independent research initiated into the question ten, fifteen, or twenty years ago, some pittance of the annual budget of $2 to $3 billion, might have made the AEC defense of itself less lame and might perhaps have provided "a basis for sound technological decisions" on water-protection policy before a hundred nukes swallowed water up and dumped it, heated and mildly irradiated, back into the rivers and lakes.

Thus, when astonishingly restrictive new radiation, thermal, and safety rules were announced late in 1971, it amounted to a contravention of prolonged previous policy and a clear response, in spite of Atomic Energy Commission denials, to the growing political power of the environmental movement. Under the new rules, anybody living in the neighborhood of a nuke would receive no more than one one-hundredth of the 500 milliroentgens of "man-made radiation" allowable previously. In actual practice, all but two or three of the twenty-three nukes producing electric power in the United States were already operating within the new guidelines, according to the commission's chief licensing administrator, Harold Price.

In addition to its imposition of explicit limitations on radioactive emissions, the commission yielded without protest—to the dismay of the whole nuclear power industry—to a landmark Federal Court of Appeals decision handed down in Washington by Judge J. Skelly Wright in the Maryland Calvert Cliffs nuclear plant case. The federal court declared that the question of thermal pollution and other nonradiological hazards, which the AEC had concluded were outside its jurisdiction, had to be settled before the commission could grant construction and operating permits. Thus, the AEC was juridically dragged into a regulatory arena it had cautiously sought to escape.

Since Dr. Ralph Lapp and others had posed some questions about reactor coolant systems and a goodly number of scientists had repeatedly charged the AEC with being altogether too casual and uncaring about long-range genetic effects of radioactivity, it was possible to conclude that the commission had suddenly become more responsive to complaints and criticism. But, according to Harold Price, such was not the case; he said that the new proposals and standards resulted from safety tests on a scale-model reactor and other studies. Long before certain AEC scientists themselves had gone before the public to charge the agency with arrogant disregard of public concerns, the commission had been exploring the possibilities for introducing tighter rules. Yet, anyone reading the AEC public relations output over the preceding years could only conclude that few possibilities for improvements were attainable or called for. The AEC was in the peculiar position of declaring that criticism of its standards was the work of uninformed or emotional critics while concurrently seeking to correct deficiencies it insisted did not exist.

With the appointments of Dr. James R. Schlesinger as chairman and of one other commissioner, William D. Doub, the AEC announced plans for a major reorganization. Mr. Doub, who filled the AEC vacancy left by the death of Theos J. Thompson, had been in the business of regulating public utilities. When Spiro Agnew was governor of Maryland, he appointed Mr. Doub, who had been defeated in a state election for public office, to serve as people's counsel before the Maryland Public Service Commission. In June, 1971, he was appointed chairman of the agency.

Besides these two new men, AEC commissioners included Wilfred E. Johnson, who moved over from perhaps the nation's leading nuclear power corporation, General Electric; Clarence E. Larson, formerly with Union Carbide, operator of the Oak Ridge facilities and beneficiary of $317 million in AEC contracts in 1969; and James T. Ramey, who had been employed for some years as staff director of the Joint Committee on Atomic Energy. Mr. Ramey was not very happy about a reorganization of the AEC that, it was asserted in public relations speeches, was going to shift its emphasis from promoting nuclear energy to protecting the public interest in nuclear affairs. Dr. Schlesinger addressed the Atomic Industrial Forum and the American Nuclear Society in Bal Harbour, Florida, seventeen days before the Cannikin explosion. He reminded the assembly of nuclear engineers and corporation managers that, thereafter, things were going to be substantially different around the AEC: "You should not expect the AEC to fight the industry's political, social and commercial battles. The AEC exists to serve the public interest. . . . From its inception, the AEC has fostered and protected the nuclear industry."

Dr. Schlesinger did not feel that the Calvert Cliffs decision, which might delay the opening of more than a hundred atomic power plants, at heavy cost to the power industry, should be appealed. He acknowledged that many people interpreted this as an abandonment by the AEC of the nuclear industry.

By issuing regulations and tightening standards to conform to the court of appeals ruling, the AEC could not deny, nor did Dr. Schlesinger deny, the presumption that it had been wrong about significant questions in the past. In promising to de-emphasize promotion of nuclear power in favor of protecting the public interest, it acknowledged the validity of a good deal of criticism of the agency.

However, with three commissioners of the old AEC still on hand and with a whole AEC bureaucracy steeped in a generation of secrecy, some skepticism about the degree of reform seemed reasonable.

The joint committee, for one thing, has been a separate power in itself in Congress. It stalled all proposals to sell the government's three gaseous-diffusion installations at Paducah, Portsmouth, and Oak Ridge. Any move to diminish AEC authority confronted a tremendous bloc of power that for many years relentlessly pursued and defended a single technology. The intent of the law to put nuclear power in civilian, not military, hands had never been properly implemented. Nuclear power remained in possession of too many inside people concerned with arms development and the profit to be gained from fueling electric power plants.

Alaska's Senator Gravel and others had proposed a moratorium on nuclear power plant construction at the end of the 1960s to allow time to study pollution and environmental issues. The proposal died in the informal discussion stage. The impression which remained around the AEC was that people fearful of nuclear power were paranoid, ignorant of the facts, and holding up development of a technology essential to national and all human development. Congressman Chet Holifield, who thought nuclear opponents were "kooks" with axes to grind, had little patience with them. Nuclear energy was, he said, "this great new good for mankind." At the other end of the dialogue scale, however, the feeling persisted that Union Carbide, General Electric, Westinghouse, United Nuclear, Combustion Engineering, and a host of corporations associated with the Atomic Industrial Forum were not necessarily in possession of all the purity and idealism so readily identified by Congressman Holifield.

In defense of Glenn Seaborg and the AEC policies that prevailed for so long, it was quite true that the scientist's confidence in extending nuclear energy to the burgeoning electric power industry was shared by people associated with it in other countries. In fact, nuclear energy enthusiasts were a confident, often impatient, breed in any country. Dr. John Dunste, of the United Kingdom Atomic Energy Authority, which had twenty-five nuclear plants in prospect, said at a United Nations symposium in August, 1970, that he welcomed public concern about environmental matters. "I'm personally glad that the public is so interested. . . . I hope this means more money and more enthusiasm to be more heavily taxed to pay to protect the environment."

At the same symposium, Dr. Chauncey Starr, dean of the School of Engineering and Applied Science at the University of California at Los Angeles, said he thought the trade-offs between risks and rewards in nuclear energy simply unnerved people. "It is commonly accepted," he said, "that everyone should have the opportunity for a natural death."

Dr. Starr sought a means of presenting the risks in acceptable terms. Since, he said, the risks that Americans seemed ordinarily willing to take in sports and transportation were about statistically equal to the death rate caused by disease, perhaps that degree of risk might become a yardstick for measuring other risks. Thus, if atomic power, contraceptive pills, and so on were within the yardstick measurement, let the risk be taken.

Concerning the risk of nuclear thermal pollution, the United Nations session heard perhaps the most comprehensive and carefully precise study of its kind reviewed by Prof. Daniel Merriman, of Yale University, who had directed it. A summary of the study was published in the May, 1970, issue of *Scientific American*, and it pretty well established that a nuclear power plant on the Connecticut River had in several years caused neither ecological damage nor harmed fish or other river organisms. Another study was to be undertaken at the huge Browns River Ferry nuclear plant in Alabama by the Tennessee Valley Authority when that 3.5-million-kilowatt monster went into operation.

The Merriman study included careful monitoring of the Connecticut River both upstream and downstream from the 562,000-kilowatt nuclear plant at Haddam Neck, fifteen miles from the eastern end of Long Island Sound, into which the 400-mile river flows. The steam condensers of the plant are cooled by the water, which is discharged at 20 to 23 degrees higher in temperature than at intake. The volume of intake and discharge is about 372,000 gallons per minute. Although the study is to continue through 1972, after five years results can be appraised.

Because the river is an estuary with tidal effects and salinity measured for forty-five miles north of the sound, the study has some bearing on what might be expected from reactors similarly situated. Moreover, thermal effects on the fishing industry were an urgent consideration in the Haddam Neck study because the migrant shad alone in Connecticut had an annual capitalized value of $7.5 million, with sport fishing providing an additional value of $14 million.

Water entering the plant is discharged, not directly into the river, but into a canal built for that purpose, which runs for a mile parallel to the river, allowing the effluent to cool 2 degrees or so before it rejoins the channel. The river flow itself ranges from a low of 968 to a high of 282,000 feet per second, a mighty variable indeed, and the factor that affects life in the river a good deal more than any other. Normal water temperature will sometimes range from 86 degrees in the summer heat to freezing in winter. The river at Haddam Neck is 2,000 feet wide, with a depth of 30 feet at low tide. The difference between low and high tide is 2½ feet.

Dr. Merriman wrote:

The calefaction [heating] of U.S. rivers, lakes and coasts is certain to increase as the power industry meets the rising national
demand for electricity. The average daily runoff of water in the
continental U.S. (excluding Alaska) is about 1.2 trillion gallons.
We use perhaps ten percent, or 120 billion gallons, for cooling the
condensers of steam turbine power plants. These plants, whether
fired with fossil fuels or nuclear fuels, are rapidly growing in number. It is possible to forecast a daily requirement of more than 200
billion gallons of cooling water by 1980 and of 600 billion gallons,
or fifty percent of all the available water, by the year 2000. If calefaction is ecologically harmful, quite a lot of harm lies just over
the horizon.

A hearing had been called in July, 1964, by the Water Resources
Commission, at which the possible effects of the plant on the river were
discussed. Dr. Merriman began to get telephone calls from anguished
citizens.

No amount of reassurance I could offer them on the improbability
of radioactive pollution of the environment lessened their concern
about a neighboring atomic plant. Not until the second hearing in
September did attention become focused more appropriately on
the effect on the ecology of the river. . . . Thereafter the fear of
radioactive pollution began to abate.

The Water Resources Commission approved use of the water for cooling on a number of conditions, one of them being a thorough environmental study before, during, and after the plant's operations. The
Connecticut Yankee Atomic Power Company had to pay for the study,
which required a staff of ten to fifteen people. From the beginning, Dr.
Merriman and the staff were counseled by an advisory committee of five,
representing several scientific disciplines. The cost of the work up to 1970
was $750,000, with another two years to run.

When the warmed water leaves the discharge canal near the surface,
it moves, depending on tides, either upstream or down. On the flood
tide, the plume of warm water becomes indistinguishable from the main
flow two miles upstream. On the ebb, the warm plume dissipates to
intake temperature three miles downstream. The shape of the plume and
the depth of it vary widely in response to velocity of flow, weather conditions, and season. Sometimes the warm water reaches the west bank
beyond the canal outlet, 2,000 feet away. Yet no thermal block has ever
been reported, meaning that the effluent never extended to the bottom
of the river, 15 to 30 feet below the surface.

For thirty months before the plant started up in October, 1967, and in the subsequent years, the river was under continuing scrutiny. Five monitoring stations—two of them located far out of range in order to serve as controls—measured rate of flow, temperature at various levels, salinity, oxygen content, and the like. The Essex Marine Laboratory installed and designed the monitoring stations.

In order to study the microbiology, larvae, and river-bottom organisms, seventeen stations were spaced four miles below and four miles above the warmwater discharge point. Samples of bottom water and silt were taken at fortnightly intervals for two years before and after plant start-up. It was found that near the intake area bottom life decreased substantially but that it increased from natural causes elsewhere. Sand and silt on the bottom were washed away by the intake velocity, leaving gravel exposed. Near the discharge canal, the bottom conformation and volume of life improved to become better suitable for a diversity of newcomer worms and larvae, on which some fish feed. Other analyses of fish and fauna covered portions of the river from the sound to Northampton, Massachusetts, ninety miles north. A total of 364 separate collections, made with seines and trawls at three depth zones, turned up thirty-six species of fish, both resident and migrant.

The fish catch generally showed little difference in the preceding and subsequent years of the plant's operations. Downstream from the discharge area, the catch showed an increase in 1969, without apparently disturbing the stability of the fish population. Six thousand fish were tagged to compute data on size, growth, and mobility. It was estimated that between 12,000 and 21,000 brown catfish and up to 7,000 white catfish made their way into the warm canal in freezing weather, apparently in search of relief from the New England winter. They paid for their preference, however, for the warm water speeded up their metabolism and the swift outflow of canal water made them swim harder to stay in it, leaving them in a somewhat run-down condition as compared with upstream brothers who did not reach the winter vacation spot.

In midsummer, a lot of fish were killed. "Midsummer kills are not uncommon in the lower reaches of the Connecticut," Dr. Merriman said. "We have observed three since the beginning of our investigations, all before the Haddam Neck plant went into operation." Kills of 100,000 and 50,000 had been measured, largely glut herring and alewives. "The kills were apparently the result neither of toxic effluents nor of a parasitic infestation," Dr. Merriman concluded. "Their most probable cause appears to be the combination of low river flow, water temperatures in excess of 80 degrees, a depleted supply of dissolved oxygen, and, in the case of summer-spawning glut herring, the stress associated with spawning activity." As for the highly favored and valuable shad, "it appears that the effluent from the plant has no significant retarding effect on its upstream progress. . . . They either pass through or under the plume without apparent difficulty or significant hesitation."

Dr. Merriman would make no concrete judgments pending completion of the studies, seven years after they began. Subtle and long-term ecological effects were not predictable. He was sorry about the exhaustion of the catfish in the canal but did not feel it was calamitous: "In the long run, the calefaction may even prove to be beneficial one way or another." He was alluding to the possibility of fish farming, using heated water without the fast flow. "It is nevertheless possible to report that the operation of the Haddam Neck power plant and the consequent calefaction of the Connecticut River in the vicinity of the plant has had no significant deleterious effect on the biology of the river."

What did the study prove? Simply that one isolated nuclear plant on one wide, reasonably swift river apparently did little thermal harm. It did not prove that a plant in the shallow bays of semitropical Florida, with an ever-present threat of algae growth, is admissible. Nor did it mean that the data are transferable to Lake Michigan, or to Chesapeake Bay, the locale of millions of shallow-water crabs, shellfish, and incomparable varieties of oysters and edible fish. The ecological stability in each area differs. And where a single isolated nuclear plant might produce only an infinitesimal imbalance, a cluster of plants might geometrically alter matters.

"Strong minded people on both sides of such problems," said Dr. Merriman, "must bend enough to arrive at the optimum balance of interests." He had also said, it must be remembered, that *if artificially heated water is ecologically injurious,* "a lot of harm lies just over the horizon." Ecology might differ, but power plants have a sameness.

Six power plants, including a second nuclear reactor, exist on the 400-mile Connecticut River, which rises in northern New England, divides New Hampshire and Vermont, moves south through Massachusetts and Connecticut, and into Long Island Sound. It is altogether likely, as in the case of the Hudson, the Ohio, the Mississippi, the Missouri, the murdered Lake Erie, the ailing and threatened Lake Michigan, that the few nuclear plants thus far have caused less danger to life and ecology than the industrial system that feeds off them. Yet, an accumulation of nuclear plants, added to the system, will almost certainly compound the problem dangerously. The villain, as the students are saying, is the system itself.

Two scientists at the Lawrence Radiation Laboratory at Livermore, California, men working in the AEC's own biochemical research program, presented perhaps the most unnerving indictment of the conduct and concepts that deal with the heart of the environmental issue. Along with Ernest J. Sternglass, professor of radiation physics at the University of Pittsburgh, they addressed themselves to nuclear technology in a manner more forceful and persuasive than had occurred in the past. The communications of Dr. John Gofman and Dr. Arthur Tamplin bear heavily on nuclear energy development and, by extension, on its diversion to the electric utilities.

John Gofman was a physicist at Lawrence Radiation Laboratory and attached to the division of medical physics at the University of California at Berkeley. Arthur Tamplin was a biophysicist at Lawrence. In a joint paper presented at the University of Minnesota in Duluth on April 22, 1970, as part of the Earth Day program, they struck out at the AEC in some of the harshest language ever used against the agency. It was directly related to any evaluation of nuclear power in national life. The following is a truncated account of their testimony before the Senate Public Works subcommittee and their Earth Day report:

First, they said, a good part of the thinking population recognized the environmental-ecologic fanfare of Earth Day as a first-class cop-out, a diversion of outrage from injustices of racism, poverty, and the idiocy of the Vietnamese war. Much of it was lip service to something called an "environmental crisis" by politicians and others who wanted the heat taken off the issue of the irrational sense of priorities and values.

Yet, as far as nuclear power was concerned, the environment issue was not a diversion but a manifestation of retribution in a society beset by instant greed. Hucksterism had created products and a diversion of energies unrelated to human needs and goals. Any optimism that the nation could survive was scarcely justified. The environment was raped by the "ultimate pollution" of the atomic era. Any intent of Congress to divert nuclear energy to peaceful uses had become a "fiasco of mammoth proportion."

The same cast of characters responsible for military application of nuclear power took over its "peaceful" development. People shuttled daily between developing nuclear explosives and testing them and protecting the health and welfare of the public. Military aspects of such work provided a "wondrous cloak or cover for any stupidity, rashness, and lack of concern." Criticism was silenced on the grounds of security. The stage was set for the creation of a superagency of government, which the AEC became. It promoted a technology capable of irradiating all living things, primarily in the civilian sector by promoting electric power. Electric usage of nuclear energy releases radiation slowly; the nuclear bomb does it rapidly.

However, it was reasoned by people with a vested interest in the matter, the rivers, the air, the oceans, and the land itself were all vast and by the "magic of dilution," the consequences of pollution could be escaped. Shipment of radioactive by-products rose steadily, and some of them got lost in transit, which was "a minor nuisance." However, benefits exceeded risks. Yet, the law was explicit: Public safety *was* to be protected. But under the circumstances, how? By studying the problem, minimizing it, and developing the concept of the "tolerance" dose of radioactivity. To do this, keep working downward from the lethal dosage, announcing with each reduction that concern for public health motivated it, meanwhile promoting increased usage of nuclear materials.

When the population has been exposed, cancer, leukemia, fetal deaths, and genetic deformities can come as a surprise, since so much care was exercised through dosage reduction. True, the nation had not reached the irreversible disaster point, no thanks to the AEC; but it was inevitable under such mentality. All radioactivity produced its "share" of death, a thesis for which Linus Pauling, for example, had been reviled and considered unpatriotic. The trick was to impugn the motives of a person like Dr. Pauling and call him a dupe of the Communists, which is what happened. Simultaneously, spread money around among scientists who could be counted upon to say that hazards did not exist or that they were being studied and guarded against. A great deal of excellent, important work was accomplished by the AEC, as everybody knew; but the thrust was always the same: Most scientists, especially if they were supported by nuclear technology, were silent about dangers, since the technology and the support money might slow down if they spoke out.

If everybody in the country received the tolerance dosage, the number of cancer and leukemia cases would increase 10 percent, adding 32,000 *extra* deaths to the annual total.

Therefore, the concept of the tolerance dose must be outlawed. If the promoters of nuclear power believe any tolerance dose is safe, let them "prove conclusively" what it is. It is *their* poison. Abolish the dual role of promoter and protector in one agency, the AEC. Institute a new principle: that pollution is a privilege to be negotiated with its victims and that polluters must prove their case in favor of it, rather than objectors being required to produce corpses to prove theirs. Let the polluter prove the benefits in terms of lives saved or improved. Then, let the public through referendum make some decisions. If the public is to be wiped out, let the people be informed of all the values and all the consequences and then vote on it.

Senator Mike Gravel, reviewing the ominous conclusions of Gofman and Tamplin, told an assembly at the University of Wisconsin that he was personally exercised by something said to him by a former head of the American Electric Power Company, whom he did not identify but who probably was Philip Sporn. Mr. Gravel quoted his informant as saying: "We're going to have some accidents with atomic plants. We don't want to have any. But we're going to."

Those apprehensions were an echo of David Lilienthal, the first chairman of the AEC and former chairman of TVA, who said in 1968: "Once a bright hope shared by all mankind, including myself, the rash proliferation of atomic power plants has become one of the ugliest clouds over America."

The AEC said that Gofman and Tamplin were wrong in their thesis that nuclear proliferation was killing people and would continue to do so on an accelerating scale. As for Dr. Sternglass, who directed a study that found nuclear radiation killing children and producing birth defects attributable to AEC testing, he was said by an AEC official to be a "fraud."

In 1969, Ernest Sternglass had somewhat bitterly opposed the antiballistic nuclear warhead program so beloved by the Pentagon, President Nixon, Secretary of Defense Laird, Vice-President Spiro Agnew, and the Cannikin crowd, who emphasized a kind of *machismo* egotism in arms policy. It was true that Dr. Sternglass allowed himself to relate the findings of a study covering some years to a politically charged controversy over ABM appropriations. But he was not a charlatan; he was an impassioned scientist who deduced that he was onto data on the death of infants caused by atom bomb testing. "The unanticipated genetic effect of strontium 90," he wrote in *Esquire* magazine in September, 1969, "has become evident from an increase in the incidence of infant mortality along the path of the fallout cloud from the first atomic test in New Mexico in 1945."

Computer calculations showed "one excess death in the U.S. per one hundred live births, due to the release of only 200 megatons of fission energy by 1963." From this, Dr. Sternglass concluded that the release of 20,000 megatons anywhere in the world (the figure needed for a first-strike offensive by nuclear warheads or for ABM defenses against them) "could lead to essentially no infants surviving to produce another generation."

The infant death pattern disclosed itself directly along the path of wind-driven fallout, Dr. Sternglass said, and was absent elsewhere. Since about 4 million births a year were occurring in the period of the fifties and early sixties covered by the study, close to 40,000 infants under the age of one year died in excess of normal expectations, he said. The figure settled to 34,000 the year after a treaty outlawed atmospheric testing in 1963.

Subsequent to the Gofman and Tamplin Senate testimony, according to Mr. Gravel, the five AEC commissioners met to review once again the

question of lowering the permissible levels of reactor pollution. On a vote
of 3 to 2, the proposal was defeated. Yet within sixteen months after that
vote, the AEC reduced radioactive emissions by 99 percent in all nuclear
reactors. Somebody, perhaps the whole protestant movement against the
AEC, pierced its bureaucracy and compelled a review that brought new
rules for operating nukes.

Mary Weik, a resident of Manhattan's Greenwich Village, and secretary of a citizens' action group called the Committee to End Radiological
Hazards, which fought all forms of nuclear reactor expansion, found her
contemporary equivalent of Moses and the burning bush in an experience
that turned her into a crusader against nuclear power. It was the story
of the New Jersey boys who discovered in 1964 a pond occupied by
mutant frogs. Two boys in Nutley, a community across New York's
Hudson River, thought they might pick up some summer money catching
the frogs and serving the limited market for *cuisses de grenouilles* in the
area of Paterson and Passaic. In one pond that harbored their aquatic
treasure, they began to find frogs with four, five, six, seven, and even
eight legs. Instead of slaughtering them for the meat they provided, they
found they could sell the whole frogs to pet shops and museums.

The incident raised certain questions for Mrs. Weik. For example,
how did the frogs get that way? It seemed that nearby industries had
claimed the pond as a dump for "unhealthy wastes." Charles M. Bogert,
curator of reptiles for the New York Museum of Natural History, told
the *New York Times* that the mutations evolved from the ingestion by the
frogs of "local deposits in the pond."

Mrs. Weik, who had been brooding about the genetic effects of
radioactive elements, was motivated to look into the phenomenon and
discovered that nuclear wastes were the probable cause of the development on the frogs of more legs than they needed. She wondered what the
presence of unhealthy wastes might do to people. She began to undertake
some research on the question, and her studies and privately published
documents thereafter produced a fairly constant stream of low-yield
radiation of their own. Mrs. Weik's organization marshaled public support opposing nuclear plants and even experimental reactors in university
laboratories around metropolitan New York and amassed substantial
material on radioactive hazards said to prevail around virtually every
federal and industrial fission operation. When, in the late sixties, a movement to erect a huge nuclear plant on Welfare Island, which lies in the
East River directly athwart Manhattan and Queens, was publicized, her
committee belabored the project as an exercise in idiocy. On the day that
word of the Welfare Island proposal appeared in the press, a long and
persuasive "think" piece was published. It had been generated by Rockefeller interests, who warmly favored the plan without dwelling on any

commercial associations they had in the nuclear industry. Nothing ever came of the project, nor did further planted press stories favoring it appear.

The state of New York, nevertheless, under the guidance of Governor Nelson Rockefeller, set up an $8-billion subsidized nuclear power program with New York utilities as its beneficiaries. A state agency, legislatively exempted from regulation, and with power to issue tax-exempt bonds, set about looking for sites. In 1963, the first privately owned atomic-fuel-processing plant was built at West Valley in the Buffalo area, which in due course began to feed radioactive materials from spent fuels into the environment. By monitoring state and federal reports that were available, usually unpublished, Mrs. Weik disclosed beta pollution at Springdale Dam, near the West Valley plant, in the amount of 42,340 picocuries per liter (pcl). This was 6,000 pcl higher than the United States Public Health Service permissible limits.

In February, 1968, a Rochester University scientist and a small cell of citizens, members of an action committee, made a foray in the nature of mild espionage. They crawled beneath a surrounding fence near the processing plant's outflow and swiped a sample of water from Buttermilk Creek, which they then smuggled to the AEC's Health and Safety Laboratory in New York City for analysis. The sample was found to contain 3,000,000 picocuries per liter of strontium 90, or 30,000 times more than the hundred pcl allowable.

A report of the test was made public, one scientist later appearing before a power plant protest meeting in White Plains, New York, to give an amusing account of the citizens' raid, followed by a chilling summary of the test. The AEC laboratory that had examined the unmarked water sample issued a press release asserting that the employee who determined the pcl count "figured wrong." One of the commandos observed that when the unidentified technician learned how to figure correctly, his prospects for a career in the AEC might improve.

Mrs. Weik's committee was held in rather low regard in official circles. Their mimeographed pamphlets were forever questioning and criticizing the "big four" corporations under contract to the AEC: the Du Pont Corporation, which ran the Savannah River plant on a 300-square-mile reservation in the South Carolina country of the late Congressman Mendel Rivers, chairman of the House Armed Services Committee; Union Carbide, operator of Oak Ridge; Bell Telephone (and its Western Electric subsidiary); and General Electric. The publications were particularly critical of solid-waste hazards around the Savannah plant, where Polaris missile submarines went to have their cores and armaments refueled.

In the spring of 1971, when, after years of planning and effort, Columbia University was denied permission to install a research reactor in a shielded building on its Manhattan campus, one of those credited with marshaling the opposition to the project was Mary Hays Weik.

Nowhere in the United States has opposition to nukes been more effective than in California, where individual efforts on the order of Mrs. Weik's resulted in a cause célèbre. Public interest in the state's 1,100 miles of coastline intensified to the level of a crusade after the Santa Barbara oil disaster, after two Standard Oil tankers collided and dumped oil into San Francisco Bay, and after the Los Angeles earthquake in February, 1971.

Two bills were before the legislature for coastline protection, including a new state authority with power to restrict oil drilling, land development, and any kind of power plants, nuclear or otherwise. The AEC responded to the uproar by asking two utilities, Southern California Edison and the San Diego Gas and Electric Company, to document exactly what would happen if a strong earthquake occurred at their San Onofre nuke, next door to President Nixon's preserve at San Clemente, and a mile from the Christianitos earthquake fault. A geological engineer, Philip J. West, employed by the companies, which hoped to establish other nuclear units at San Onofre, said nothing much would happen at all, and that the fault was not capable of any "significant" surface movement.

Whether Mr. West's deductions were accurate or not, he was not widely believed because of the power companies' loss of credibility and because other geologists, working with protesting organizations, challenged him. The state's Public Utilities Commission clearly resented public intervention in its affairs. The president of the commission, V. K. Vukasin, retorted that many of the protests were "irresponsible, insincere, and anti-Establishment." Another commission member, Walter J. Cavagnaro, denounced the prospects of any curtailment of nuclear plant construction. It would result, he said, in a serious power shortage in California.

In the early 1960s, public outrage had forced the Pacific Gas and Electric Company to abandon plans for erecting a big nuke at Bodega Bay, north of San Francisco. Subsequently, another proposed plant at Malibu was stopped. Only two plants were operating in the nation's most populous state in 1972 (the one at San Onofre and another at Humboldt Bay), but a third was under construction and the utilities had plans more or less in motion for half a dozen others.

California organizations have demanded that nuclear plants be subject to state and local referendum. They had been impressed with a referendum in Eugene, Oregon, in 1970 when voters canceled a nuclear plant there and forced adoption of a four-year moratorium to allow further study of nuclear hazards.

Elsewhere, in fact almost everywhere in the land, the situation was remarkably similar. Lee C. White, former chairman of the Federal Power Commission, observed that the dialogue between the environmentalists and the utilities, which for seventy years or more have been able to do pretty much what they pleased, had shifted. It was no longer a case of the public asking a power company to move a proposed plant to another site, said Mr. White. The new dialogue demanded to know whether the construction of additional plants anywhere could be justified, whether, in fact, the nation's commitment to ever-increasing power supplies was itself defensible.

13

The Hazards of Power
and the
New Revolution

NOTHING IS as inexorable as the law of chance. Anything that can happen will happen sometime. The failure of a relay box in Ontario in November, 1965, is a case in point. The failure of an entire sequential fail-safe system at a nuclear reactor in Windscale, England, is another. An area of 160,000 acres (twelve times larger than Manhattan Island) has been inadvertently "contaminated" by radioactivity in the Nevada desert.

In the Christmas season of 1971, a Delta Air Lines jetliner, carrying a leaky cargo of radioactive isotopes, became an airborne equivalent of Typhoid Mary and spread toxicity to eight airports in five states before the mishap was discovered. The AEC said passengers and luggage from eight flights probably were not contaminated to the extent that a health hazard was involved. The leakage had occurred in one or two lead-lined containers dispatched by Union Carbide from New York to Houston.

A week later, at the Navy submarine base in New London, Connecticut, a nuclear-powered submarine "inadvertently discharged" 500 gallons of reactor coolant water into the Thames River. The accident occurred as the radioactive fluid was being transferred from an attack submarine to a tender. A Pentagon information officer said the radioactivity amounted to less than limits set by federal and international agencies. It was learned that "a few" such leakages had occurred previously at the base. A policy of secrecy prevented their disclosure to the public. Newspaper reporters just happened on the latest incident.

Accidents are, of course, sometimes unpreventable. In the world of fissionable materials, they have occurred across the scale from the inconsequential to the Fermi reactor on Lake Michigan and the destruction by fire of an AEC plutonium installation in Colorado. No one with an interest in staying alive is intentionally clumsy or reckless in the care and handling of fissionable fuels. Yet, lapses have occurred in safeguarding people and nature from the effects of radiation.

Increasing amounts of highly radioactive materials are being hauled around the world in airplanes, ships, trains, and trucks and are being stored in unlikely and, it is presumed, inaccessible places. After ninety years of commercially produced electricity and a quarter of a century of development in the nuclear energy business, the two have become combined in a tandem process for creating both power and deadly wastes on an inconceivable scale.

No one in a position to assess the matter believes that accidents and operation failures of enormous range and consequences have been entirely eliminated by watchdog computers and remorselessly perfect sensors. Nuclear administrators and utility managers rely on their technicians and scientists to prevent, at all costs, a major or maximum-predictable accident, knowing that failure at this level might jeopardize the whole heavily capitalized industry.

Even though nukes cannot really explode with the force of an atom bomb, they can explode at lesser levels of energy and release radioactivity under certain circumstances. A bomb requires the amassing of enriched fuel in a precise conjunction not possible in power plants and mathematically unlikely in any imagined similar situation. But they can be sabotaged, and they can discharge radioactive material. There are scientists who make it very clear that trained, armed guards should surround every locale that harbors fissionable material every hour of every day.

A leading and, in old atomic energy circles, respected advocate of the fastest-possible development of nuclear power in America is Dr. Alvin M. Weinberg, director of the Oak Ridge National Laboratory and winner of the in-group Atoms for Peace Award in 1960. Dr. Weinberg is an insistent and articulate proponent of power expansion as, possibly, the world's primary defense against the population explosion. For a scientist, his faith in certain subjective aspects of human nature is remarkable.

Conceding that there are extraordinary problems inherent in unrelieved power expansion, Dr. Weinberg nevertheless is at odds with scientists convinced that limitless power itself poses conditions too dangerous to tolerate. He has said:

> There is the spectre of catastrophic failure of a large power reactor, of its engineered safeguard systems, and of its containment

vessel. If such ever happened, it would be a catastrophe indeed. Surely the chance that such an event will happen is very small. Yet one cannot prove negative propositions of this sort.

The best prospect of a gigantic failure never happening at all, Dr. Weinberg feels, "is the stake the whole nuclear community has in avoiding it." All people associated with the industry—the Joint Committee on Atomic Energy, reactor manufacturers, utilities, engineers, scientists— "realize that their futures, their aspirations, in a sense their whole lives, depend on avoiding such an incident. This is the best practical reason I can offer for believing that such a catastrophe is unlikely."

Dr. Weinberg's exceptional faith in good intentions allows him to be somewhat scornful of criticism that suggests that power generation technology has a momentum and force all its own, that this force exists in relative isolation from the rest of society. He does not accept the argument that technologists sometimes simply are intent on fulfilling their own aspirations: "It is true that modern technology has certain inner imperatives to develop and proliferate, imperatives that stem from the sense of excitement and desire for achievements. . . . Critics consistently make an error that is a mirror image of the one they accuse the technologists of making." Critics, says Dr. Weinberg, are forever talking about dangers of technology and environmental damage; whereas the technologists have their eye on the benefits and the progress that society will reap. As Dr. Weinberg sees it, the critics and proponents of nuclear power are responsive to different probabilities. Some people see it one way, some another.

With the creation of plutonium in large volume in breeder reactors, the danger will become increasingly likely and increasingly lethal. When the day arrives on which fifty or sixty plutonium-producing plants are scattered about the land, the security control over material, a few pounds of which could produce utter havoc over a vast area, will exceed anything ever required to guard money, diamonds, narcotics, or state secrets. And any reasonably competent nuclear physicist, with a little assistance and a proper place to work, can put together a workable bomb with the destructive capacity to obliterate a metropolis. It was beyond probability, of course, in the early stages of technology, but it is becoming more possible and, therefore, more likely each year. Considering what a hijacker can do with a gun, a knife, or a few sticks of dynamite, the opportunities open to a dissident group with a satchel full of nuclear explosives is not hard to imagine. And power plants by the hundreds will be producing or stocking such material all over the world, all the time.

Over the years, and up to about 1970, official comments on the probability of theft of nuclear material and the likelihood of lethal danger from stored radioactive wastes were uniformly expressions of confidence. Questions raised in Congress and in public forums were answered in reassuring terms. There was simply no possibility of unauthorized persons acquiring, transporting, and concealing fissionable materials in the first place. And in the improbable event that enriched material could somehow be diverted from monitored stockpiles, the hardware and expertise, the machinery and technology required to convert it into a controlled bomb explosion made it likely that those who stole it would kill themselves in the process. Radioactivity might be momentarily harmful to innocent victims, but control factors superseded the probability of any runaway danger. After all, it took the United States government years of intense effort and the combined labor of thousands of scientists, not to mention $2 billion of public money, to explode the first experimental bomb at Trinity. No commune of hairy crooks could duplicate that.

But after some years, such spokesmen have begun to hedge a little, then concede that perfection in safeguarding nuclear materials has not been altogether developed, and that just possibly, under the proper manipulated conditions, certain low or criminal types might be able to trigger a nuclear bomb. And the best chance of such a dreadful event occurring comes with the nuclear power plants, the processing of enriched uranium, and the breeding of plutonium in the forthcoming generation of reactors.

Airliners have been captured in flight and diverted to destinations thousands of miles away. Speeding trains have been commandeered by bandits, and as much as $2 million has been carried off under the noses of armed but subdued or intimidated guards. Armored trucks transporting gems and cash can be highjacked, and a good many have been. Even safe-deposit vaults of banks and hotels can be invaded. The FBI and the CIA, supported by armed might and 10,000 loyal agents, cannot protect the persons or the secrets under their care in all instances. Who could develop the faith and the confidence that in a world full of power plants busily producing explosive and radioactive substances at tonnage levels some of it will not be on occasion diverted or stolen?

Theodore Taylor, a protégé of the Cornell University physicist Hans Bethe, has helped design bombs for the Atomic Energy Commission and, like Bethe, hopes that uranium and plutonium will, by virtue of their destructive capability, make peace preferable to war under all circumstances. As a scientist with a sensitive conscience, he thinks peaceful uses of atomic energy can redeem the world from poverty and despair. Dr. Taylor thus welcomes extension of nuclear energy to electric power, conditional upon balanced usage and the careful management of nuclear fuels. It is the latter problem that worried him.

"I am quite alarmed," he said,* "about how easy it is to make an atomic bomb. You could do it in your cellar. The materials are obtainable. You need only enough to form a critical mass and a way to contain it for a microsecond. And a way to shield yourself from it, of course."

Dr. Taylor, president of the International Research and Technology Corporation in Washington, appeared before the annual sessions of the American Association for the Advancement of Science in Philadelphia on December 27, 1971, to repeat his warning and express concern over safeguard procedures he thought altogether too casual. "Crude but highly destructive nuclear explosives" could be put together by any group determined to do so, if it obtained the necessary materials. Milton Shaw, AEC director of reactor development, as usual took a milder view of such a possibility. Although the threat of theft was perhaps a problem, nobody could go around stealing it like candy; it was "too hot" and too dangerous to prospective thieves.

Arthur Tamplin, the AEC engineer who, with John Gofman, had castigated the agency for alleged indifference to radioactive hazards, disputed Milton Shaw and declared that a nuclear-detonating device could be assembled with 5 kilograms of plutonium, some dynamite, "and a mad nuclear scientist." Adequate safeguards against theft and blackmail by fission bomb did not exist. Dr. Taylor had found "many situations . . . where quantities of fissionable materials sufficient for several nuclear explosions are not protected by armed guards, major physical barriers, or intrusion alarms." He advocated a protection system designed to incorporate reserve units of armed men at nuclear power plants and fuel-processing installations.

On occasion before he left the AEC, Glenn Seaborg had indicated that he thought fissionable-materials-control efforts are inadequate for the time when power plants will be turning out twenty-five tons of plutonium a year. Dr. Ralph Lapp has suggested that the loss of even 1 percent of MUF (the Atomic Energy Commission's acronym for "material unaccounted for") "will be enough to obliterate us all." Moreover, a good deal of motivation to obtain such material exists among terrorists, insurrectionists, small aggressive nations, countries interested in bargaining leverage with superpowers, and just plain opportunists. The latter can scarcely be expected to abjure developing a black market for a substance that has a value thirty times or more that of gold.

The stuff is in transit to and from processing plants on a round-the-clock basis, shipped overseas by air in open invitation to hijackers. Normally, it is not readily convertible to high-energy nuclear explosives,

---

* In a tape-recorded conversation with the author.

being insufficiently enriched; but plutonium is another matter entirely. A containment vessel with the masses separated beyond critical proximity, a timing device to bring them together at a given moment, an explosive charge to trigger it, and one has a bomb. Dr. Taylor has said that $270,000 worth of plutonium, a fraction of the amount transportable in a single truckload, including shielding and containers, would be enough to put together a device adequate to blackmail or terrorize a nation.

In 1969, at the University of Chicago, where Enrico Fermi and his associates brought the nuclear era to reality in 1942, Dr. Albert Wohlstetter said that "an essential trouble with nuclear plowshares . . . is that they can be beaten into nuclear swords. . . . Expanding civilian use in general makes it easier, quicker, and cheaper to get bombs."

One company, founded by a group of men who had worked with the AEC and who knew a civilian opportunity when they saw one, was heavily fined for "losing" 220 pounds of enriched uranium. This was enough to put together a half-dozen atomic bombs. The Nuclear Materials and Equipment Corporation (Numec) was assessed more than a million dollars for material that had "disappeared," some of it in a paper-work tally. An unestimated quantity, it was said, was simply dispersed through vents and tracked away on the shoes of workmen. In any case, it did not appear that safeguards had worked very well.

When a writer for *Esquire* magazine, Alan M. Adelson, happened to mention to an official of W. R. Grace & Co. at a cocktail party that he was somewhat concerned about unarmed trucks carrying plutonium across country, the man responded: "Who in the world would ever want that stuff? What would they ever do with it?"

Mr. Adelson, who reported the incident in an article in the magazine in May, 1969, thought of Nasser, Castro, and a number of others.

An unidentified official of another atomic industry had a different reaction to the shipments. "My God," he said, "if that stuff is really going unguarded like that, we're dead."

The penalty for disposing of fissionable material "with intent" to injure the United States or help a foreign power is death. But if the intent is only to make a killing in the marketing sense, like peddling contraband, the penalty is five years in prison, a sentence imposed at times for the simple act of possessing a joint of marijuana. The movement to increase the penalty for peddling plutonium and to modify the sentence for sharing a bit of pot would seem to be understandable. It is about time, it seems, that some distinction was made between blowing one's mind with a mild intoxicant and blowing up a city.

It is equally understandable that an electric utility board chairman,

already concerned about commandeering sites, thermal effects on waterways, control procedures for radioactive materials, and the like, welcomed the prospect of being retired from the power business by the time
his company has to deal with plutonium. He would be just too worried,
he said, about accidents of a possibly irreversible nature. Meanwhile, of
course, he felt obliged to do what was necessary to provide power, give
stockholders a return on their investment, and hope that a sane and
balanced federal policy would evolve that the industry could live with.

As for accidents, the certainty of their occurrence has been conceded.
More restrictive safeguard legislation is under study within the AEC and
the Congress, but privately, people in the nuclear sector of industry and
in the private utilities acknowledge the inevitability of the law of chance.
The safeguard factor may seek perfection, but it is not, in a changing
process, attainable. In a world of increasing danger from many sources,
however, the danger from nuclear operations may grow, in a relative
sense, proportionately less.

Dr. William D. Jackson, principal research scientist for the AVCO
Everett Research Laboratory and an authority on plasma phenomena
and magnetohydrodynamics (MHD),* has said that large-scale accidents
in nuclear-fueled power generation are "probably inevitable." Making
allowances for the fact that he had sought unsuccessfully for two years to
persuade the federal government to inaugurate research into forms of
power generation less volatile than nuclear energy, Dr. Jackson feels
that opposing industrial interests have forced compromises of a harrow-
ing nature. As a scientist, an employee of a large corporation, and a
humanitarian, he, like isolated industrialists in the electric utility industry, feels that the government for too long has been responsive to
pressures rather than to meritorious ideas. The good ideas and the
pressures do not always conflict, of course, but as a rule, they have. Thus,
the initiative for research into new and less toxic methods of generating
power, like research into new and less toxic forms of vehicular and mass
transportation, will be motivated less by their merit than by the political
and economic power of those forces demanding them. The nuclear industry cares little for MHD.

Said Dr. Jackson:

I could be fired for saying this, I suppose, and of course I
trust not, but one has a low level of confidence in many depart-

---

* Dr. Jackson and the author engaged in a full day of taped discussion at the
MacDowell Colony, Peterborough, New Hampshire, early in 1969. MHD is a
form of power generation referred to later in this chapter.

ments of the government. . . . This worries me. The calibre of scientific and engineering people is low . . . people who presume to make judgments in fields they don't understand. It is awfully difficult to believe that one can make intelligent decisions based on ignorance. It isn't true elsewhere. . . . This idea that they can weigh the evidence and make a decision! I don't see this as a decision-making process.

Dr. Jackson, a Scot turned into an American citizen, thought it was the government's obligation

to look down the road a piece, to see what's in prospect ten, fifteen, twenty-five years from now. The long view would surely dictate federal funding of research into power generation that might be more efficient, discharging far less heat. MHD research offers promise. But there is a conspiracy to promote nuclear power. In any country where the politics of the AEC is absent, there is an MHD program. We need coal research, too, for converting it to gas for use as relatively non-polluting power plant fuel. Milton Shaw, who used to work with Admiral Hyman Rickover in developing reactors before he got into promoting nuclear reactors for the AEC, is a negative service to the public interest. He made a statement that all research into MHD must cease. How in the hell can he be sure?

The Interior Department has barely struggled away from the pork barrel stage. The AEC introduced the greatest energy development since the first flame, then tried to give it away to private industry as fast as possible. The Federal Power Commission is symptomatic of too many lawyers, not enough scientists and engineers. Never mind about the environmental implications. Engineering is an afterthought. TVA is close to a very large private utility and not much given to research, either. It is run by the same kind of people who run private utilities.

There are all sorts of technological innovations possible in nuclear power but the AEC has turned most of these off or reduced them to such trivial levels that nothing is happening. They've decided in their infinite wisdom that this is the way to go. Once you've made such a decision, you chuck everything out because it's contrary to the decision. But is this the right way to organize— where we're only just beginning? I'm sure it isn't. If we don't get the power situation under control, we're in real trouble. That damned war in Vietnam has stalled research.

Dr. Jackson felt the nation was passing over an extraordinary opportunity by failing to develop the low-pollutant, high-efficiency MHD technology and forms such as thermionics,* solar cells, coal conversion, on-site power processes independent of transmission systems, and geo-thermal phenomena (heat beneath the earth's crust, which is used to drive steam generators in Mexico and California and to heat homes and buildings in Iceland). In France, a fascinating experimental power plant is operated with heat from the sun, collected and focused from multiple reflecting mirrors—a completely pollution-free system that, to be sure, functions only in the daylight hours when the sun is shining.

All these systems and other exotic forms scarcely beyond the theo-retical stage of development offer possibilities for increasing efficiency, reducing emissions, dispersing dependence on any one system across the spectrum of power sources.

Magnetohydrodynamics (MHD) was described in the notes and diary of Faraday. It was adapted to the dynamics of power and propulsion in rocket engines. It involves either a fluid at high temperature serving as an electric conductor or a gas mixture in a state of expansion passing through a magnetic field. MHD invariably depends on a high tempera-ture containment and is, or can be, powered by igniting powdered coal mixed with preheated air. When it is dispatched to a combustion chamber, very much like a solid-fuel rocket engine, it passes through a nozzle and is accelerated across a magnetic field. With MHD, the 30 to 40 percent efficiency factor in fuel plants could be increased to 60 percent, with pollutants largely recovered or removed as salable chemicals.

Philip Sporn and Dr. Arthur Kantrowitz, a Cornell University pro-fessor, joined an AVCO division for a time to try to promote MHD through government research. Although not projected as a primary base-load power factor, MHD (like a pumped storage plant) would be highly suitable for peak-load generation, quickly started up and instantaneously admitted to a power network. The aerospace industry developed the technology, advanced in Hungary before World War II. Dr. Jackson, Sporn, AVCO scientists, and a good many others were confident that a research commitment of $50 million would speed the technology forward and provide operating experience essential to make it significant. Why did such research not go forward?

---

* In March, 1971, the Soviet Union announced, in a guarded statement, a sensa-tional development in a thermionic method of generating electricity. The method involves the use of nuclear fission, without a reactor, emitting electrons to a col-lector that discharges energy of "several kilowatts," according to *Tass*, the Soviet news agency. This is a direct conversion of fuel into electricity without steam to drive a turbine generator. Dr. Jackson, who has inspected some of the experimental plants on a visit to Russia, suspects that the Russians are devoting talent and resources to such direct conversion methods of energy production and are doubtless far ahead of the United States in the field.

"There's no immediate money in it," said Dr. Jackson. He feels that nuclear plants will get too big, in the pursuit of the economy of scale, and dump excessive waste heat in each of many places. A power plant ought to be limited by the conditions and location of the site to optimum heat discharge—optimum, not maximum, something below harmful levels, even if it means trimming the scale to a size commensurate with environmental acceptability. Dr. Jackson said AVCO's own stake in MHD was related to its hope of realizing return on certain patents, thus acknowledging a vested interest in the matter. Why, then, did the corporation itself not allocate $50 million as a development risk? Because research requiring heavy expenditures, as in the case of nuclear energy itself, ought to be an expression of the national interest.

Vast pools of talent, sometimes the kind of talent not readily available in even the largest corporations, must be recruited and paid. Detachment from vested interests gives talented researchers opportunities to undertake imaginative and theoretical projects. Private interests seldom combine to impose a new technology on the market for altruistic purposes and indeed cannot do so once a heavy capital commitment has been made to a given goal. They must press forward, sometimes in the wrong direction, in search of a return, perhaps discarding aspects of a research project that cannot be translated at once into dollars and profits. Power is a national, a world problem, not a corporate one. Public policy and universal well-being are involved. The total environment and ecology of the earth are involved. In research efforts of such dimension, corporate beneficiaries might be made to pay their portion of research and development costs, but the direction ought to be primarily governmental.

If somebody is going to impose new methods of generating power on the market or methods of making fewer kilowatts of power per capita or for making less power provide more energy service, it is not going to be the electric utilities and their money that initiate such developments. It is in this respect that the utilities and the auto makers, as prime national polluters, are kin. They cannot be expected to march into a future in which their diminishing business is joyfully accepted because they no longer pollute. If they can avoid pollution and not frighten people with the implications of their growth and technology while concurrently growing at a rate of 8 or 9 percent a year, they are quite willing to contribute to the qualitative upgrading of life.

The costs and initiative for changes of great magnitude will have to come, not from within the power industry (or the automobile industry, in the case of a steam car), but from the country itself, from the people, from their government. Emphasis is directed to automobiles and electric power in this context, but it is no less valid for all industry and services;

nothing less than radical, perhaps revolutionary, departures from previous methods of persuasion and enforcement are essential to any resolution
of the energy crisis.

Proposals for radical departures from the past or present lead inevitably to charges from James Roche, from utility managers, and from
their counterparts that socialism is being called down on the heads of
the people, that corporate responsibility is being demeaned, and that free
enterprise as the nation has known it is being threatened by a political
ideology. And that might even be true, at least to the extent that free
enterprise is involved or that industrial responsibility is exercised. It is
where necessary change does not occur and where failure to change is
dangerous to the public interest that radical departure from policy and
practice takes on urgency and significance, whether it is identified as
socialism or simple necessity.

Enthusiasts of MHD trying to get the government to launch research
and development assaults on electric power problems did not feel that
they were proponents of socialism, or at least not much of it. The United
States Senate, in approving a guaranteed loan of $250 million to bail out
the Lockheed Corporation in 1971, was hardly adopting socialism. It was
a radical act, however, to give a faltering corporation $250 million simply
to keep it going, an enormous welfare payment that stands as a landmark
development in government-industry relations. Why, then, was it any
more radical, considering the range of public well-being and environmental implications involved, for the government to lead the way in
research and development that might help human beings cope with the
proliferation of electric power and automobiles?

There is, of course, a crucial difference between government intervention in research and in corporate management. Where personal rewards
for judgment, initiative, and recompense for doing a good job are concerned, governmental intervention is not indicated; but the decision on
the power sources to be developed (nuclear, pumped storage, MHD, and
the like) has the best chance of being formulated when detachment and
the absence of corporate pressures characterize the program.*

* The need for and prospects of developing electric power in other countries of
the world is analyzed in a comprehensive report published by the United Nations
Economic and Social Council on January 11, 1971 (U.N. document E/C.7/2/Add.2).
The report examines carefully the issue of world-wide pollution, power production
to help minimize it, power produced by tidal action, hydroelectric possibilities, and
especially geothermal sources for converting deep underground heated water into
electricity. The report proposes continental and hemispheric transmission grids.
Surprisingly, Soviet Premier Aleksei N. Kosygin, in an economic report to the
twenty-fourth Soviet Communist Party Congress in Moscow was the first leader
of a world power to respond favorably to the United Nations proposal. Kosygin
proposed the construction of an electric power grid encompassing Europe that
could save considerable expenditures in individual countries, a grid similar to that
proposed for the United States by the author in this book.

What is needed, Dr. Jackson thinks, is a better response to national situations, with a more forthright and candid form of communication between the government, industry, and the public. Too many problems have been solved by default for too many years. "The response of the public to a national situation ought to be something more appropriate than sticking American flags on their cars," he said, citing one manifestation.

> Let's start getting things done *before* a crisis. Let's get a National Energy Commission, but not some superagency committed to a single direction, manipulating superficial response, playing games. Let's keep the direction in view, keep corruption low or nonexistent, and get our tasks accomplished as a mature country. If we are to respond to crisis situations, let's respond with determination to solve it, not divide into support teams which determine, by their size and strength, policy decisions. An example of that sort of thing is the supersonic transport project.

The more enlightened of private utility administrators would doubtless approve of Dr. Jackson's critique in general, wincing perhaps at the prospects of putting emphasis on processes not immediately applicable to the crisis in which they find themselves. The utilities have been soundly condemned for not engaging more extensively in research, and justification for the criticism exists. But in complex modern technology, it is a good deal harder for a hundred widely dispersed corporations to get together on an effective research program than it is to respond collectively to wisely conceived government research criteria related to the public interest that is only peripherally concerned with problems of a power system.

The aggravations and service requirements of an electric utility in the plains and mountain states of the West, where transmission lines extend over vast distances, with customers scattered in a thousand communities, differ to a degree beyond comparison with an urban utility serving millions of customers. A rural cooperative of 17,000 consumers on 1,800 square miles of the Eastern Shore of Maryland has little in common with Consolidated Edison's problems in metropolitan New York, where more than 1 million of its customers are on welfare and confined to derelict, congested housing. There are sociological, technological, economic, and political problems in providing electric service. Only a national policy with high standards of reliability and management, with controls over fuels and seminal technology, can provide the denominator of common interest. A national grid will provide a beginning of such a policy, but a new and unfamiliar kind of governmental and industrial mentality will have to emerge before anything like that can occur.

And perhaps a world-wide energy policy, as United Nations studies time and time again have proposed, would encourage superpowers to share the energy-producing resources they command with their technology, armed might, economic power, and management skills. On a planet of 58 million square miles—more than 37 billion acres, with the United States comprising 2 billion of them—it is no longer fair or peacefully possible for giant nations to take command of resources as Rome took command of the old world.

Somewhere along the path to the future, an accommodation has to be made to the reality that the resources of energy, of electric power, simply cannot be appropriated by one or several nations at the intolerable expense of others. Nor can the fear that an underdeveloped country like China or India, where per capita consumption is less than 60 kilowatts a year, may grow and prosper a little justify grabbing and control of resources that somehow and at some time have to be shared.

14

Assumptions

of

Power

SOMEWHERE SHORT of the foolishness and corporate make-play that in-
duces the wanton waste of resources for such purposes as Disney World,
somewhere this side of an industrial policy that devours the earthly
habitat in the process of its own growth, a philosophy of moderation in
the use of man-made energy is waiting to be born.

The years since World War II, the most fertile period in history
for industrial advancement and the universal application of electric
power, have clearly demonstrated that ecologically science and technology are a failure. With the development of computers, now emerging
into what will become the largest and richest industry on earth, with the
advent of the 1-million-kilowatt (and soon the 10-million-kilowatt) power
plant, with the application of war-born science to consumer-product
consumption, the world becomes each day less fit to inhabit.

Even nuclear energy is a failure when measured against its original
intended purpose. It cannot be used successfully in an assault against a
superpower or in defense against its use. Military application of nuclear
warheads against an enemy nation would produce such immediate re-
taliation that the distinction between attacker and defender would be
lost in a common obliteration of the property and citizens of opposing
powers. Thus, the expenditure of hundreds of billions of dollars in many
lands to develop nuclear arms has been an irretrievable, monumental
waste except, perhaps, to the extent that it can be adapted safely and
with restraint to meeting human needs. And the needs will have to be

redefined to separate them from human desires, which as often as not are inimical to necessity.

A philosophy of restraint, of examining the long-range purpose of the use of energy, must reassess some old and common assumptions. One assumption at least open to question and applicable to electric power production especially is that the inventive capability of the power industry can be relied upon to correct the environmental problems it caused in the first place. Any confidence that the fuels and power industries, which constitute a formidable economic bloc, might initiate reforms leading to modification of energy consumption is misplaced.

Thus, President Nixon's proposed plan for solving and alleviating the environmental crisis, if not completely without merit, seemed rather like a continuation of business as usual. He intended, he said, to reverse the destructive trend against life-support systems by mobilizing the talent and resources of those industries in which it has been standard practice to use the skies, the waters, and the lands as disposal dumps for their wastes.

Since technology is in large measure to blame for the environmental crisis, which is inseparable from the power crisis in America, elementary wisdom dictates, as Dr. Barry Commoner wrote persuasively, that the nation learn how the inventive genius of industry failed to identify or ameliorate the problems it caused. At the very least, the shortcomings of past performance ought to be overcome before the future survival of mankind is entrusted to technology's faith in itself.

For example, an aluminum company can present itself to an investing public as a highly attractive prospect for dividends and stock growth accruing from the manufacture of aluminum cans. Its consumption of electric power, processing of materials, and wide distribution of a nearly indestructible throwaway container can be seen as a miracle of conversion of energy and elements into a useful and publicly welcomed product. Understandably, the assumption then develops that manufacturing aluminum cans is a great idea and another example of industrial accomplishment. It is also, measured by different criteria, an ecological disaster.

Aluminum production requires fifteen times more fuel and energy for its production than steel, even more for glass, and one hundred fifty times more than lumber. The aluminum and chemical industries in the United States consume more than 25 percent of the total national output of non-residential electric power. When it is remembered that a glass bottle can be reused from eighteen to forty times and that the lowly aluminum beer can, even making allowances for differences in weight, takes more than six times as much energy to produce as a steel can, the assumption of convenience and advantage in favor of the aluminum article fades away.

This is especially true when it is understood that air and water pollution at aluminum plants is extremely difficult to control despite significant efforts to do so. About the only advantage the aluminum can has over other containers is the money it makes.

Power companies like to serve aluminum companies, of course, because they consume enormous quantities of electricity at comparatively low service cost to the utilities. But the assumption that increased power production, caused by growth of the aluminum industry's can and container market, strengthens the economy is inaccurate. A technology burning up six to fifteen times more fuel and energy to replace a recycled bottle made by a thrifty use of energy, is an ecological freeloader.

It is not intended and not fair to single out aluminum makers, since similar examples could be cited in nearly every major industry in the generation after World War II. The intention of such examples is to show the falsity of assumptions on which a good deal of American industrial practice is firmly, but one hopes not irrevocably, based.

Another assumption which must be doubted in its past and present impact concludes that the growth in population has produced the power and pollution crisis. There is a shred of truth in this that must, however, be isolated from a torrent of misconception. The presence of 42 percent more people in the United States in 1971 than in 1946, each of them using on the average two and a half times more electricity than people used before World War II, contributed to the expanded output of power. The use of more electricity by these newborn additions to the American populace significantly aggravated but by no means caused the environmental crisis.

While the population was growing by 42 percent, pollution of the air, water, and land increased in some instances at more than forty times the rate that population alone might have explained. The contribution of electric utilities to environmental deterioration, although substantial and always visible insofar as smokestack emissions are concerned, is fragmentary indeed compared with new industrial offenders.

It was not the newly born and their families, or even the concentration of people in the cities, but the products and services they were persuaded, or compelled for lack of choice, by American industry to buy and consume after World War II that altered the character and volume of toxicity in human environment. It was fossil and radioactive fuels, chemicals and petrochemicals in abundance, chemicals not previously released in nature that posed the threat of human degradation or extinction. And all these were released into the habitat by the limitless supply of electricity.

The assumption that the population explosion has been a primary cause of the wasteful and polluting conditions is only marginally valid.

But the assumption that is valid is that a continuation of the explosion into the next two generations presents a future that can scarcely be contemplated without horror.

But whatever stress, famines, plagues, or unimagined problems the increasing population may impose on the future, it was not the 42 percent increase in the twenty-five years after World War II that caused the environmental and ecological crisis of the 1970s. The cause of *that* crisis, aggravated indeed by the explosive growth of the electric power industry, was a brutal, economically aggressive form of industrial and marketing disorder which the nation had been conditioned—mistakenly, as it developed—to believe was liberating, healthy, a revelation of national genius, and a triumph of science and technology.

It was in this period of industrial and technological expansion that nearly every pollution problem of consequence developed. While the country grew and prospered, regardless of the millions who remained impoverished or locked out of upward mobility, the most affluent middle- and upper-class society in history shared in the boom times, in the profits and wages, and in the rewards. But the growth of the gross national income to $1 trillion was, to a depressing extent, dirty money. So many of the industries and products that brought unprecedented affluence to more than half the nation's populace imposed so much pollution and such a heavy burden on the environment that its reclamation may not be possible.

Barry Commoner and his staff in Saint Louis have shown a cause- and-effect correlation between specific commodities and manufactured products and their destructive impact on life. In the generation after World War II, phosphate production increased 700 percent to 300 million pounds a year. Nitrogen oxides from automobiles (which make smog) increased 630 percent; lead in gasoline, 415 percent; mercury, 2,100 percent; synthetic pesticides, 270 percent in the seventeen years after 1950; inorganic nitrogen fertilizer (which is used on farms and which leaches into water and pollutes it), 789 percent.

The mountains of nondecaying plastics, radioactive materials and emissions, the millions of tons of detergents, synthetic fibers, DDT, and the successful effort by automobile manufacturers to persuade people to buy new and more powerful cars every one, two, or three years all combined to lay across the continent a measureless quantity of poisons, filth, and litter; of eroded and destroyed or paved land; of congestion and concentration and consuming ugliness. Behind it all—what made it all possible, often promoting it and of course profiting from it all, energizing and feeding on it all—were the electric utilities and their sole service and product: power. They polluted as they generated and transmitted power; they could not do otherwise. And every kilowatt of power they produced, consuming energy and creating energy, in one manner or another, at its generated source or in the uses to which it was put, polluted, too.* Energy and power were life. Their abuse and excess were death. Yet, the abusive and excessive use of energy and power since the 1940s has been a concomitant of the modern industrial system. The deduction that seems to follow, then, with irresistible logic is that this commitment to energy expansion makes American economic and industrial life self-destructive. And so it may be.

The possibility that the course and character of industry and technology cannot or will not be changed to accommodate essential conditions for endurable life leads to another popularly held assumption in need of review. This is the belief which seems reasonable enough at first glance, that because all people, regardless of wealth, status, sex, race, age, or mentality, for the most part treasure their own lives, a consensus on the necessity for preserving and protecting the earthly ecosystem ought naturally to develop. Right-wing lunatics and pointy-headed liberals of the left share with radlibs, commies, hippies, and homosexuals a concern for the elements that sustain life. How could a political issue arise over such a one-sided question? Even the people who might polarize into separate camps over motherhood, the flag, J. Edgar Hoover, or the innocence of infants could scarcely be expected to favor foul air, screeching noise, radioactivity, poisoned water, and the like. Or so it seems.

But because any modification in energy policy or determined enforcement of restrictions against major polluters tampers with economic factors, threatening production cutbacks and loss of jobs, the ecology and environmental issue by 1972 had become suspect. When priorities and enforcement procedures favoring preservation or reclamation of the environment clash with traditional values, such as jobs and growth, the issue becomes at once charged with acrimony. Although most people agree in general that the issue is important and want the ruination of the air and water stopped, their right to work for good incomes in dangerously polluting industries or factories will be abridged if, as has happened in isolated instances, management elects to close down operations when unwilling or unable to comply with newly applied laws.

In other instances, management has elected simply to defy the law, as many corporations have done with impunity for decades, depending on public support and hesitant enforcement policy to remain in production and to keep employees at work. Consolidated Edison in New York was charged by the city's Environmental Control Board in December,

---

* Excluding the disruptions and ecological damage sometimes caused by their condemnation of land and construction, hydroelectric plants, of course, do not pollute at the generating source.

1971, with twenty-two air-pollution violations when the power company refused to limit its coal-fired generators at a Staten Island plant to 200,000 kilowatts. The city had ordered the reduction from 500,000 kilowatts "in accordance with duly enacted laws to control the operation of utilities to the extent that such operations may affect the health and safety of their citizens."

While the city, through Environmental Protection Administrator Jerome Kretchmer, threatened to levy $100-a-day fines on each count of pollution, Consolidated Edison concluded that the health and safety of the citizens would be more imposed upon by power shortages or failures that might occur if production was curtailed. The utility simply challenged the ruling and kept the heavily polluting plant in operation.

President Nixon was quick to make things perfectly clear when it became evident that environmental protection policy, even when gingerly enforced, was on a collision course with industry's production practice. His administration launched an offensive against a water-pollution-control bill (which Senator Edmund S. Muskie was trying to propel through the Senate) that would commit the government to cleaning up all rivers and waterways by 1985. William Ruckelshaus, administrator of the federal Environmental Protection Agency, said he thought the goal of no pollution at all in American waters was "ridiculous" because it took little account of all the implications. What would such a goal do to the increased needs for power? And to the problem of solid wastes, and so on?

Admittedly, the old law passed back in 1899 had not accomplished anything in the way of water-pollution prevention, but that was no reason to try to impose unrealistic standards now. John T. Connor, chairman of Allied Chemical Corporation, in a speech before the Synthetic Organic Chemical Manufacturers Association, declared that the Muskie bill would burden the taxpayers excessively. In addition, he felt that water-pollution legislation should be taken out of "the inevitable politics of an election year." Mr. Connor quoted Governor Nelson Rockefeller of New York as his authority for the statement that eliminating all polluting discharges from the waters of that state alone would cost the taxpayers $230 billion. On the other hand, Mr. Rockefeller's record for accuracy and planning on pollution issues has been rather poor. He had persuaded the voters of New York to approve a $1.5-billion bond issue in the 1960s that, he said, would go a long way toward purifying state waters. Apparently the money has, indeed, gone a long way, for it has not reappeared as evidence that purification has occurred.

Mr. Connor, who was Secretary of Commerce in the Lyndon Johnson administration and who has become one of the highest-ranking leaders of the chemicals industry, spoke for much of the industrial community when he expressed irritation at the prospects of the environmental movement going too far and too fast. From the highest councils of government, finance, agriculture, and industry come laments and warnings against zealots trying to get the system changed and spreading fear about mankind surviving.

Dr. Schlesinger of the AEC declares that the commission will not let itself get involved in the question of whether society "ought to curb its appetite for energy and electric power." But he suggests that "responsible environmentalists" probably recognize that if there are brownouts, blackouts, and power interruptions, the environmental movement will pay a severe price for perhaps stalling the construction of new installations. It is not, however, up to the AEC to become "entangled" in policy issues relating to the merits or dangers of electric power expansion. That is the public's decision to make.

President Nixon soothed the disturbed auto manufacturers, somewhat alarmed over the prospects of having to make the internal combustion engine conform to what was thought to be impossibly strict air-pollution standards, when he visited Detroit before Christmas, 1971.

"We are committed to cleaning up the air and cleaning up the water," he said. "But we are also committed to a strong economy and we are not going to allow the environmental issue to be used sometimes falsely and sometimes in a demagogic way basically to destroy the industrial system that made this the great country it is."

In nearby Midland, Michigan, a good deal of grass-roots opposition had developed against such groups as the Sierra Club and the Saginaw Valley Nuclear Study Club, which were contesting the licensing of a large nuke to supply energy to the Dow Chemical Company. The reactor would supply both steam and power to the chemical complex in the first such dual-purpose operation. Employment at Dow had dropped from around 12,500 to a little over 10,000 in a three-year period, and a good deal of apprehension developed over the rumor that thousands more jobs would be lost if the nuke was not built.

The town of 35,000 rallied to the nuclear cause, and people gathered in a public demonstration to urge the Atomic Energy Commission to issue the construction license. The citizens delivered to Washington a ten-by-twenty-foot billboard decorated with the signatures of 15,000 persons in support of the plant. It was probably the first demonstration of its kind in which the public fought for, rather than against, nuclear power in their community.

From the hushed quarters of the Rockefeller Brothers Fund there emerged a small book under the name of Fred Smith, long associated in one manner or another with Rockefeller enterprises and services and a perennial personage on public bodies reflecting Rockefeller connections with conservation. Mr. Smith had served on the Advisory Commission of the Hudson River Valley Commission, which was administered by one of Governor Rockefeller's cousins, and which concluded in a report that a six-lane expressway along the Hudson River in Westchester County was a perfectly appropriate exercise in conserving natural resources. Nelson, David, and Laurance Rockefeller favored the expressway along the riverfront, and Nelson, as governor, had gotten the law and funds approved by the state legislature. This doubtless explained Fred Smith's zeal for the project. After six years of litigation and protests on the part of the public, the expressway was abandoned. Mr. Smith moved upward to become a consultant to President Nixon's Citizens Advisory Committee on Environmental Quality, a role in which he might make an important contribution if called upon to pass judgment on the conversion of riverbanks into highways and similar environmental-improvement projects.

The Smith booklet, which went into three printings in 1971, was distributed free through business channels and mailed from the Rockefeller Brothers Fund offices in New York to those who responded to offers of free copies in business newsletters and other channels. Its title was *America Is a Growing Country*. The book is a self-serving, sugarcoated tribute to a vision of America and its economy commonly held in the era of boosterism that preceded Herbert Hoover and Franklin D. Roosevelt. The booklet's importance lies in its reflection of the old-line Establishment position on environmental questions and the imputation of evil design to militant and critical people (among whom must be numbered scholars and scientists of good credentials and renown) convinced that industrial society is approaching a cataclysm.

In the Great Depression of the 1930s, writes Mr. Smith,

> the old American philosophy of self-determination was in full retreat. Nobody ever said, anymore, that America was a great, growing country filled with opportunity for the alert; that its best years lay ahead of it. . . . Today we are reliving that old experience; we've been this way before.
>
> Our system has let us down, we are hearing; industry is wrongheaded, worthless, and endlessly damaging to society. . . . Do away with growth, curb technology, they say. . . . A few opportunistic lawyers, supposedly acting in the public interest, indulge in a kind of publicity-rich legal guerrilla warfare to put a stop to anything anybody doesn't like, anything that makes a profit or smells of success. As a result, the confused public is once again ready to believe anything that sounds reasonably logical, especially if it also sounds frightening.
>
> It is widely held these days by environmentalists that we've

"got to get off this growth kick" . . . if we are to survive. We are told to put a stop to "progress." No more power plants, especially nuclear power plants. No SST. No increase in the Gross National Product. . . .

I have had a considerable amount of first-hand experience with industry and industrialists during this environmental era, and by and large I would give them good marks. Most of them are as much concerned about pollution, for example, as the most adamant environmentalist. Most want to move as fast as technology and economic feasibility permit. But because their destinies are determined by consumers, they are more sensitive to the effects of cost than the affluent environmental enthusiast who says, "Do as I say."

Too many environmentalists are impelled by "an all-too-human desire to pass the buck, to point the finger, to find a culprit. And the media have not helped: they have sought out controversy and nourished it at every turn. . . . It sells papers and increases audiences. But it doesn't solve anything."

This viewpoint is strongly reflected by Earl L. Butz, a former director of the Ralston Purina Company, a vast fertilizer and agricultural products empire, and director of a farm machinery manufacturing company, whom President Nixon named Secretary of Agriculture late in 1971. Mr. Butz is a leading spokesman for agribusiness, meaning the corporation farm operator as differentiated from the individual or family-owned farm. Since agriculture has been dramatically altered by petrochemicals, pesticides, herbicides, and an array of fertilizers and chemicals, it emerged after World War II into a major land and water polluter. With the extension of electric power and gasoline and diesel-fueled machinery to all farms, agriculture has become over the years an energy-consuming business; that is, it has become resources-intensive where once it had been labor-intensive.

In a speech before an agricultural advertising and marketing seminar on April 26, 1971, Mr. Butz said:

It's a typical American characteristic to over-react to crisis. Before the hunger and malnutrition binge we were on, it was integration and segregation and we were all hepped up about that, you recall. And the people who are really suffering from this environmental binge we are on now are the integrationists. Their money's dried up, the support is dried up. These fellows are really hurting because we've forgotten about that. Well, right now I think we're at the crest of what I would call the agitation curve of this environmental binge.

It could easily be argued that the harsh views of Mr. Butz made him something of an extremist himself, but his knack for equating such social

issues as hunger and malnutrition, racial integration, and ecology with
a cycle of binges doomed to lose their appeal to the public conscience is
disquieting. Especially if his evaluation of the depth of the appeal of
these issues is correct. But even when assessments of the issues are
more reasoned and compassionate, nowhere in government and only in
circumspect and rare commentary within the community of electric
utilities does a vision of the future appear that encompasses restraint or
moderation in the proliferation of man-made energy.

In a report that is as authoritative as it is chilling, thirty-three leading
scientists in Great Britain called in January, 1972, for drastic measures
to discourage population growth and charted a collapse of the planet's
life-support systems "possibly by the end of the century, certainly within
the lifetimes of our children." The population of Great Britain, 55
million, has to be reduced to about 30 million for the long future's sake.
The exponential depletion of resources and damage to the ecology require an end to building highways, stabilizing existing ecological demands, a freeze on raw-materials usage, and the development of labor-
intensive industries to halt the spread of resource-intensive production.
The report, entitled *Blueprint for Survival*, proposes a 100 percent tax
on products designed to last a year and nothing on those designed to last
a hundred years.

In Washington, Sir Frank Darling, vice-president of the Conservation
Foundation, called the blueprint "the sanest popular statement thus far
produced on the environmental crisis." The blueprint calls for curtailment through taxation of electric power. Statements supporting the blueprint and its findings have been issued by V. C. Wynne-Edwards, Regius
Professor of Natural History at the University of Aberdeen and chairman
of the British government's Natural Environment Research Council; Sir
Julian Huxley, the biologist; C. H. Waddington, professor of animal
genetics at the University of Edinburgh; and others.

On the other side, Dr. Milton Friedman, economist and presidential
adviser, offered his contribution to shore up the expanding industrial
growth policy. He published an article asserting that public drives to
influence corporate decision making at inner-policy levels, if successful,
would bring on "pure and unadulterated socialism." The fundamental
responsibility of a corporation remained, as it had always been, to
increase profits:

> In a free enterprise, private property system, a corporate execu-
> tive is an employee of the owners of his business. He has direct
> responsibility to his employers. That responsibility is to conduct
> the business in accordance with their desires, which generally
> will be to make as much money as possible while conforming to

the basic rules of the society, both those embodied in law and those embodied in ethical custom.

With the plutonium power era taking shape, in a time when the environment has already been half destroyed, with rigged markets devoid of competitive free enterprise, the Friedman thesis is dangerous. Economists looking at the American petroleum industry, the four automobile manufacturing corporations left from eighty-four in business fifty years ago, and the electric power monopolies and observing in them an interplay of free enterprise lack credibility if not the ability to see straight.

At the highest levels of politics, government, and industry, the overwhelming threat to the ecosphere and national life simply is not identified or defined. Cosmetic, largely superficial programs calculated to treat symptoms of the threat are welcomed and to some modest extent here and there are effective in diverting certain excessive discharges from the air and water. But the essential cause of the threat is gross economic growth in which excessive use and waste of resources and energy is socially and financially rewarded.

It should have become apparent long ago that the uncontrolled proliferation of electric power and the energy abuses it provoked and ultimately institutionalized would have to be brought under some form of jurisdiction, if only to provide social and more rational guidance for its use. Yet in a process of social development characterized by a general lack of objective analysis, gross growth and the cumulative waste of energy have come to be thought of as progress, something to be sought for its own sake. Senator Mike Gravel has said that the word *progress* itself ought to be redefined to make its meaning more explicit in an industrial society. Appealing for repeal of legislation that freed electric utilities from liability in the event of catastrophic accident, Senator Gravel was challenged on the question of whether a legislative move against nuclear energy was an obstruction to progress. "Progress in technology," he said, "might be defined as something which enhances human health and survival. The one technology which has the ability to pollute this planet permanently is hard to consider as progress."

The legislation the senator sought in this instance would have repealed the Price-Anderson Act at once, rather than waiting for its expiration date in 1977. It is this act that makes the government largely responsible for damage and liability in any of those "maximum-predictable" nuke accidents that the AEC and electric utility people talk about.

It is the extension of atomic fission and the plutonium-producing plant to the power industry and to civil life that has aroused public aware-

ness, so long in coming, on the whole question of energy. This aware-
ness, the questions raised, and the protests in Congress and in public
forums have come close to stalling nuclear power development. In the
United States, 23 nukes were operating (unless Indian Point is shut down
again) in 1972; 110 or thereabouts were under construction or are likely
to be in a few years. They will all be built, and more will come, for the
industrial society in its pursuit of gross growth is trapped in a dilemma
of materialistic success and inertial force from which there is no turning.

Those few managers, a small minority within the largest business in
America, the electric utilities, who know that both the government and
the power industry itself are unlikely to unite in some new, more effective
control program have observed the developing crisis with a good deal of
pain. Unable to slow down the accelerated rate of power expansion
because they are obliged to respond to the need and unable to meet the
demands made on them to supply it on so vast a scale, they have their
own dilemma of extraordinary magnitude. Like a protagonist in a Greek
drama, a utility is compelled to contribute to disaster in the pursuit of
any course open to it. No agency, no arm of government, no single sector
of the economy, no one has power over power.

Jay Forrester, a scientist with expertise in several disciplines, including original work in computer technology at M.I.T., has taken the
measure of the American industrial dilemma in his book *World Dynamics*. He believes that the country must be brought to a state of
equilibrium and the quality of life stabilized by the incredibly early
date of 1980. In order to achieve this goal, pollution will have to be
reduced by 50 percent; capital-investment generation, by 40 percent; the
birth rate, by 30 percent; food production, by 20 percent; the rate of
consumption of natural resources, by a staggering 75 percent.

It is altogether impossible to accomplish even one-tenth of what Dr.
Forrester hopes, and he offers no consolation for partial achievements,
anyway. The only solace permissible in appraising these out-of-reach
goals lies in the hope that with all that data at hand and with all those
great computers that absorbed it, Dr. Forrester and his electronic brains
somehow got it all wrong.

Dr. José Delgado, a noted Yale University physiologist long engaged
in research involving electrical stimulation of the human brain, has
questioned whether mankind any longer can handle the world's accumulation of knowledge. Perhaps people, like the dinosaurs, are incapable
of adapting to their environment. They did fairly well in adapting to
the environment inherited from the natural processes and phenomena of
nature. But they seem to be botching up the job of adapting to the environment they have been developing for themselves.

What people have accomplished in ninety years of electric power is awesome testimony to their ingenuity, their ambitions, and their success-ful search for comfort, material security, and status. But the conditions that, in the process, people have brought upon themselves and on their habitat are revealing testimony to their frightening failure to devise a social organization, including government, that gives priority to the prevalence, the value, the inner delight, and the survival of the most ulti-mate of miracles: life itself.

If there is substance to such a gloomy truth, are there any corrective, restorative remedies that can be devised and applied to arrest the course on which our broken-down social organization is propelling us?

There are, indeed, but they require in some abundance a new kind of human being—*new* in the sense that such people may become newly noticed and newly ascendant to power, for they have been here all along. They want life affirmed, life sustained, life cherished; and they do not need accumulated wealth, necessarily, nor do they aspire to power for the sake of power. They want to rescue the planet Earth, their own environment, from the grievous, nearly fatal wounds inflicted upon it, heal those wounds, let the life flow back into it, and let it, and every-thing on it, live again. The wrong kind of people, too often, have come to power; and the price paid for their accomplishment and for the popular acceptance of that accomplishment has been nearly lethal.

15

The Power
to
Change

A PRIMARY PREREQUISITE to the revolution in attitudes that would make a sane power policy acceptable, which is essential to its effectiveness, is the emergence in larger numbers of citizens ready to demand reforms in the economic and political systems.

For although it is quite true that the reckless waste of energy, with all it implies, can be reversed only after reevaluating what is sanctified in a materialist society, it is equally true that the distortion of values is sanctioned by political and economic power. It is safe to say, in fact, that the political and economic sectors of national life honor, perpetuate, and outrageously exploit a hoary translation of the national interest that disallows healthy heresy.

Barry Commoner concludes in *The Closing Circle:* "What is real in our lives is the apparently hopeless inertia of the economic and political system; its fantastic agility in sliding away from the basic issues which logic reveals; the selfish maneuvering of those in power."

Robert Townsend, a former corporation manager and writer (*Up the Organization* and some good essays and articles), wrote in the *Center Magazine* early in 1972:

> It is no exaggeration to say that all the big company managements I am familiar with are basically engaged, whether they are conscious of it or not, in screwing their stockholders, employees,

customers, and the general public as well, while living off the fat of the land themselves.

In my judgment, the government is not going to do anything about it; neither are the labor unions.

But certainly a president who built a constituency and a political power base on twenty-five years or so of relentless opposition to Communist China only to discard his principles when they became unpopular could detect the validity of a "survival binge," as Earl Butz might describe it, if enough people seemed to be in favor of it. And it does seem that public interest in national and global survival is increasing. But one has to be sure. The issue has to be a winner.

It was not exactly a case of the lion and the lamb taking a nap together, but something more than symbolic evidence of opposing forces approaching reconciliation occurred early in 1972 between power company leadership and some of its most determined and articulate critics. A task force established by the Sierra Club, a formidable and highly respectable conservationist organization of 140,000 members, recommended the creation of a national energy planning agency. The recommendation and report followed months of discussions around the country culminating in a three-day conference in Johnson, Vermont, with 350 nuclear physicists, electric utility managers, ecologists, lawyers, power equipment manufacturers, economists, and government representatives participating.

Twenty or more electric utility officers took part in the conference. It was an unprecedented confrontation. They did not lose their composure, even when it came to the point where the panel recommended that the new federal energy agency provide for public participation in selecting sites for power plants and share in the decision making with regard to generating equipment and transmission facilities. Whatever the outcome of the forum and others that will surely follow, it was an interesting exercise in the examination of questions that defy one-sided answers.

Charles F. Luce, of New York's Consolidated Edison, was on hand to report on his company's program to encourage customers to curtail electric power use. Although the program had not been very effective, it seemed to indicate support for the conservationist position that utilities ought to stop promoting increased per capita use. Mr. Luce even told an amusing story about Con Ed's power load increasing by 200,000 watts (the total output of a good-sized power plant) when the populace turned on their television sets by the millions to watch Tiny Tim get married between commercials on the Johnny Carson show. If that strange wedding ceremony had been telecast for the entertainment of the people on a hot summer afternoon when Con Ed's load was at its peak with all reserve power in use, Mr. Luce said it would have been "a tragedy." As it was, it was only a waste of power.

"I think both sides are beginning to realize they've got to sit down and reason with each other," the press quoted John R. Dunigan, vice-president of the Public Service Company of Indiana, as saying.

Keith Roberts, a San Francisco lawyer, chairman of the Sierra Club's energy policy committee, and chairman of the panel, said the Sierra Club did not want to have its responsibility doubted and "we don't want to be in the position of arbitrarily blocking every new electric power plant that comes along."

The panel's report was prepared after the conference listened to twenty-four papers that were to be published subsequently in book form. No position was taken on the divisive issue of fossil-fuel versus nuclear power plants pending a determination on the part of the entire Sierra Club membership, but the thirteen-member task force came directly to grips with important issues. They called for a reexamination of real and reasonable needs in the area of energy growth, land-use policies, fuels usage, the economics of digging and drilling for fuels, and disposal of wastes. They urged both stringent safeguards around nuclear plants and vastly improved prevention of pollution in all power plants. Somewhat to the relief of utility executives, the panel report conceded the necessity for an accommodation between contradictory goals.

But if the power-generating technology existing and expanding in America can somehow be brought under effective and sustained control, other industries, all of them being really extensions of electric energy, must be contained, too, in some system of regulated growth commensurate with what life-support systems can tolerate.*

The limitation on household consumption of electric power can simply be a control at the meter so that growth and expansion can be regulated to 1 or 2 percent a year. At a given point, with appropriate exemption in hardship cases, a utility customer would be allocated for the year the kilowatt total he had consumed the previous year, plus a 1 or 2 percent increase allowed for the subsequent year. He would be allocated, for example, 10,000 kilowatt-hours to use for any purpose he cared to choose. Presumably, he would look upon his allocation as he

---

* The per capita consumption of electric power in the United States will exceed 10,000 kilowatt-hours in 1972, five times what it was in 1950. Industry consumes 43 percent of the annual generated output; commercial enterprises, 22 percent; and residential customers, 31 percent. Traditionally, consumers of the greatest volume of power pay the least unit cost, an invitation to excessive consumption that any energy policy, unless government again yields to industrial pressure, must change.

would his income. With just so much currency, in the electrical sense, he would expend it as necessity and choice dictated.

If a household's occupants decided to install a new appliance, it would be necessary either to cut back on some other electric usage or to wait a year until the staggered increment permitted the purchase, very much like decisions have to be made with respect to the purchase of new carpeting or a sailboat. It would be decided upon when it could be paid for or when an anticipated increase in income, combined with cutting down elsewhere, allowed sufficient redeployment of power to increase the meter measurement. No one need be denied the minimum for light, hot water, and basic appliances; but the decision to load electric usage to the maximum of one's ability to pay for it would be denied.

Promotion of electricity usage would become, then, not the function of the electric utility but of the manufacturer whose product consumed electricity. The manufacturer would have to present his case in terms of the desirability of his product *over* others, rather than *in addition* to others. Since electric service is metered in kilowatt-hours consumed, the basic regulatory factor is already part of the system. Where this is not the case, as in apartment dwellings where the owner pays one electric bill and prorates it among tenants, the system would be easily adaptable.

As for commercial and industrial consumers, some aspect of the controlled disbursement of power would apply, with appropriate variables allowed. But even there, annual expansion would be equated with public policy, with deferrals and exemptions permissible according to necessity and existing capacity. There is no question that the door would be opened, as in the case of oil quotas, import tariffs, and the like, to corruption and the exercise of political preference. One has little doubt, for example, that a fifty-dollar bill attached to an exemption application might expedite a decision that would otherwise languish in an unopened drawer. Nevertheless, such a system would constitute a beginning in the process of imposing some controls on the expansion of electric energy.

With limits on the amount and, at industrial levels, on the purpose of electricity, there is little doubt that given new motivation, manufacturers of high-profit, energy-consuming devices would search for improved, more efficient designs. Wasteful air conditioners, which sometimes consume two or three times the amount of power to produce the same cooling capacity as a maximum-efficiency model, would disappear from the market. They would cost too much, not at the point of purchase necessarily, but in terms of using up the electricity budget. Someone might even reinvent forms of light reflection, like those found in old lighthouses in which a lantern, reflected from crystals and mirrors, increased il-

lumination a thousand times more than a single flame. Instead of increasing the wattage of bulbs in every home, as Edwin Vennard used to
like to do, wattage might be reduced or stabilized while candlepower
reflected from multiple sources increased. The electric companies would
not necessarily be in danger of losing money because with population
increases assured for years to come and an annual allowable expansion
of power, business would not regress. The runaway character of power
growth, though, would be deterred.

If anything can be said for free enterprise and technological ingenuity or for the idea that necessity is the mother of invention, it is
conceivable that some regulation of energy at its source would generate
a new concept of problem solving related to the balanced use of resources, rather than to the exploitation of them. And that would surely
be a stupendous advance in social organization.

In addition to source energy control, which is a form of rationing,
there remains taxation of energy for any newly established policy commission to consider. It offers one means by which emphasis might be
shifted to job-intensive means of production and economic development
from overpowered automated forms of technology that have come close
to eliminating people in all roles save that of consumer.

In order to extend the effectiveness of electric power control at the
meter and to dispatch power to any section of the country from any other
section, the nation needs a coast-to-coast transmission grid, preferably
built by the federal government or a public service corporation. It is
wholly inconsistent with optimum design and efficiency for each utility
to own its transmission lines exclusively in all cases. It would be comparable to steel or coal companies owning their own highway or rail
systems over which to ship products to their customers, although the
analogy is, of course, loosely drawn. Electric power is weightless and
invisible; it is the power company's only product; and there is no fundamental reason why unneeded generating capacity in one region should
not be dispatched through a national network to a region where power
is in short supply.

There are some technological issues to be resolved; a system for funding construction and maintenance of the costly project would have to be
devised; and procedures would have to be developed for allocating costs
for use of the grid. None of these problems is beyond solution. Probably
the strongest pressure against a national grid comes from the private
utilities themselves and from the great credit and finance institutions
that put up the capital for plant expansion. Any utility hooked into a
grid and, therefore, in a position to receive power in emergencies or in
special peak-load periods from generating plants hundreds, perhaps a

thousand, miles away would have less need for continuously constructing facilities to provide for all the electric energy needs predicted over a given time in its own franchised area. Thus its capital base and, consequently, its base on which rates are computed would not expand as fast as they normally would in the autonomous monopoly state.

One of Donald Cook's ideas for electric power efficiency has long been a coalescence of generating companies into twelve to fifteen regional conglomerates capable of capitalizing and operating on a higher level of efficiency and economies of scale. Unwelcome as Mr. Cook's concept is in terms of corporate development, which would make the whole country dependent on a dozen or so operating systems of gigantic size, the idea of transmission grids designed to shift large blocs of power from areas with good reserves to deprived sectors has always been a good one.

Donald Cook says a national grid would not work. But the United Nations found that a grid covering all Europe would work fine, if only the countries it encompassed would permit its construction. The Soviet Union liked the idea of a European continental grid for reasons that might bear scrutiny. One reason was that the Soviet Union is developing all kinds of power-generating resources on a vast and accelerated scale, and it would not be particularly astonishing if the Russians supported a grid simply because they might in time be able to sell power all over Europe. Moreover, having the nations of Europe even partially dependent on Russian electricity would put the Soviets in a sweet bargaining position as economic union and development grows apace in Europe.

But granted that a wait-and-see attitude has some justification in Western Europe at least, what justification exists for the United States, which could sanction corporate satellite developments and turn the postal system over to a form of corporate management, to make absolutely no concerted effort to link the whole nation together in an interconnected power grid? The question has never been satisfactorily answered, and it never can be. The grid should be put together, Donald Cook to the contrary, if only because it is not the same old kind of a world anymore. The "survival binge," which is not exactly an intellectual diversion or a show that will close when the audience runs out, seems to prove that.

An overall energy policy cannot ignore, obviously, the problems caused by the concentration of fuel ownership. New York Democratic Congressman Richard Ottinger and Republican Senator Charles Goodell, also from New York, jointly tried to raise this issue in the election campaign of 1969, the only instance in the country of electric power and utility fuels breaking out into any campaign. Goodell declared that in a move to slow down energy-fuel consumption, electric utilities should

make large industrial consumers pay more on the theory that the more
energy used, the more it should cost per unit. Ottinger said the Department of Justice should take antitrust action against the oil companies.
Their opponent in the New York race for a Senate seat, archconservative
James L. Buckley, said nothing. Buckley, heir to a family oil fortune,
won. Buckley had an enormous amount of help from Governor Nelson
Rockefeller, who is a little oily himself.

Talk of prosecuting the oil companies and establishing an energy and
fuels policy was unnerving to petroleum interests, even though it should
have been perfectly clear that with Mr. Nixon at the helm and important Senate and House committees safely guarding against legislation
frowned on by the fuels industry, they had little to be alarmed about.

Frank N. Ikard, president of the American Petroleum Institute, declared that the federal government alone was responsible for insufficient
energy fuels because for sixteen years it had held down natural gas
prices. The coal question was not raised by Mr. Ikard, which is perhaps
just as well, since coal production, substantially in the hands of the oil
industry, has fallen short as sky-high prices and new high-speed strip-
mining technology have produced both inflationary and environmental
problems. Coal is a commodity completely unregulated by government,
but as a free and open market commodity its fate is, if anything, in worse
shape than oil and gas.

Mr. Ikard said the petroleum corporations were battling for a principle and that the doleful talk about pricing and profits was only peripherally relevant. All gas at the wellhead, he contended, is a commodity and
as such should be priced solely by the interaction of supply and demand.
No price regulation on gas is justified unless public subsidy is offered.
He disregarded the fact that federal leasing and import policies, not to
mention tax and depreciation benefits, add up to a subsidy of several
billion dollars a year.

Mr. Ikard took no account of the geological fact that fossil fuels are
distinguished, as a commodity, from potatoes, peanuts, or grain. A fossil
fuel, cooked up over 4 billion years and marketed by a few great energy-
producing corporations, bears scarcely any comparison to the interaction
of supply and demand on crops produced on private lands by thousands
of agricultural businesses and individuals.

Occasional but never concerted pressure for a national energy policy
and stricter controls over oil corporations has appeared at intervals on
both the domestic and the international horizons. It has become increasingly disturbing to many that the cash flow and gross income, and hence
the economic and political power, of fifteen or so conglomerate corporations exceeds the gross national product of many sovereign powers. In
Singapore, late in February, 1971, Dr. Malcolm Caldwell, a British

scholar at the School of Oriental and African Studies in London, expressed angry concern about the power of international corporations in general and the influence of petroleum interests in particular. He said:

> Standard Oil of New Jersey, for instance, has a bigger annual turnover than the gross national products of Indonesia, Malaysia, and Singapore combined. In fact, the Standard Oil Group as a whole stands third only to the United States and the Soviet Union as an economic entity. American oil companies generate up to three-fifths of the American gross national product and it is not surprising that they can dictate foreign policy. . . . This kind of economic inequality is extremely dangerous because these vast industrial empires answer only to a handful of leading shareholders. Yet they can—and do—make and unmake governments all round the world, and lead nations into war. It is in the interests of the giant conglomerates to buy up elites subservient to their purposes wherever advantage is to be gleaned.

However great the need for the establishment of an energy board, past experience and present realism warn that it could very likely become simply another casual, industry-oriented regulatory body. The primary safeguard would be to have the majority of members of the energy policy board chosen by methods substantially different from those used in the past. Assuming, of course, that the new energy board *is* to have independence from the petroleum, finance, nuclear, electric power, and related businesses. If such detachment is not a requisite qualification for at least half the members on the board, it will go the way of just about every other regulatory and policy-making institution since the theory of regulation became an adjunct of popular government. For example:

A House Banking and Currency Committee has shown that forty-nine of the nation's largest banks hold interlocking directorates with thirty-six of the major electric utilities, twenty-eight gas companies, fifty-eight coal-carrying railroads, and twenty-seven companies supplying electrical transmission and distribution equipment. The same study showed that the Mellon National Bank and Trust Company, the bank of the Gulf Oil family, which holds 52 percent of all bank deposits in the Pittsburgh area, has directors on its board who also have interlocking-directorate connections with Consolidation Coal Company, General Electric, Westinghouse, and three major private utilities in Pennsylvania and Ohio.

An energy policy board should contain the kind of people a conventional president would not dream of appointing to it. And no president should be authorized to appoint the majority membership on such an agency, anyway.

Assuming that an energy policy board is composed of thirteen members, six of them could be appointed by the president, with or without the approval of the Senate. They would be drawn from the patronage pool, from the energy-fuels industry, the electric utilities, from the fields of law, government, or finance, pretty much as in the past. Six others would be chosen by a nominating and electoral process involving the membership of the chartered conservationist and environmental protection organizations, people recognized by their educational credentials or by their activism. The thirteenth member and chairman of the agency would be elected by the others. Such a method of selection would tend to strike a balance and perhaps redress the appointment of board chairmen of polluting corporations to presidential environmental advisory boards or the appointment of an executive of an international company under antitrust indictment to a commission recommending revision of the laws that caused the indictment in the first place. Conceivably, such a mix on an energy agency would establish public confidence in the decisions reached as the best reconciliation possible between inherently contradictory issues.

If this should lead to public dialogue and official review of the validity of expending enormous energy resources in enterprises similar to Disney World, or aluminum beer-can manufacture, or nuclear plants that might not be necessary if a national grid served the nation, or the senseless waste in the design and fueling of overpowered automobiles, or the production of plastics and biologically destructive chemicals inimical to life, a better definition of progress would have an improved chance of acceptance.

No control and rationing of energy and the natural resources required to produce it will, independently of other necessary reforms, produce a panacea for the phalanx of ills that plague the American industrial society. The problems of environmental pollution are about the same wherever concentrations of people, technology and industrial development, electric power, and expanding use of fossil fuels exist. As one Atlantic Richfield Company institutional advertisement pointed out in February, 1972, it is not uncommon for the air in large industrial cities of every continent to be officially unfit to breathe on at least one day of any given week.

In the United States, a program of regulating the expansion of energy production and consumption in some sane and fair manner requires corollary regulation at levels of industrial management and national policy beyond the question of energy alone. To do this, the country needs a good deal of specific information about itself and its interlocking economic and industrial power that is either not known or is hidden away in inaccessible reaches of government and the financial community. With all the investigative resources of the Congress, its agencies, and committees, a good deal of ignorance prevails among regulatory bodies, sometimes simply because the mechanisms for channeling information to the regulators fail to function or are not invoked.

"We knew what we were trying to regulate," Charles Ross, former FPC commissioner, has said, "but we didn't know *who* we were trying to regulate." What do the superrich families really own and what, through their interlocks with corporations and institutions they do not own, do they influence or control? What are the person-to-person, sequence-by-sequence links connecting the government-developed nuclear industry with the petroleum, coal, and gas industries, and in turn connecting *them* with heavy-equipment manufacturers, the great banks and investment houses, strip-mining firms, electric utility companies, privileged universities holding vast securities in the American corporate kingdom, and so on and on?

What is very much needed is a reincarnation of a fact-finding institution established in the early period of the Franklin D. Roosevelt administration. It was called the Temporary National Economic Committee (TNEC), and it still provides a rich source of research and data for thesis writing among political science and economics graduate students. For a couple of years, TNEC hearings and investigations gave the country an unprecedented insight into the councils of money and economic power. Whatever might emerge from a new TNEC-style study and investigative program could only help the country to, and perhaps provide the necessary impetus for, change. The capacity to change is vital to national life, and a number of imaginative, forceful proposals for change were in the air as the 1972 presidential election descended on the country.

A movement pressed by Ralph Nader and his associates and, astonishingly, supported by strong elements in the legal and industrial community, was calling for federal charters for corporations, especially those in interstate or international trade. The state charters—notably those of Delaware, New Jersey, and Nevada—are all but meaningless insofar as any inhibitory or regulatory controls are concerned. A federal charter could spell out more clearly the dimensions and limitations under which the privilege of corporate business is defined and protected. Competing companies would be subject to identical charter provisions. No manufacturer, for example, should be required to install pollution-abatement equipment, which requires capital outlay and adds no value to his product and no likelihood of increased income, unless all manufacturers of the same product are required to do the same thing at the same time.

Robert Townsend, maverick corporate manager of Avis car rental fame, proposed a radical innovation guaranteed to upset Milton Friedman, President Nixon's resident economist, who believes corporations should content themselves with the sole objective of seeking maximum profits, subject to law and custom. Townsend thinks big corporations need close scrutiny on a day-by-day basis, with professional monitors quartered in general corporate headquarters with access to every secret and detail of policy, operation, and management. But because there is no existing way to select representatives of special-interest or public-interest groups, no means providing them with a power base within a corporation, a way has to be devised.

As a working formula, every industrial corporation with $1 billion in assets, of which there were 110 in 1970, would be required to hand over $1 million a year of the company's money to a public director. The director, man or woman, would take $50,000 in salary and spend the rest on scientists, engineers, lawyers, accountants, investigators, or whatever category of expertise was needed to develop answers to questions that the company was not asking. No doors or files would be closed to the director, and notices of all meetings would be given and all meetings would be opened to him. The director would be required to call two press conferences a year and report on the company's progress or lack of it on issues of interest to the public.

Townsend, acknowledging that directing boards often do not do much or even question management, has suggested that "out of sheer shame" boards would be compelled to help the public director pursue relevant questions. Some managements, he felt, might find the idea so distasteful that they would prefer to spin off enough subsidiaries to get below the billion-dollar mark. This would be fine because although the company would not have a public director, it would have a healthy effect on increasing tax income, since the tax laws are drawn to favor conglomerates, subsidize acquisitions, and in general sanctify open-end bigness without regard to reason or merit. If the public director was really experienced, intelligent, and energetic, he would be aware of corporate efforts to put phonies on his staff, to swamp him, to shove him into dead-end assignments; and being aware of them, he could overcome them. Townsend wrote:

> My guess is that he would get help from a lot of people in the company—people below the top management level who are turned off by what top management is doing or failing to do. He would find a lot of friends and a lot of sources of informal and valuable information if he were there all the time and especially if he gave out his home phone number to enough people.

Other changes under examination and quite seriously proposed would nationalize such corporations as Lockheed and Penn Central, which are suffering from indescribable mismanagement, giantism, and what appears to be palpable corruption. Either they should be allowed to revive or to sink, according to their own efforts, or they should be nationalized, not bailed out with hundreds of millions of dollars of public money that socialized the losses and individualized profits until there were likely to be none.

Thomas B. Mechling of Larchmont, New York, a management consultant and associate of Eugene McCarthy in the 1968 presidential campaign, spent many months developing and expects to have the Public Equity Corporation (PEC), a project which has received a good deal of notice and publicity in the United States and abroad, organized and chartered in 1972. The corporation would be funded in a public underwriting, with proper warning to its stockholders that the quest for profits in PEC would be subordinate to more important corporate goals. In fact, the prospectus to be examined by the Securities and Exchange Commission would clearly warn: "These securities involve the highest degree of risk."

Mechling, something of a maverick himself, had been an executive for IBM and Xerox after very nearly becoming United States senator from Nevada. His idea for the Public Equity Corporation, one of the most imaginative and antithetical corporate concepts yet devised, could have a creative regulatory effect on every electric utility, telephone, manufacturing, and agricultural corporation in the country. It might, now and then, even make some money. The basic product of PEC would be litigation: class action suits. Its operational mode would be to work explicitly within the system of law that, ideally, is supposed to serve with equal justice all citizens but that, in fact and reality, serves wealth and power. The function of PEC is to move in on injustices or situations where derelict corporate or government practice causes damages to the environment or people and to seek treble damages in antitrust actions or punitive damages in lawsuits or criminal contempt proceedings.

For example, the Atomic Energy Commission regulatory staff in January, 1972, recommended that the Indian Point Number 2 reactor of Consolidated Edison be allowed to begin operations at 50 percent capacity. The 873-megawatt reactor was expected to be producing power in time to relieve the summer crisis. At the same time, the AEC Division of Reactor Licensing conceded that operation of the reactor would suck striped-bass larvae into the plant's cooling system and destroy "up to twenty-five percent" of all the eggs that passed into it. Moreover, about 600 pounds per day of white perch and other fish would be trapped in the screens of the cooling apparatus. Since these young fish weigh about half an ounce each, it can be expected that 18,000 or more of them will be chewed up daily. A year of operations could thus expect to eliminate

6,570,000 young fish and one-quarter of all the striped bass unlucky
enough to be in the egg stage of their development as they pass the
coolant intakes on the Hudson River.

As the Public Equity Corporation views the matter, or might view it
in a class action damage suit brought, let it be assumed, by commercial
fishermen or sportsmen, this is a great deal of both personal and environmental damage. What is it worth? PEC would institute the litigation and
in due course the utility and possibly the AEC as well might be ordered
to part with millions of dollars which might become, minus some portion
disbursed among abused fishermen, corporate income for PEC.*

The Nevada Cement Company was directed to pay eighty-five residents of the hamlet of Fernley, Nevada, thirty miles east of Reno,
$1,800,000 in 1971 for damage to their homes and belongings caused by
stack pollution from the company's operations. The company, owned by
a Dallas concern, failing to persuade the judge to order a new trial, then
appealed to the Nevada Supreme Court to set the decision aside or ease
up on the penalty, which awarded an average of $21,000 to everyone in
town. Mr. Mechling said there are so many hundreds and perhaps thousands of cases where neglect, arrogance, and willful circumvention of law
make remedial litigation possible that the Public Equity Corporation has
either an extraordinary future or none. It has no prospects, of course, if
no one invests in it. "I am betting that the United States doesn't run one
hundred percent on profits," he said.

As a public affairs consultant to a number of corporations and investment services, a former executive with the National Association of Manufacturers, and confidant of financiers and industrialists, he is acutely
aware of their desire to be esteemed, their ambitions, the ambivalence
of the management position in having to justify injustice and socially
damaging results as the cost of producing necessary goods. Just as
electric utility managers joined the Audubon Society and the Sierra Club
while building nuclear power plants that the organizations went to court
to try to stop, Mechling feels that PEC might provide an original and
needed public service attracting investors, some of whom would disap-
prove of some of the results.

The Public Equity Corporation would have been laughed at a few
years before it was designed. It took the Nader movement and the environmental crisis, coming on top of the human and civil rights turmoil,

* This example of the type of case that the Public Equity Corporation might get
involved with is the supposition of the author, deduced from my understanding
of the work it might undertake. It is not intended to suggest that Consolidated
Edison or the AEC should be sued for damages for building or licensing the plant.
The projections of fish destruction are somewhat fanciful anyway, since the life
cycle would not deliver the same number of fish to their doom day in and day
out, all through the year.

to make the beginning of a new system of values acceptable. PEC's plan to sell 480,000 shares at five dollars each would, in all probability formerly have been decried as fraudulent. But things have changed to the point where there is reason to believe that the profits desired by part of the investing public do not have to be money itself but can be the introduction of a new ethic, a code of justice and responsibility in the industrial and governmental system that the old institutions have failed to develop. Changing attitudes suggest that completely new concepts of regulation and social controls are in the process of formulation. The Public Equity Corporation and subsequent variants of it could give these new attitudes power far in excess of the numerical strengeh of people expressing them.

In the heart of the power industry, at the center of its development and management, are men who *know* that the electric utilities are in substantial part the cause of, and a possible hope for modifying, some of the degenerating conditions that have become palpably obvious to everyone. They do not know how to reverse the course of ruin, but they know that somehow it has to be done. With little enthusiasm, and perhaps out of reflex and habit developed in years of expansion (an increase in gross growth from $100 billion in Franklin D. Roosevelt's time to $1 trillion in the Nixon years), they seem to depend on larger markets and new technology to solve their problems or, at least, defer their accounting indefinitely. They do not blame themselves as individuals, since "no managerial fault" can be specifically attributed to them.

No utility system by itself can make changes, make repairs that will alter the national course. Theirs is not the initiative to take.

In private conversations, Lee Sillin expresses hope that some government action and some new, as yet unproclaimed, technology will absolve the utilities of their responsibility for environmental damage and reward them for the generation of enough power to meet national needs without harm to anyone, with blessings for all. When Sillin speaks or writes of the role of electric utilities in the years ahead he foresees an abundance of "clean" energy in such supply that no economic, social, or environmental problem need elude solution. He speaks of a thirty-year plan for "pollution-free energy sources" promised by research and development.

But there can be no "clean" energy, ever, even if nondamaging methods of generating it are devised. For as it is transmitted and consumed, it will always, whatever it energizes, pollute. The laws of thermodynamics guarantee that energy in use ends as heat, and excess heat alone will change the character and climate of the earth.

Charles Luce, speaking at a forum observing the fiftieth anniversary of the Federal Power Commission in Washington on June 3, 1970, said "yesterday's verities are today's apostasy" and all but conceded that constantly expanding energy and growth make no ultimate sense.

Mr. Luce did not, he said, believe any longer that the balance between growth and the natural environment "in the long run" could be served. Society would simply have to protect itself with some

> new environmental ethic . . . a willingness of individuals to take a somewhat lower standard of living . . . to forego some of the frills such as big autos, throwaways, and conspicuous consumption —and a willingness to pay higher prices for goods and services produced with due regard for environmental protection, and to pay higher taxes for public facilities to combat pollution. . . . If we do develop that kind of ethic, we can slowly, by discussion and teaching, make the changes in our life style that will protect our natural environment. . . . And perhaps the intellectual change they will present, and the self-discipline they will require, will be good for all of us.

What Charles Luce did not say, because a $150,000-a-year utility executive in search of capital and trying to maintain cordial relations with major stockholders could not say it, was that investors could not expect to go on collecting their tax-exempt dividends in the same old way, either. The dual character of so much of management life was exemplified in what Luce was saying. Profit in environmental destruction cannot go on indefinitely, but it cannot be stopped. That lower standard of living cannot, and will not, be tolerated by those already at the bottom of the economic waste bins.

Aubrey J. Wagner, director of TVA at an annual salary equal to what Charles Luce is paid every couple of months, observed the creative impact of electric power in the loop of states along the Tennessee River and reviewed the change with parochial enthusiasm. This region of once-terrible poverty and despair was elevated, with the presence of low-cost electricity in enormous volume, into a region of promise and vitality. A half-million acres of lakes and waterways, thousands of acres of newly verdant pastureland, 600,000 new jobs, and the lowest power rates east of Saint Louis have been provided with relatively limited damage to the environment. Reduction of poverty alone, a social achievement previously unparalleled in America, justified this investment in human betterment. There can be no cutting back of power, said Mr. Wagner, no curtailment, yet "the leadership of the present world must avoid the waste of resources." How can it be done if the ever-consuming monster of energy production and use cannot be curtailed and perhaps limited to useful purpose?

What Messrs. Sillin, Luce, Wagner, and their colleagues in the world of public and private power invariably see is the endless necessity for more energy. In searching for and hoping to devise the means of producing "clean" energy, they consume their own energy working on the wrong problem. What is even more necessary than new sources of power, clean or otherwise, is the control of demand for its use. This control of demand is the one splendid gift the twentieth century can give the century that follows.

Even if thermonuclear fusion is perfected as a method of creating harmlessly produced power, and even if mankind never needs to fear that there may never again be enough, its limitless use will remain a fatal evil. Energy will have to be used for those purposes that are useful to life and its continuity and withheld for purposes to the contrary. The need to change and the power to change, like the future itself, is upon us.